Child Study and Guidance in Schools

A. W. BOLGER

Child Study and Guidance
in Schools

CONSTABLE

LONDON

To Inez, my wife, who made it possible
and my children Andrew, Fergus and Victoria

First published in Great Britain 1975
by Constable and Co Ltd
10 Orange Street London WC2H 7EG
Hardback ISBN 0 09 460090 2
Paperback ISBN 0 09 460460 6

Set in Monotype Times New Roman
Printed in Great Britain by The Anchor Press Ltd
and bound by Wm Brendon & Son Ltd
both of Tiptree, Essex

Contents

1 Child Study and Guidance 9

2 Observation and Measurement 19

3 Keeping and Using Records 35

4 The Habitat of the Child 51

5 Anecdotal Records 61

6 The Use of Tests in Child Study 74

7 Studying Physical Development 84

8 Studying Intellectual Development 98

9 Studying Social Development 117

10 Studying Personality Development 135

11 The Interview in Child Study and Guidance 158

12 Helping Children with Problems: The School 170

13 Helping Children with Problems: The External Agencies 182

14 Helping Children with Problems: A Strategy for Teachers 194

Bibliography 219

Appendices A Training Courses in Counselling, Guidance and Pastoral Care 229

B Examples of School Record Forms 232

C Examples of Observation Schedules and Checklists 236

D Tests for Studying Aspects of Intellectual Development Suitability 245

E A Perceptual Survey Rating Scale 253

Name Index 264

Subject Index 267

Illustrations

Plates

1 The family relations test   *facing page* 54

Figures

1   The aims of education and their guidance implications   13
2   Developmental tasks and the aims of education   15
3   The expanding habitat of the child   53
4   NFER categories of tests   78
5   An observation schedule in physical development   87
6   Example of an audiogram   92
7   Diagrammatic representations of an island, as completed
       by some 18-year-old students   109
8   A model of creative thinking   112
9   Progress assessment chart   124
10 Member roles in groups   128
11 A sociometric test   129
12 Sociometric summary sheet   131
13 Individual sociograms   132
14 The influence of heredity and environment on personality   137
15 A schematic representation of personality and its study   143
16 Personality and the theory of temperaments   147
17 A personality rating scale   148
18 Bogardus test of social distance   150
19 Complete-a-sentence test   155
20 Tell-a-story test   156
21 Different kinds of interviews   160
22 A pyramid of need   171
23 Systems of guidance or pastoral care in comprehensive
       schools   178
24 Guidance services outside the school   183
25 Child guidance and the school psychological service   185

26 The organisation of local authority social work before and
       after the 1970 Act   188
27 A strategy for teachers   195
28 Guidance   201
29 Age and referral basis in guidance   203
30 Multiple reference   204
31 Group work   206

Grateful acknowledgment is offered to Miss Eileen Beard who
took the photograph which appears opposite p. 54 and Miss Eileen
Young who recorded the anecdotes on pp. 70–73.

1

Child Study and Guidance

It has become a truism in education to point out that the chief concern of teachers should be not the subject they teach but the children they teach. At a general level this statement would be almost universally accepted by teachers, certainly by primary-school teachers, and would be incorporated into their educational aims:

> When we asked our witnesses for their views on the aims of primary education we found a wide general measure of agreement, though many of the replies seemed to have as much relevance to other phases of education as to primary. The heads of junior and infant schools laid emphasis upon the all-round development of the individual and upon the acquisition of the basic skills necessary in contemporary society. (Plowden, 1967, p. 497)

In practice, having made obeisance to educational theory, many teachers return with relief to educational aims of a more limited, specific kind and their concern with individual children tends to decrease with the number of years the child spends in school. I have been disheartened many times by meeting teachers prepared to express, privately and publicly, their belief that their job is to teach children not to study them. As if the one task could be divorced from the other. One teacher put it even more bluntly. I was discussing the behaviour of children in groups with a large number of senior teachers when he interrupted: 'There is only one thing I need to know about kids, whether they're bright or whether they're dull!' He was unusual in being prepared to expose his views publicly, but, judged by the murmur of approval his words received, not unusual in his views.

Yet educators have been stressing the importance of child study at least since Quintilian, in the first century A.D., who said, 'The skilled teacher, when a pupil is entrusted to his care, will seek to discover his ability and natural disposition' (Quintilian, 1938, p. 30).

The Plowden Report has come out more recently in support of child study:

> At the heart of the educational process lies the child. No advances in policy, no acquisitions of new equipment have their desired effect unless they are in harmony with the nature of the child, unless they are fundamentally acceptable to him (para. 9).

and again

> Knowledge of the manner in which children develop, therefore, is of prime importance, both in avoiding educationally harmful practices and in introducing effective ones (para. 10).

The purpose of this book is to put the emphasis back on to 'the heart of the educational process', the children we teach. It is based on the firm beliefs that consideration of children as individuals is a central part of the teacher-training process, that skills in child study are an essential requirement of efficient teachers, that full acceptance by teachers of a pastoral care and guidance role is necessary if teaching is to be truly a profession and that child study itself is barren unless the knowledge we gain of individual children can be translated into effective helping.

Teacher training

Let us first consider teacher training. The three-year course in a college of education and the one year of post-graduate training are very full and are tending to become even fuller. Different subjects and different experiences compete with each other for inclusion in the course and, in the process, the child can, all too easily, disappear from view. Although this is understandable it should not be allowed to happen. Whatever else is sacrificed it should not be the child. Yet, does a greater emphasis upon child study necessarily imply that other training interests should suffer? I do not think so. What is needed is a re-interpretation of teacher training to remove the traditional division between content and method – a division which is even less appropriate in colleges of education than it is in schools. Postman and Weingarten have this to say about the way in which teacher training perpetuates the division:

> To our knowledge, all schools of education and teacher-training institutions in the United States are organised around the idea

that content and method are separate in the manner we have described. Perhaps the most important message thus communicated to teachers in training is that this separation is real, useful and urgent, and that it ought to be maintained in the schools (Postman and Weingarten, 1971, p. 29).

What follows from this, they suggest, is that teacher training should abandon its traditional separation of content and method if schools are ever to treat their pupils as whole individuals.

Perhaps this applies equally well to teacher training in this country.

This book does not provide the occasion for going into detail about how content and method may be merged in colleges of education nor to explore fully how this procedure could help teachers to better understand children. It is possible, however, to look briefly at some of the implications of merging content and method, particularly for the study of education and educational psychology. From the beginning of their course students would need to study themselves, their past development, their present functioning, their future potential in both objective and subjective ways. They would need to look at the ways in which they communicate with others, the 'games' they play and the quality of the relationships they form. Since the teacher's work is most frequently with groups, the student teacher would need to study group behaviour from his position as a member of various small groups, work groups, discussion groups, sensitivity groups. Through role-playing simulation and communication exercises, he could develop some skill in reading human behaviour and so improve his capacity to understand and communicate with his pupils. From the beginning this will mean close contact with children as individuals and in small groups rather than in large classes and it will mean plenty of opportunity for interaction with fellow students in learning situations. Students could observe children as they learn in school instead of having lectures on theories of learning; they could carry out Piaget-type experiments with them to study their concept development and give them intelligence tests to discover the uses and the limitations of intelligence tests. They could carry out sociometric surveys and plot the social interaction within groups of children. Above all they could listen to children as they talk about themselves and their problems, and develop their own little used faculty for 'total listening'. Their observations could be written up into case notes which they would need to communicate to others orally, in case conferences, in written case studies and in reports and then translated into helping programmes, remedial or otherwise, which would be useful both to the student himself and to the child whom he is observing. One of the 'extras' which it is urged should be put more extensively into the initial training programme is instruction into methods of teaching reading. This lends itself very well to the approach we are describing. The students themselves should undertake a programme in reading improvement since research has shown that everyone can be a better reader. Each student should also be given responsibility for one, two or three children in local schools whom he would study and to whom he would teach reading over a protracted period (perhaps the three years of the course). This will benefit the children, the students and education in general.

All of these activities assume an understanding of methods of child study and skill in using specific techniques. This would need to be begun early in the student's course and should take the form of actual case study work so that students could learn the techniques at the same time as they study children. This is one of the purposes of this book, to describe the methods of observation and the tests which are available so that students in training can be helped in the preparation of child studies.

Child study, pastoral care and guidance

The other beliefs on which this book is based, that child study pastoral care and guidance are essential aspects of education, need to be considered as a whole. Figure 1 indicates the relationship between the objectives of the school, the roles that teachers play, child study and guidance, and will be used as the basis of the discussion which follows. The objectives of the school have been expressed in general terms as 'the all-round development of all children' since this agrees both with the philosophy of the writer and that of the Plowden Report. This very general aim may be broken up into subsidiary aims using, for example, the notion of developmental tasks (see Fig. 2) and then into specific teaching courses or strategies. If the teacher is to achieve the general and specific aims of education and employ appropriate teaching strategies he has to perform several contrasting functions. The most useful way of conceptualising these functions is through a description of the sub-roles which teachers play in the classroom. It is possible to draw up varied lists of classroom roles.

Sorenson *et al.* (1963) suggested six principal sub-roles: adviser, counsellor, disciplinarian, information-giver, motivator and referrer. Others have made different lists, for instance, Policeman, Clerk, Librarian and Planner. Hargreaves (1972) talks of two basic sub-roles: instructor and disciplinarian. These are 'descriptive' terms. The role titles I have chosen are 'prescriptive' since they have been derived from theoretical consideration of the objectives of education.

FIGURE 1. THE AIMS OF EDUCATION AND THEIR GUIDANCE IMPLICATIONS

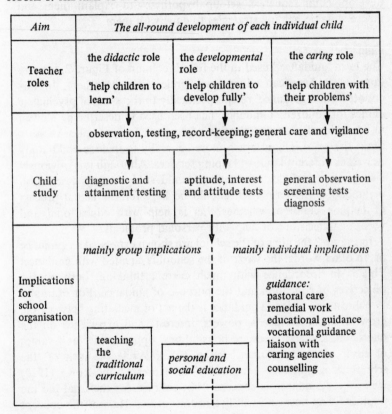

Aim	*The all-round development of each individual child*		
Teacher roles	the *didactic* role 'help children to learn'	the *developmental* role 'help children to develop fully'	the *caring* role 'help children with their problems'
	observation, testing, record-keeping; general care and vigilance		
Child study	diagnostic and attainment testing	aptitude, interest and attitude tests	general observation screening tests diagnosis
Implications for school organisation	*mainly group implications*	*mainly individual implications*	
	teaching the *traditional curriculum*	*personal and social education*	*guidance:* pastoral care remedial work educational guidance vocational guidance liaison with caring agencies counselling

Therefore the three terms I have used – 'didactic, developmental and caring' summarise not only what teachers are doing but what they ought to be doing. The didactic role can, it is true, be sub-merged in the developmental since helping children to learn is part of the process of helping them to grow up. It is given separate identity, however, because teachers value this role so highly and spend so much of their time playing it.

These three roles all demand that the teacher should know the children for whom he is responsible and should employ child study methods. To fulfil his didactic role he will need to assess the child's abilities, evaluate his learning style and diagnose his learning difficulties. For the developmental role he will need to observe the child's level of maturity, physical, intellectual, emotional and social and, for the caring role, be able to observe anomalies in this developmental sequence, set up hypotheses to explain them and devise suitable helping strategies to cope with them.

Guidance

The term 'guidance,' used in the fourth column of Figure 2, is more familiar in American educational circles than it is here. In this country 'child guidance' refers specifically to the work of psychiatric clinics for children. 'Guidance' has been used to describe help given in educational matters, selection of courses, for example. At other times the word is used much more generally to include child study as well as different kinds of helping services. Although it is obviously necessary to include techniques of child study in any description of guidance, the term itself should be kept for the actual process of helping children, whether this is help with educational and vocational decisions or help with personal problems.

In Figure 2 the aims of the school are shown expressed as guidance or, in other words, the work of the school is equated with guidance. This is in accordance with much current thinking, both on the objectives of education and the purpose of guidance. For example:

'Education viewed as guidance is the act of mediating between the growing child, his needs, powers, interests and experience on the one hand, and the needs, responsibilities, opportunities and values of adult life on the other.' (NFER 1953). While the idea of 'the school as a guidance community' is expressed by Rowe (1970) who says, 'Guidance is concern – but concern for the total life the pupil is living now and will live in the future.' He sees the concept of guidance as embracing the whole of the life of the school. As he says in his Foreword, 'Guidance is not direction. It is a concept which should in the future be used to cover all the things of impor-tance that go on both in the curricular and, when a teacher is present, in the extra-curricular life of the school.' It is in this sense that the term is being used in this book. Blocher *et al.* (1971) use the analogy of a guidance system in a missile to describe the function of a school guidance system. It helps to keep the individual 'system'

FIGURE 2. DEVELOPMENTAL TASKS AND THE AIMS OF EDUCATION

General aim of education	Specific aims based on the concept of developmental tasks	Strategies	
		Group curriculum	Individual guidance
	Examples only (See ch. 10 for a complete list of developmental tasks) *Learning to read*	*Reading readiness programme Developmental reading programme Remedial reading programme Effective reading programme*	*Checking reading readiness* by observation and testing *Keeping records of reading progress Diagnostic testing Counselling interviews Liaison with parents Liaison* with educational psychologist, school medical officer, etc.
The all-round development of each individual child	*Developing a sense of identity by learning appropriate masculine and feminine roles*	*Personal/social Education programme* including, the biology of adolescence, the psychology of adolescence, personal relationships, youth and the community *Physical education programme* including activities designed to increase self-confidence, improve body image and co-ordination, health education	*Child study*: general vigilance and diagnostic skill. *Pastoral care*: belonging to someone who cares and who is responsible *Individual and group counselling* *Liaison with parents* *Liaison with external agencies*

on course. The course in the individual pupil is determined by his own aptitudes and interests rather than by external criteria. The guidance system also acts in a similar way on the school system, providing feedback to keep it on course, that is to help it to achieve its objectives. This idea of guidance, as being, not an agent of adjustment maintaining the *status quo*, but an active agent of change within the school environment is one which I fully support.

A list of the guidance activities within a school would include the following activities:

Educational guidance
This covers all kinds of help given to pupils in the selection of subjects and courses, the diagnosis of problems in learning and assistance with these problems.

Remedial work
This is not usually considered as guidance but inasmuch as it is individualised assistance intended to bring the pupil 'back on to course' it is as much guidance as any of the other activities listed here.

Personal and social education
This covers all experiences planned in the curriculum to help individual growth and development. Emotional and social development are particularly emphasised because these are the most neglected aspects in conventional education. When the curriculum is planned with developmental needs in mind, then personal-social education takes its place as of equal importance with cognitive-physical. (See Figure 2).

Vocational guidance and vocational education
Properly speaking, these activities need to be co-ordinated with and incorporated into personal and social education. The pupil's vocational maturity, his ability to consider realistically his own aptitudes and interests against the background of the world of work should grow with his emotional and social maturity. Experiences to foster this growth should be included in the curriculum from an early date, certainly from the beginning of secondary school.

Counselling
This term is used here to cover all attempts to help pupils to solve

their own problems or to gain fresh insight into their own behaviour, mainly by allowing the pupil to talk through his difficulties. At some stage in the relationship between counsellor and pupil, practical steps may be suggested to help the pupil overcome his difficulties. These steps may include any of the guidance activities described previously, other helpful activities within the interview situation like role-playing or modelling, manipulation of the environment, such as changing class or school, or referral to other helping agencies outside the school. Counselling will be carried out at some time or other by all teachers concerned with the individual welfare of their pupils but, if children are to receive the help they need, when they need it, a trained and designated counsellor is required in each school. Most counselling encounters tend to be one-to-one interviews but counselling with small groups may be the most effective form of help with some people or some problems. Counselling is described more fully in Chapter 11.

Therapeutic and social work services outside the school
It is impossible for the school, no matter how dedicated and concerned, to cope with all the problems of all its pupils. Many of the difficulties experienced by children are the product of social or emotional conditions over which the school has little or no control. It is necessary, therefore, for the school to use and to be familiar with a range of helping services, e.g.,

The school medical service
The school psychological service
Child guidance
The educational welfare service
The social services department
The probation service
The youth employment service.

Liaison should be maintained with these agencies and it is better for this liaison to be made on a personal basis by a small number of school staff members. The school counsellor is an obvious choice for this job, but house masters, year masters or some specially delegated senior teacher could be assigned to the role. In primary schools it is usually the head teacher who takes on this task although there is no reason why another teacher should not be appointed to do it. There are a great number of specialist roles within these agencies and teachers should understand what these are. An example of some of the personnel involved with school children are: psychiatric social workers, educational welfare officers, family and community social workers, educational psychologists, child psychiatrists, play therapists, psychotherapists, speech therapists, school medical officers, school nurses, health visitors, careers officers, probation officers. Details of the work of these people and the agencies they serve are given in Chapter 13.

Reading matter

There are many good books on child and adolescent development (e.g., Pickard, Jersild, Cole etc. listed alphabetically in the Bibliography at the end of this book), and this book is not intended to replace any of these. The emphasis will be put on techniques of child study and guidance but it is felt that to describe tests or other methods of observation without giving some picture of the background in which they are administered and the insight which they are expected to give is to produce merely a guidance cookbook. It is planned, therefore, to introduce methods of child study within the context of a description of child development. It is hoped therefore that the book may be used as an introduction to child development as well as a handbook of child study methods. In addition an overview of guidance and counselling is given. Books on these linked topics are rare in Great Britain and most of them concentrate upon proving the need for counselling or describing what it entails. This book describes guidance and counselling in the context of the general objectives of education, and as a necessary part of both the developmental and the caring roles of teachers. Guidance and counselling are no longer suspect innovations but a necessary part of every teacher's repertoire of skills. It is hoped that this book can be used both to give this overall picture of the guidance side of teaching and as a manual of child study, and that it will be useful both for students in training and all teachers who recognise that they have a guidance function to perform.

2

Observation and Measurement

Introduction

Child study is based very firmly on observation and the history of
child psychology is very largely the history of the refinement and
systematisation of observation. Teachers are in a very good situation to be observers. They are in a group and yet apart from it.
They are in a position of authority so that they can require co-
operation and yet have a relationship warm enough to ensure that
this co-operation is received. It is important, however, that the
observation which teachers make incorporates the advances in
child study which have been made in the last century or so. The
random, informal, unsystematic observation in which teachers
inevitably are involved can become, with care and study, a means of
understanding and helping the children they teach. In this chapter
we shall consider what is involved in observation and the different
methods which have been developed to make it more effective.

The development of a scientific attitude towards human behaviour

It is hard to adopt a scientific attitude towards human behaviour.
To do this demands a detachment, a dispassionate approach towards fellow-beings which traditionally men have found to be
difficult if not distasteful. It is, after all, like asking us to treat
people as if they were things – stones or trees – rather than objects
of love or hate. Furthermore, such an attitude demands that we
achieve a considerable degree of objectivity about our own mental
processes, that we stand outside ourselves, as observers, and, as on
the first occasion of hearing our own voice on a tape-recorder or
seeing ourselves on a screen, this can be a disturbing experience. It
is not surprising that a science of behaviour arrived very late on the
scene nor that, having arrived, it should be fiercely opposed in many
quarters even today. The emotional reaction to lectures on behavi-
ourism, that theory of psychology which explains behaviour in
mechanistic terms, has to be experienced to be believed.

In spite of human reluctance to study human behaviour there

have been many attempts to conceptualise personality in objective terms. From earliest times some men, observing natural phenomena – sun, rain, wind – have drawn analogies to human behaviour. Hippocrates, the 'Father of Medicine', explained personality by the proportion of natural elements, heat, cold, moistness and dryness, within the individual. These elements he located in body secretions: blood, phlegm, yellow bile and black bile. A preponderance of one of these elements determined the individual temperament. Today we still speak of the sanguine, phlegmatic, choleric and melancholic individual. Galen, in Roman times, elaborated this simple formulation into a complete theory of temperaments, assigning different proportions of the four basic elements to explain the wide variety of personality types. This theory of temperaments persisted right through the Middle Ages and an adaptation of it is used today (see Figure 16 on p. 147).

From this time speculation about human behaviour increased although it was usually expressed in theological terms. Such concepts as grace, free will, original sin, were used to explain differences between individuals and differences within the individual. The scholastic philosopher, Erigena, for example, explained individual differences according to the doctrine of original sin. The true man is the Idea of man in God and in this Idea all possible individual human beings are eternally contained. Original sin caused separation into male and female, black and white, tall and short, good and bad. Once started, this process of separation was said to continue inexorably (Gilson, 1955, p. 123). Adam and Eve sinning meant that the whole reality sinned, and, as this reality exists throughout time each member of the human race is charged with original sin. When a child is born, no new substance is formed but just a new property of the reality already in existence. Human differences appear accidentally on the surface of humanity in the way ripples appear on the surface of a pool.

With the Renaissance, awareness of individual differences and a readiness to explain them in objective terms increased. Most commentators seemed to want to connect conduct with physiology. Vives, for example, used differences in the temperature of the blood to explain differences in behaviour, hot blood went with courage, cold blood with caution. Leonardo da Vinci studied facial expression, Juan Huarte explained individual differences as arising at the time of conception, the result of differences in the temperature of the seed, the mode of copulation and the moral state of the conception. With the empirical tradition, however, emphasis shifted to environmental influences. From this period dates Locke's famous description of a young child as 'white paper or wax'. This dictum gave support to an extreme environmentalist position which did not really represent Locke's view but has been credited to him ever since. Once the view is accepted that human nature is produced by environmental circumstances, the value of studying human behaviour becomes apparent. Yet, until the end of the nineteenth century, there was little attempt at purposeful observation and psychology was still largely introspective.

One elaborate attempt to produce a pragmatic system to explain human behaviour and individual differences was phrenology. Gall, an anatomist, believed from his observation of human skulls that the shape of the head determined the way in which people behaved. Phrenology developed from his writing, being based on four assumptions; the first was that the mind can be analysed into various faculties, the second that specific faculties were located in specific areas of the brain, the third that the size of each area of the brain determined the relative strength of the faculty and the fourth that the configuration of the brain was observable in the outward shape of the skull. We now know that this line of enquiry leads to a dead end but it was, for that time, a good guess and, what is more important, it satisfied a need in society. Character readings became fashionable and the phrenologists' emphasis on the importance of exercise in the development of mental faculties led to increased interest in education. For example, in 1848 a phrenologist, Howe, founded the first school for retarded children. Phrenology was characterised by careful measurement and consistent attempts to link these measurements with observed behaviour.

The time was ripe for those methods of observation which had proved so successful in physical science to be applied to mental science. Bacon had in fact laid down guide-lines for such an approach. In his *Advancement of Learning* he described a way of classifying learning, a classification which set out a basis of scientific method. This included 'human philosophy'. It was only a matter of time before his approach was adopted. For example, in education the Jesuits prescribed the keeping of cumulative records on all pupils, and other writers on education emphasised the importance of child study. Alongside this very practical approach was a growing tradition of careful observation with the object of determining general rules of behaviour. This was to develop into the laboratory approach to psychology but it was not until 1869 that methods of observation were applied to measure how individuals differed from each other rather than how they were similar in their reactions. Then it was Francis Galton who, by applying mathematics successfully to the study of individual differences, provided the techniques which psychologists in the future would use to make sense of their data.

The next big advance in the study of children came with Alfred Binet and the construction of the first intelligence test which could be used practically. Charged with the task of developing an instrument which would differentiate children who needed special educational treatment, he departed from the sensory measures which preoccupied so many of his contemporaries. He divided mental functioning into ten processes: memory, mental imagery, imagination, attention, comprehension, suggestibility, aesthetic sense, moral sense, persistence and motor skill (Binet and Henri, 1896) and then proceeded to devise tests to measure these processes. At the same time he laid down the general conditions under which mental testing should be performed and a very comprehensive list it was. He suggested that tests:

1. should be of wide variety to embrace the greatest number of psychological faculties,
2. should test the higher faculties (that is higher order mental operations as distinct from sensory processes),
3. should not exceed one and a half hours' duration to prevent fatigue,
4. should be varied for the same reason,
5. should be appropriate to the subject's environment,
6. should not necessitate complicated apparatus.

With Simon, Binet devised a scheme in which a number of short tests were given. These increased in difficulty, starting from the lowest intellectual level and ending with average intelligence. After the first revision in 1908 tests were re-arranged in order of difficulty and grouped into age levels which were determined as the age at which the 'majority of children succeed in them' (Binet and Simon, 1908).

From this arose the concept of 'mental age'. For example, if a child of seven years answers correctly items which the 'majority' (defined as 59 to 78 per cent) of children aged nine answer, then he is credited with a mental age of nine years. Binet avoided tests which measured psychophysical characteristics like reaction time and tests which were too influenced by instruction since he wished to measure the level of 'natural intelligence' but, between these limits, he devised a wide range of tasks for a wide age range. His tests have been translated into several languages and have been revised several times since then, the last time in 1960. They still remain as the yard-stick by which other tests are judged.

Since that time a 'test explosion' has taken place and the current *Tests in Print* lists thousands of tests covering a wide variety of psychological variables. Child study does not depend upon tests alone to obtain its data. A wide range of techniques has been employed from the early baby biographies to sophisticated time studies recorded on videotape. All these techniques, simple or sophisticated, depend upon one basic scientific tool – observation.

Observation as the basis of child study
All science has been built on the technique of observation. Weather, rocks, stars, chemicals, plants, animals, people – all study of these must begin with observation. Child study relies equally on observation whether it is the precise study of psychologists watching children through a one-way vision screen or the purposeful scrutiny of a teacher looking at her class at work. Observation can be either formal or informal. Formal observation, including tests and specific measurements, has its place in classroom child study while informal observation, provided it is carried out within an appropriate frame of reference, can be a valuable source of information about children. Formal observation has developed from the gradual refinement of informal observation as psychologists have devised techniques to study children. Many of these techniques can be adopted by teachers to refine their own observations and make it more effective.

The refinement of informal observation
Whenever we make an observation we are involved in making judgments. If we observe children playing in a nursery school we must make judgments about their behaviour. We must, for instance, decide on the kinds of play we are observing. What do we call it when two or three children combine together in the house corner to play mothers and fathers? What name do we use when we see young Alan riding his bike on his own, Betty standing watching a group in the sand-pit, or Jane and Helen painting companionably side by side? Having decided upon a frame of reference in which to consider these situations, that is when we have formed a hypo-

thesis about the nature of children's play, it is necessary to decide
upon the terms we shall use. It is of little use if different workers use
different terms, so agreement upon terms must be reached. Let
us conceptualise play as a social activity which develops from
solitary play to fully co-operative group activity. Then we shall
need terms to describe different kinds of play between these two
extremes. One set of terms which has been used to describe play in
this frame of reference has been used in several child studies.

The scale of play was:

solitary play, parallel play, observer play, associative play,
co-operative play.

When we have settled the terms we are going to use we must
agree upon the way in which we shall quantify, that is, attach
numerical value to our observations. If co-operative play is considered to be more advanced, from a developmental point of view,
than solitary play, it could be given a higher score. Then our observations, when summarised, will represent the increase in complexity
of the play we are observing. The studies previously referred to used
weighted scores on a scale:

solitary play		co-operative play
−2	0	+2

The points on the scale could have been weighted differently, e.g.,

1	2	3	4	5

and whichever we use may well affect our interpretation of our
observation. On the other hand we might be more interested in the
number of social contacts that children make in each category
rather than in assigning value to the kind of play we observe. In
this case we could give each observation equal value although
then we would run into the difficulty of taking into account the
length of time spent on each type of play. A child who stayed at
one kind of activity for the whole of an observation session could
not be compared very easily with a child who moved rapidly from
group to group. The final score scale to be used would have to be
settled after a period of observation and trial and error. This serves
to illustrate the problems involved in quantifying observation.

Not every bit of classroom observation will have to be treated this way. Very often the quantification has been done before in a previous research or by a test constructor or no quantification is necessary beyond recording of frequency of occurrence. Teachers are, however, inveterate quantifiers. They attach numerical value to all kinds of observations which they make in the course of their work – number of words spelt correctly, number of sums completed correctly, position in class, number of pupils present on a particular day, marks in geography, performance in art, the merits of an essay. They use these numbers in many different ways, very often combining and contrasting, quite unjustifiably, numbers arrived at in different situations. The common practice of averaging scores arrived at on different examinations, when these scores have not been stand-ardised, and comparing children on the basis of this average is quite unjustified from a statistical point of view. Yet teachers, even mathematics teachers, are prepared to make decisions about the future of children based on this aggregation of unstandardised scores simply because it is the traditional way of doing things. There will be a discussion of test marks and their significance in chapter 6. At present it is sufficient to make the point that numbers are not always as straightforward as they seem to be and we should think carefully about what they are representing before accepting them at their face value.

One thing we need to do if we wish to improve the reliability of our observation is to increase the number of observations which we make. We may observe a child in school who acts in a very unco-ordinated way, perhaps stumbling when there is nothing to stumble over. Commonsense will tell us not to jump to any conclusions on the basis of one observation. In scientific child study the number of observations are increased many times in order to reduce the possi-bility that what we observed was an isolated event. In classroom study a series of careful observations would be made until the teacher was certain that she was actually observing unco-ordinated behaviour. Even then of course she would not know *why* the child was unco-ordinated.

In the study previously described where children's nursery school play was observed, observation had to take place over an extended period. At different times in the day the pattern of children's play changes. There are quiet periods where they listen to a story, group periods where they sing or dance, periods of noisy boisterous play on the outdoor equipment. A sample of play taken at one of these

20050

times would not be representative of play in general. Sometimes the children's mood is different or their level of fatigue and, as every teacher knows, the weather can have a profound effect upon children's behaviour. This means that the observations cannot be restricted to one day, however carefully observed, but must be spread over a longer period. What we are doing with our observation is sampling the child's behaviour. We cannot encompass all that he does, even in one narrow field of activity, say arithmetic. We must take a sample of his behaviour so, in this instance, we draw up a test which represents, as far as possible, the total of his arithmetic experience. We are sampling his knowledge of arithmetic. In our nursery school study we observe play for a period long enough to be representative of the children's play but not so long that the developmental dimension becomes important and the children's play changes as they grow older.

The word 'sampling' is used in two ways principally to describe the number of individuals which need to be studied in order that the results be representative of the whole population but also to describe the number of observations which need to be made in order that our observation should represent the class of experience which is being studied. It is this second use of the word with which we are concerned at present. In practical terms teachers must be careful to take a series of observations before arriving at any conclusions since any one observation may not be typical.

A further method of refining observation is to increase the number of observers. If a number of different people make observations of the same behaviour this increases the total number of observations in the way we have just discussed. In addition the reliability of the observation is increased since independent judgments, when averaged out, avoid the extremes of any single observer. In the classroom a teacher increases the number of observations made on a particular child when she uses standardised tests. Observations have been made during the standardisation of the test on a very large number of children and the teacher relates her test results to these and thus increases the number of observations on which she bases her conclusions. In a lesser degree she can increase the number of observers when she consults other teachers or looks back at record cards. Systematic errors in judgment can creep into any observation. The so-called 'halo effect' can affect all judgments. Children who are bright and successful can be judged to be braver, better behaved or more sociable than others who are not so bright and successful. That is, one type of observation can affect other kinds of observations when they are made on the same subject. This kind of distorted perception is a familiar phenomenon to child psychologists. Children choose value loaded objects as being bigger than non-value loaded objects. For example, coins are said to be bigger than plain discs of the same size. I witnessed an example of this recently when a spastic boy being tested by a colleague chose a 10p piece as bigger than an old penny. Value was perceived as size. This halo-effect can distort judgments made by single observers or by a number of independent observers. Anyone studying children has to be alert to the possibility of these and other systematic errors creeping in.

Observation can be made more accurate not only by improving the judgment but also by improving the conditions under which these judgments are made. Judges can be trained to be more precise and this is one of the aims of this book. The reliability of judgments made by different judges can be improved by practice and by critical appraisal. This has been demonstrated by many studies of judgments made on such diverse aspects of behaviour as teaching efficiency, play, and examination responses. If teachers marking the same examination spend some time on establishing criteria and comparing marking standards, their inter-marker reliability is increased considerably. Accuracy of recording is another essential condition for the improvement of observation. This is translated into classroom child study by the keeping of careful records. Test results need to be entered in a brief but unambiguous way. Information gathered about children from general observation and interview situations needs to be recorded in such a way that future questions can be answered. For example, if we have an entry IQ 87 for a particular child we need to know when the test was given, by whom, under what conditions and even more importantly what test it was. The entry would then read like this:

Test Scores:
Mar. 1973, IQ 87, AH4 [name of test], J.B. [initials of test administrator], rout. grp. [routine administration to group in school].

Anyone reading this item would be able to place the test score in the context of the child's school life and would be able to avoid either treating it as a label or discarding it as worthless information. Similarly a record, 'parent visit', would acquire meaning only if it were amplified to describe the date, occasion and outcome of the visit.

Records can come in many different forms. They may have been written by the subject himself as in the case of autobiographies, essays or test responses. They may be written by the observer as in many individual tests or in anecdotal records. They can come in the form of lengthy verbal documents or as simple check tests. More recently child study material has been recorded on film, videotape or sound tape. While such techniques are more appropriate to the specialist researcher than the classroom situation it is worth while keeping in mind audio-visual methods of recording child behaviour since schools have the facilities for such studies.

We can now classify child study methods according to the degree of control which is brought into the situation in which the child is being observed. If we observe children through a one-way vision screen and they play naturally, unaware of being watched then we can say there is no control of the situation. If we have a child seated opposite to us at a table and ask him first to pour liquid from bottles into different sized glasses and then to tell us which vessel has the most liquid, we are controlling the situation very strictly. Between these two extremes there are a wide range of observations we can make in which the situation is more or less controlled. For convenience we can divide the observation of children into two main categories – one in which there is little or no control over the situation and the other in which the situation is strictly controlled.

Observation without control over the situation
In the first category we can place narrative records of all kinds. These include the earliest kinds of child studies, the baby biographies in which the day by day behaviour of small children was carefully recorded. One example of such observation begins in this way:

Born in a Nursing Home.

19 days	– Eyes followed light. Removed from Nursing Home.
6 weeks	– Smiled; observed staring at trees.
2 months	– Held rattle
3 months	– Turned on side.

4 months — Crawling movements noted; pulled mother's hair, made monosyllabic sounds.

5 months — Transferred toy from one hand to the other; distinguished between parents and strangers; splashed in bath; shouted.

6 months — Ki-ki, da-da, r-r sounds made; turned over from back to chest; tore sheet.

7 months — Ma-ma (when fretting); rolled over on side; first tooth; crept; showed expectance of feed and walk.

8 months — Sat up in pram; blew whistle; said na-na (negative meaning).

9 months — Energetic crawling; ti-ti added to repertoire; weaning commenced.

10 months — Smiled at another baby; understood 'no'; said ga-ga (dog), bi-wi (bus) (first words).

11 months — Climbed part of stairs; understood 'are you hungry?', 'biscuit', 'going for a walk?', 'no'.

12 months — Weaning accomplished; 8 teeth; walked with support; climbed 10 steps without support; later climbed 22 steps without support.

1 year 2 months — Stood without support; da-da, ta-ta-ta, bu (bird); took two steps alone; showed delight in company.

1 year 3 months — Walked 10–12 yards alone; vocabulary – 23 words by end of month.

1 year 4 months — Showed interest in gramophone; vocabulary – 27 words.

1 year 5 months — Vocabulary – 200 words; 'Look – moon – sky' first sentence.

1 year 6 months — Memory – at least for three months.

1 year 7 months — Counted 2.

1 year 9 months — Interest in colours shown – distinguished and named green, yellow, red, blue and grey; distinguished gramophone records by different marks on labels; showed interest in fitting things.

(Bowley, 1942)

Narrative records were made more comparable by observing children at specific times, during playtime, for example, or at meal times. When recurring situations were observed fully it was possible to study changes in behaviour resulting from the development of the children or alterations in the circumstances. For example these observations of children's fears:

> Andrew, aged 4, was often really terrified because an older boy used to tease him by pretending that he could run an electric current through his body by touching him with a bit of wire. This game had to be stringently prohibited by adults because it caused so many tears.
> (Bowley, 1942)

Time sampling was another method which added precision to observation. By observing fully for limited periods, chosen randomly or systematically, detailed records could be made and the bias of unconscious selection avoided. A splendid example of careful observation using both situational and time sampling has been filmed in James Robertson's 'A Two Year Old Goes to Hospital'. A little girl entering hospital for a minor operation was observed before, during and after her hospitalisation. Although the presence of the cameraman undoubtedly changed the situation to a certain extent this is very largely the filmed record of child study employing observation without control of the situation. It has led to many changes in the attitude of hospitals to the visiting of child patients.

Another way in which this type of observation has developed since the early biographies is in reports and ratings of child behaviour. One well-used example of a report form is the Bristol Social Adjustment Guide (Stott, 1956 and 1971). The teacher reports on the behaviour which he has observed in the classroom, classifying it according to criteria laid down in the Guide. Classroom behaviour is described in objective terms.

> e.g., Persistence (classwork): Works steadily/too restless ever to work alone/works only when watched or compelled/can work alone but has no energy/varies very noticeably from day to day.

The teacher is asked to underline the most appropriate statement.

By such means it is possible to make comparison between one child and another and to refer to normative data. Another example can be seen in the 'Pre-primary Profile' at present being tried out in Gloucestershire by the Science Research Associates. Here it is the mother who is being asked to report on her child's behaviour, and, when she rates him on such characteristics as:

Behaviour	Not yet	Just beginning	Well	Very well
Hops on one foot				

she has been found to be a reliable observer.

It is possible, therefore, for the trained observer to state the criteria of his observation in careful objective terms in order to enable the untrained observer to make valid judgments about children's behaviour.

Another way in which observation can be carried out on children in the classroom without affecting the situation is through the keeping of anecdotal records. Here the teacher makes a full verbatim report on incidents she observes. Since value judgments are excluded she can use the material at later times to confirm or disprove hypotheses she may have formed.

Personal products including documents, drawings and models have long been considered a source of information about child behaviour. Essays and other written material can be analysed in many ways looking at style and content. At the simplest level children's written work can prove a source of information about home conditions, parental attitudes, as well as children's interests, vocational aspirations, self concepts and value systems. Just consider how fruitful essays on 'My Family' can be in helping teachers to understand the children they teach. At a more sophisticated level studies have been made of written material to assess the use made of verbs or adjectives, the complexity of syntax or the level of vocabulary in order to test some hypothesis about language development. Story-telling both oral and written comes very close to the projective material described below.

Children's art work presents another indirect way of observation. Again the content can be analysed for what it tells us about the child's inner life, e.g., a child who persistently represents a large mother and a tiny father is telling us something about the way he perceives his relationship to his parents. The standard of technique used can give us information about the child's cognitive development and in fact 'The Goodenough-Harris Drawing Test' is a reliable measure of intelligence (Goodenough and Harris, 1963).

Observation with control of the situation

The other class of observation is that in which the situation is materially affected by the action of the observer. Into this broad category would be put any specific measurements of school work. Since we are altering the children's behaviour in order to obtain our measurements this observation is of a different type from that previously described. We could include in this category such measurements as the number of sums done correctly, the number of spelling mistakes, the time taken to complete a task, and all examination results. Standardised tests differ from these in having been carefully prepared in such a way that results can be compared from one child to another and from one occasion to another. A test is tried out on a large and representative sample of children of the age for whom it is intended. From these results 'norms' are set up and other children's performance on this test can be compared with these norms. The more sophisticated of these tests are known as psychometric tests and they can measure capacity, aptitude and attainment. A good psychometric test must be administered under standard conditions, scored objectively and interpreted in relation to norms from a large and representative sample.

Sometimes the situation in which we are studying children is manipulated experimentally so that we can measure the affect of one variable. Much educational research could be placed in this category. If we were to try to find out the affect of one teaching procedure as compared with another, e.g. the use of an individual reading scheme, like the Science Research Associates (SRA) Reading Laboratory, compared with a more usual group reading scheme we should need to adopt an experimental design. Two groups would be set up, a control group which would use the conventional approach and an experimental group which would use the new reading approach. Each group would have to be matched very carefully to make sure that they did not differ in other important ways, other variables such as teacher differences would have to be controlled and then the reading programme would begin. At the end of the period set aside for the programme the relative merits of the two schemes could be assessed in terms of the difference between the improvement in reading of the control group and the improvement in reading of the experimental group. If we had been successful in eliminating, or at least substantially reducing, other variables, and if our samples had been representative of school children of that age then we could arrive at conclusions about the two schemes. Any differences we found would have to be tested statistically to discover if they were, in fact, significant. It can be seen, even from this superficial description of a hypothetical piece of research in education, that it is no easy matter to set up the kinds of control over the situation which are necessary if we wish to draw precise conclusions from our observation.

There are other kinds of observational techniques used in child study which need to be mentioned. A whole class of situations vaguely called 'projective tests' or 'projective techniques' have been used by psychologists and psychotherapists. Many of these, like the famous Rorschach or Inkblot Test are very specialist and have little practical interest for the teacher. The aim of the projective technique is to arrive at an understanding of less easily accessible aspects of a child's personality, his unconscious motivation for example. In order to study these aspects of the child he is presented with stimuli which are indirect, for example, ink-blots, pictures, patterns, dolls and his reactions to these are recorded. Usually it is verbal reaction that is studied, 'Tell me a story about this picture', but sometimes non-verbal reactions are studied, for example drawings. One useful projective technique used in this country is the Family-Relations Test (Bene-Anthony, 1957). Here the child and the examiner play a game together setting up a number of cardboard figures mounted on a sort of money-box (see plate 1, p. 54 f) to represent the child's family. He is then given a number of cards which make statements like 'This person gets very angry with me', and posts these in one of the boxes. At the end of the time the examiner can sort out the cards in each box to arrive at an impression of the relationships existing in that particular family (see Chapter 4 for further details). The difficulties which exist in the interpretation of these results are much less than in more open-ended situations where, for example, the child has to tell a story about a picture of some animals in a domestic situation. Even so, we can never be sure of the reliability of an individual's responses in a situation like this nor of the degree of importance that we can place on any reliably reported relationship. Such a technique may be very useful however, although it is not likely to be employed in the school situation. The teacher is more likely to use quasi-projective material like essays on 'My Autobiography', 'My Family', or paintings and drawings of stimulating subjects like 'Fear', 'Ambition'. Some projective tests can be adopted for use in the classroom, however, and these will be described later.

B

Many other measures of personality are based on self-reports and self-ratings. Children are asked to classify their previous behaviour or to report on its frequency. Questionnaires use these methods and also multiple-choice situations in which the child is asked to choose, from a number of statements, the one most appropriate to his own circumstances. One example is perhaps appropriate at this stage:

Which would you rather do.
a. visit a zoo *b.* uncertain *c.* go up in an airplane?
(Example from Jr-Sr HSPQ, Catell, 1962)

A great deal of work has gone into many personality questionnaires on the market at present and they may well be placed in the category of psychometric tests.

A simple procedure which has great relevance to the classroom situation is the sociometric 'test'. In this the children are asked to respond to a simple question like, 'Which three children in this class would you most like to have sitting next to you?' The names they quote can be used to assess the social relationships present within the class. There are several different sociometric techniques and these are discussed in detail in Chapter 9. The results can be summarised in the form of a sociogram so that the teacher can observe the friendship groups and leadership patterns within the classroom. Another way of analysing the results is to arrive at a popularity score from the number of times the child is chosen by his peers.

Most of the techniques of observation which have been briefly described were developed by psychologists in laboratory situations. They have been used successfully by teachers carrying out educational research, by educational psychologists studying problem children, by reading consultants dealing with remedial readers and by teachers and counsellors interested in individual children. Many of the techniques described can be learned (without difficulty) by interested teachers and the interpretation of these observations can be made realistic by reading appropriate books and discussing their implications with other colleagues, teachers, psychologists, doctors and social workers.

It is contended that a knowledge of appropriate methods of child study is essential if the teacher is to ensure the harmonious development of individual pupils. The most appropriate techniques and the way in which they can be used will be dealt with in later chapters.

3

Keeping and Using Records

The need for cumulative records

As a very young teacher I took up an appointment in a school in a depressing industrial area. On my first morning I reported to the headmaster, a harassed man trying to cope with queues of parents and constant interruptions. I waited a long time to see him. The bell for classes to begin had sounded before I entered his office. He had very little time to spare for me. 'Bolger? Oh yes I had a letter from the office to say you were coming. About time too! 3c have been without a teacher for a week. You'd better go there right away and take charge. Come with me and I'll show you.' He took me by the arm out into the corridor, bustled me around a corner and pointed.

'The third door on the left. You can't miss it. They are the ones making all the noise.'

He scuttled back around the corner to the safety of his office. I stared after him, bewildered and apprehensive and then made my way to 3c. He was right. I couldn't miss the classroom. The noise was frightening. I opened the door and went in. The sudden silence was even more frightening. . . .

In this way I began my acquaintance with 45 thirteen-year-olds. I was given no information about my pupils. I did not know what work they had been doing nor what they should have been doing. There were no syllabuses, no schemes of work, far less was there information about individual pupils, their special abilities and disabilities, their problems, their achievements. I had to find out everything from the boys themselves. Starting with their names, I looked at their exercise-books and textbooks to determine the programme they had been following and their individual success at this programme. It was hardly a very efficient means of collecting this information but it was the only means that was left for me.

This experience may not be typical of the way in which teachers find out about their classes although I suspect that many new teachers are still pitch-forked into the classroom situation without sufficient preparation. I feel, however, that the anecdote illustrated a widespread weakness in our schools – the lack of adequate records. While cumulative record systems have been established by most local education authorities, the records are usually brief, omit much important information, present what has been recorded in a way that is not easily usable and are administered in a way that makes the retrieval of information difficult. Many teachers are sceptical about their value, object to spending time entering up record forms and reduce what value the present systems have by irregular entries and thoughtless or routine comments. Very often teachers are unduly influenced in their comments on pupils by remarks made by teachers in previous years. Insensitive comments like, 'Johnny is very lazy', are repeated from year to year long after the behaviour which prompted the remark has changed. This justifies the criticism frequently made by teachers that records merely help to 'give a dog a bad name'.

Record systems do not need to be like this, however, and their value should not need to be spelled out. No enterprise can be carried out efficiently, whether it be in business, research, war or education, without the maintenance of clear and concise records. Without these records it is impossible to evaluate progress or plan for future development. In this book our particular concern is the individual child. We feel that by studying children as individuals we can, among other desirable outcomes, become more efficient teachers. Classes are too large to allow the benefits of individual child study to affect the whole class unless records of that study are kept and used. If we are to maintain concern for the individual, know each child's strength and weakness, then it is essential that we keep records of what each child has achieved. Otherwise the individual is bound to be overlooked in the full-time job of teaching a group.

The point is sometimes not made clearly enough that studying children is different from studying adults in at least one very important respect. There is an extra dimension in child behaviour, the dimension of time. It is possible to study adults as static, treat them entirely in the 'here and now' but children must always be considered as in a state of 'becoming'. They are developing organisms subject to constant change. This change is different from that of adults who obviously are changing, slowly as they age or suddenly as circumstances affect them, in that it is part of the programme of development, a constant programme at the same time both individual and subject to regular laws. This time sequence in child behaviour can only be appreciated if our records are cumulative. Only by taking notice of the sequence of records can discrete observations become meaningful. John's 'laziness' (recorded in less judgmental terms, we hope) can achieve meaning when seen in the sequence of reading failure in earlier years and lack of reinforcement to follow. Isolated incidents reveal a pattern of behaviour when looked at in the context of cumulative records. A puzzling outburst of aggression in a usually passive child acquires meaning when it is seen that similar outbursts in previous years have coincided with his father's absence on business trips.

The uses of school records

Cumulative records, once established in a comprehensive form and maintained by teachers who are both sympathetic to the idea of records and efficient in completing them, become the means of all-round improvement in education. When a teacher is taking over a new class, the information is there for him to study so that from the beginning the pupils may be seen as individuals. Instead of teaching a new process to the class, assuming them all to be at approximately the same stage, or setting a test to determine just what stage they are at, the teacher with access to adequate cumulative records can use these to decide where each child should begin.

When a child behaves in an unusual and worrying way the teacher is not faced with an isolated situation but is able to refer it to the child's past history and can find possibly an explanation there. In the same way the experience of each child which the teacher accumulates throughout the year of his responsibility is not lost completely when the child moves into another class at the end of the year. Some of the information is on record so that the teachers who are responsible for the child in subsequent years can benefit from it. Full informative records are invaluable to the teacher who is carrying out parent interviews. The importance of liaison with parents is clearly recognised in education today although as Young and McGeeney (1968) point out the reality is often very different from the theory. But even in schools where 'parent-teacher co-operation' consists of one meeting a year at which the parents of the children who least need help come to the school to meet their children's teachers, information is invaluable. I can remember occasions on which I have waited to meet my son's teachers only to find that they know very little about him. Their vagueness, the educational clichés used, made it clear that he was little more than a name and a set of marks to them. If they had possessed adequate cumulative records and had used them properly they would have had a picture of him as a person which would have made the conference a valuable one. Again the population is becoming increasingly mobile and this means the pupils change schools frequently. Unless informative school records accompany these moves much educational momentum will be lost.

These are examples of the type of educational guidance in which all teachers are involved. There are many other occasions upon which guidance needs to be given in a child's school life. Learning problems occur: reading failure, difficulty with spelling and handwriting, number problems, failure in secondary subjects. Guidance must be given in choosing among the wide selection of subjects offered to students in big comprehensive schools and, in giving such guidance, access to records containing information about the child's ability, special aptitudes and previous attainment, is essential. Vocational guidance is seen now to be something more than an attempt, late in a child's school life, to fit him into an appropriate job. Vocational decision needs to be based on understanding achieved by the pupil throughout his schooling, understanding of himself as a person, his special aptitudes, his general ability, his personality strengths and weaknesses, understanding of the basis of choice, interests, values and needs, together with understanding of the world of work. In order to give this kind of guidance, careers teachers and counsellors need to have available comprehensive records which show the development of the pupils' vocational aspirations.

When we come to the field of personal guidance the need for records is even clearer. The information available should include details of the child's home background, his medical history and his educational history as well as records of personal development. Taken together these should add up to a comprehensive picture of the child's total development to date. With records such as these accessible to him, the teacher concerned in personal guidance is able to begin from a position of understanding and sympathy denied to those who are denied such records.

There is a final practical use to which records can be put. Teachers are continually being asked to act as referees, involving the writing of reports and testimonials on students about whom they often know very little. The possession of full cumulative records means that past pupils can be recollected as three-dimensional people rather than fading images. This is not to suggest that the content of records should be divulged to all who ask but that the pupil's cumulative record should be used by the teacher to help draw a fair and accurate picture of him as he was known to the school.

Not all teachers are convinced of the value of keeping records. Sometimes their opposition is based upon the inadequacy of present record systems and the trite and trivial information which they contain. At other times their opposition stems from a feeling that they wish to judge the child for themselves, they do not wish to be influenced by the opinion of other teachers. This is an understandable point of view, but it is based, I feel, on an underestimation of themselves as professional people and a misunderstanding of the purpose of records. On the one hand, teachers should be capable of holding a realistic view of a child, uninfluenced by other people's opinions. It is not a matter of liking or disliking a child, the teacher is as subject to these emotions as everyone else but they are irrelevant to his job as a teacher. It is a matter of understanding. 'To know all is to forgive all', and understanding arises in part from properly maintained records. On the other hand records which consist only of a series of derogatory remarks do not provide the criteria for understanding and teachers who have experienced only such records are understandably sceptical of their value.

One example of such a negative record is quoted in 'Helping Teachers to Understand Children' (Commission on Teacher Education, 1945, p. 7).

Grade 1: Frederick does not show much interest in school. Rather indifferent to work which others are doing. Is agreeable when urged to take part but *has to be urged to work.*

Grade 2: Frederick is a good pupil in school. Gives no trouble. Very quiet. Likes to read but is careless in other work.

Grade 3: Absent minded. Reads much of the time. Is not working to the best of his ability.

Grade 4: Inattentive. Reads much, otherwise shiftless and lazy.

Grade 5: A good pupil if he would be more attentive. He could do well in school if he applied himself.

Grade 6: Tends to sit quietly and do little. Consider him lazy. Does passing work in reading which he seems to enjoy. Will not put forth effort in other subjects. Have tried everything I know to get him interested. Frederick seems not to care what happens. Attends irregularly.

Grade 7: Retained. Since Frederick was unprepared for seventh-grade work he was retained. Work is some better. Still reads much. Could help with discussions but will not talk. A very queer boy . . . Moved away at Christmas.

It is a sad record and on reading it we cannot help but realise that Frederick was a boy with a problem. His problem was un-recognised by his teachers, however. Only one of his teachers saw him as a good pupil and then, apparently, because 'he gives no trouble', otherwise he was condemned as lazy, forced to repeat sixth grade and so he left that particular school with his problems still unresolved and unrecognised. The American terminology should not lead us to think that it could not happen here. It could and it does.

Another more valid reservation that teachers and others have about cumulative records lies in the question of confidentiality. It is clearly undesirable that information gathered about such private subjects as the child's family, his health or state of mind should be widely accessible. Such information should not be the subject of gossip, in or out of the staffroom. Nor should con-fidential records be accessible to non-professional people. On the other hand it must be assumed that all teachers are professional people who will use the records for the good of the child only. This assumption must be made because professional growth depends on responsibility and the opportunity to exercise responsibility and in my experience such opportunities lead people to behave in a professional manner. The same assumption must be made about student teachers carrying out supervised child studies in teaching practice. It is necessary for their professional growth that they be given access to records and that they should be expected to use them in a professional way.

The best way to ensure that school record systems are used in a manner that ensures their confidentiality is to discuss their use at staff meetings. If free discussion is allowed, all points of view will emerge and methods of ensuring the accessibility of records while preserving their confidentiality will be worked out. Some schools, for example, have found it useful to separate factual information from more personal details. The latter is kept by the member of staff concerned, housemaster, personal tutor or school counsellor and other members of staff who need this type of information are referred to this individual for it. The question of respect for the individual and the confidentiality of his personal life should be a topic discussed during teacher training. In these ways the extreme views expressed by some teachers – on the one hand it is improper to investigate any of the child's life outside the school and on the other that the *in loco parentis* role of the teacher denies the child any right to a private world of his own – can be reconciled.

The characteristics of good records

Good record systems should be comprehensive, accurate, concise and easily accessible. Let us look at these characteristics one at a time.

Records should be *comprehensive*, covering all aspects of a child's life: physical, intellectual, emotional and social. This means that positive and negative aspects need to be equally reported. A child's achievements, his hobbies and interests, his successes in sport and study are equally as important to record as his failures, the trouble he has given in class, his appearance in Juvenile Court.

What information is needed if a record is to be comprehensive? I shall list the topics which need to be covered and the details which desirably ought to be recorded.

1. Identification details

These should include all the basic information necessary to identify the child. The precise information, the order in which it is put and the manner of recording need to be decided by the particular school or system but most of the following should be included:

Full name
Date of birth (Chronological age on the 1st September of each year is a useful detail)
Sex, number of brothers and sisters and position in family. A useful way of recording this is:

B   G | G | B   (The date on which the record was made
15 13 | 11 | 9   should be clear.)

Parents' names. A way of recording whether the child is living with both or one of the parents is necessary to save trouble and embarrassment. In this section, however, details of family history should be avoided.
Parents' occupations and availability during school hours.

2. Home environment

Very often the child's address will tell you much that you need to know about the child's home and its immediate neighbourhood. Such information as to whether the home is in a rural, urban or suburban district, or on a housing estate can be helpful. Records can be kept of some of the significant details which are learned from parents or on home visits including whether a house is shared, whether the child has a room of his own for sleeping or homework and the general standard of care and maintenance.

3. Health history

It is important to know about the child's previous and present health and this information will be available in the records of the school medical officer (SMO). These should be accessible to the teacher but since some SMO's prefer to keep the cards in their own offices it may be necessary to transpose some information. This could be done under the following headings:

Illnesses and Accidents particularly those requiring hospitalisation (e.g., 'hospital hernia, aged 3 years').
Physical handicaps including hearing and eyesight (e.g., 'asthma, to age 10').
General physique including body-build, posture, muscular co-ordination, stamina and day-to-day health (e.g., 'subject to colds').

4. School history

This needs to contain a record of the child's previous schools, a record of the classes he enters in the present school and his attendance, subjects taken when choices have existed, a record of test and examination results, a note of any special achievements he has made including club and team membership, school visits, camps etc. Notes of the child's intellectual development may be appropriate here, particularly in the earlier stages of schooling when this may be expressed in teacher ratings (e.g., *Language development*, 1970):

v. advanced	advanced	average	slow	v. slow
_____	__✓__	_____	_____	_____

5. Social and emotional development

This is not so easy to document and much information on these aspects of development will already have been recorded in previous sections. For example, home environment, hospitalisation and club membership may all be important clues to social development. The results of social adjustment guides and sociometric tests will be entered in this section together with personality tests (if used) and observations made by the teacher. Behaviour problems as they have arisen will have been noted as well as the steps taken to help the child (e.g., Child Guidance from 3/75 to 8/75) and any records of parents' contribution to the understanding of the child's emotional development.

6. *Vocational development*

This may be expressed in terms of vocational aim at various stages in the child's school career together with the results of interests and attitude scales, records of works visits and interviews with careers teachers and careers officers.

To assemble this comprehensive record of a child's life may sound like a formidable task, but it must be understood that such records are built up over a long time. A form is designed which allows the information to be inserted at the appropriate stage by the appropriate person. For example a form teacher interviewing the child's parents will be able to insert relevant information following the interview. This may mean simply writing a few words, ticking a space or writing a descriptive sentence. Again the careers teacher, after setting the child an 'interest blank', will summarise the results on the form or, alternatively, include the blank in the cumulative record.

Accessibility of information

Accuracy and conciseness should be a main consideration when designing the record form. For example, if records of parent interviews are going to be kept – and much valuable information will be lost if they are not – then the framework of the record should be printed to allow this information to be entered easily. The date of the interview, the persons present and the occasion could all be provided for as well as space for extra information and expected outcomes. A sheet could be printed with appropriate headings and spaces for writing under them. This sheet could be included in a cumulative record folder or a space could be left on a record sheet for these observations to be transposed. If the record sheet is vague and the purpose of an entry unclear then this will result in in-accuracy and waste of time.

Ease of accessibility

If cumulative records are seen as information storage systems then it is important that information stored away can be recovered easily, whenever it is required and by all who are qualified to use it. Many school record systems are kept under lock and key in the headmaster's office and are virtually inaccessible to the classroom teacher. The records are locked up to ensure confidentiality but confidential records which are not used defeat their purpose. It is essential that form teachers, tutors and housemasters should be able to refer quickly and easily to records whenever they need to help individual children, interview parents, write reports or references or, in fact, add to the information store new facts as they are learned or judgments as they are made. If this is to be reconciled with the demand of confidentiality then it will be necessary to separate the data. Information which is needed generally, by any member of staff, school secretaries and professional visitors must be kept where there is easy access. Other records including psychological reports, personality ratings, interview records, case notes need to be kept separately, preferably by the staff member who is going to have most use of them.

How do the record systems in operation in schools measure up to these standards? It is difficult to say. The only thorough investigation in record systems in this country was carried out by the National Foundation for Educational Research in 1954 (Walker, 1955). At that time two-thirds of local educational authorities in England and Wales were using a cumulative record system in at least one stage (infants, juniors or secondary) and of these, two-thirds had all-age records. This meant that something like one half of all local educational authorities had record systems covering both primary and secondary age levels. The adequacy of these record systems was more difficult to assess. One quarter of the records used were record cards supplied by the NFER. These had been designed by the Foundation and came at the end of many attempts by educational leaders to launch cumulative records systems in Britain. Perhaps the first (in this as in many other educational innovations) came from Sir Cyril Burt who described in a book on delinquency how to make and keep case study records (Burt, 1925). In 1934 the Teachers' Advisory Committee of the Wiltshire Education Committee decided on a scheme of pupil records and received help from the London Institute of Education.

A number of educationists worked together to produce a report on cumulative records which included a record form. This was finally published (Hamley *et al.*, 1936). Early in the war Valentine drew up a record form to be used with evacuees (Valentine, 1940) and in 1944 Professor Hamley wrote a series of articles on the subject in one of which he described a record system (Hamley, 1944). As a result of this the newly formed National Foundation for Educational Research set up a committee which designed a cumulative record system (Fleming, 1945). The 1944 Education Act implied that cumulative record systems should be used and in 1947 Circular 151 spelt out the issue:

> Whenever a pupil ceases to attend the school and becomes a pupil at any other school . . . adequate medical and educational information concerning him shall be supplied to persons conducting that other school or place.

In spite of this, eight years later one half of all education authorities had not adopted cumulative record systems for all age levels.

The position fifteen years later is very hard to estimate. Some recent writings on school reports and records are far less professional in tone than the works I have just quoted and individual schools, particularly secondary schools, are still setting up or thinking about setting up cumulative record systems. A survey made by the head teachers of one local educational authority two years ago came to the conclusion that although 'under grant regulations we are obliged to pass on records from one school to another this is more honoured in the breach than in the observance.' They estimated that 'in terms of transferable records' the proportion of pupils served in 1968 was less than that in 1954. Their survey showed the great variation in records in use, from basic information cards to bulky personal folders. Another point made concerned the frequency with which entries in records petered out in the child's progress through the school.

Forms of record systems
Let us examine some of the forms which record systems take and estimate their value.

The dossier method
This is the method I adopted when I set up a record system in a school so that I have a certain vested interest in it. A folder is kept

for each child. Into this folder is put, in order, all relevant papers gathered about the child during his stay in the school. At the front goes an information sheet containing identification details obtained when the child first enters the school. Behind this goes test forms completed by the pupil, records of interviews, copies of reports, correspondence etc. It is comprehensive but often fails to meet the other criteria of conciseness and accessibility. The sheer bulk is a weakness in itself, in terms of storage space and difficulty of locking, and it may also prove difficult to find precise information at a glance. Another serious criticism, and this is made by the head teachers I have mentioned above, is that mixing routine and confidential matters may make the latter too widely accessible. In spite of this I feel that there is a place for cumulative personal files of this kind if a counsellor or some other interested and knowledgeable person is prepared to maintain them or, rather, supervise their maintenance.

A variation of the dossier is the loose-leaf folder in which are kept annual reports rather like a comprehensive collection of personal documents.

Neither of these methods work very well unless they are accompanied by a brief cumulative summary which may be used for day-to-day reference and which avoids the over-accessibility of confidential material.

Folded cards
In this form the cumulative summary comes as a manilla folder, usually quarto in size, in which the most important of separate documents, e.g., Psychologist's Reports may be kept. The cover itself is printed so that the cumulative summary can be entered on it. This kind of record is easily stored and is accessible for quick reference. It can never be as comprehensive as the dossier.

Unfolded cards
Such records are usually stiff cards of varying sizes and different colours – often pink for girls and blue for boys. Some authorities use a series of cards to cover different stages of education. This system allows for easy storage and reference but there is no provision for retaining other relevant documents and there is limited space for entries which must of necessity be stylised, and are therefore perhaps not very informative.

Book records
Another method is to use stiff-covered books containing pages arranged either chronologically or according to different developmental areas. Some schools add an envelope to the back cover to contain important documents. The book record is bulky, difficult to store and rather intimidating. It has the disadvantage of keeping all information, confidential and otherwise, in one package which cannot be divided.

Examples of record systems
It may be useful to have a look at some record systems which have been set up in different circumstances. This may give readers the opportunity to compare with arrangements in their own schools and evaluate their suitability.

Counsellor records
A group of school counsellors working in a local authority set up a working-party to consider a record system for their schools. Their record is a double-page foolscap sheet. Page 1 has spaces for identification details, a first-year photograph and a fourth-year photograph, family details, medical details, test records, special interests, attendance and previous schools. Page 2 is arranged for personality assessment by the staff. Characteristics such as reliability, co-operation and personal drive are assessed on a five-point scale, such as:

Leadership: constantly leads; usually leads; occasionally leads; seldom leads; never leads.

Place is made, economically, for these assessments over five years although it is difficult to see how successive assessors could avoid being influenced by previous assessments. Space at the bottom of the page is left for rather freer comments. Page 3 is kept for a record of attainment and progress by subject and year, followed by a record of courses outside school and work experience. Page 4 has spaces for standardised test scores, activities, representation, interests, etc. An interesting addition is for follow-up information on employment and further education with a final space for subsequent history.

This record booklet is comprehensive and concise, concentrates upon positive aspects and is suitable for personal, educational and vocational guidance as well as being useful for research purpose. It has the disadvantage of including all material on one form which restricts its usefulness for quick reference by the staff in general and it does not easily adapt to hold incidental documents referring to individual pupils. What is most important, however, is that it meets the needs of those who are going to be using it most frequently and this is the most important single criterion.

Tutor records

Another record system which commends itself to me arose out of a re-organisation of the pastoral care in Tolgus County Secondary School. The staff decided that their needs in pastoral care would be met best by a family tutor system in which each child is attached to a tutor on entering school and stays with that tutor throughout his school life. A stable staff allows this system to work and thus ensures a continuity of concern for the child. It was decided that information was needed at two levels. The first is that of subject teacher and school secretary who may need to refer quickly to a child's records. For this purpose a school card was evolved on which is maintained a summary of basic information about the child. This card is maintained by the tutor and is kept in the general office. In addition to this the tutor keeps his own card which contains more detailed information of the confidential kind. Periodically information is transferred from the tutor's card to the school card to keep it up to date. Personal documents relating to the pupil, school reports, notes from parents, notes about clothing allowances etc. are filed with his primary school record card in a large envelope in the headmaster's room.

The headmaster in making an assessment of the system evolved in his school says that in general it works in the way it was intended and that no serious amendments are contemplated. He has two reservations about its use. The first is that 'some tutors, in their enthusiasm to complete their paper work, regard the compilation of the record card as a first duty'. The view of the staff in general is that 'it comes very much second to the establishment of the right personal relationship' and 'information should be obtained informally where possible rather than by formal interview or questioning'. The second reservation is that the records are deficient on the educational side as compared with the welfare side. He suggests that a programme of testing would help to make up this deficiency.

Although these records may be criticised in detail it is a flexible and reasonably comprehensive system which takes full account of the principle of confidentiality. What is most important is that this system developed out of the expressed needs of the school, was designed by the members of staff themselves and is maintained by each one of them as family tutor.

An experimental 'all through' record system
In Gloucestershire an experiment has begun into the maintenance of cumulative records from pre-school onwards. The records are begun when the child first enters nursery school or pre-school play group. At this time a questionnaire, based on Gesell's longitudinal studies of child development, is given to the child's mother. This questionnaire is supplemented by a report from the health visitor. The mother's responses are then summarised on the second page of the Cumulative Summary folder, the Pre-primary Profile as the questionnaire to the mother is called, is kept in the folder along with the health visitor's report. In this way a cumulative record begins. The teacher makes a further assessment of the child at a later stage using the same scale as the mother and this is also recorded on the Cumulative Summary. Professional workers are often unwilling to trust mothers to be strictly objective about their own children but one person who has worked closely with the mothers of severely handicapped children thinks differently, '. . . we have found mothers to be careful and sound observers of their own children and they are, besides, absolutely stark realists. The trouble is that hardly anybody listens to mothers.' (Doman, 1964).

The profile includes sections on self-care, classroom management, skill development, language development, previous experience and 'notes to my child's teacher'. Space is kept for records of parent-teacher conferences and for notes on development. These records are being kept under controlled conditions so that the value of information gathered so early can be estimated.

Making use of cumulative records in child study
I have described types of cumulative record systems which may be found in schools today so that those who are studying children may be able to find their way around them, or, where adequate records do not exist, help to establish them.

There are three main uses to which records can be put in child study. The first and simplest is to find out, or check, precise bits of information, date of birth, name of junior school, marks at 'O' level. The second is to check some particular hypothesis which arises from observations of the child's behaviour. For example, he is observed to be clumsy in his movements. There are a number of possible explanations of this behaviour and subsequent observation may decide which applies here. The record card may help in checking these out. Perhaps his clumsiness is the result of physical handicap of a minor kind, some slight disturbance of the motor area of the brain, poor eyesight, crossed laterality. Perhaps it is a developmental factor, poor motor co-ordination following rapid body growth or the self-consciousness which often accompanies such growth. Perhaps it is the result of more permanent personality factors, crippling shyness or lack of self-confidence.

The record card will help his teacher to check these possibilities. Does his medical card have any record of motor or perceptual weakness or any accident which may have caused damage? Do records of height and weight give any evidence of a rapid growth spurt? Has he been described as shy or self-conscious or in similar terms? Have such comments been constant throughout school or has there been a recent change? Do standardised tests or exam results show any pattern which may indicate motor or perceptual difficulties?

The third way in which record cards can contribute to child study is in writing case histories. The case worker can assemble the information on record into a coherent account of the subject's past life. What is important in this process is that, where gaps in knowledge exist, these should be frankly acknowledged rather than the gaps bridged by speculation. When a case history written up from records is supplemented by retrospective descriptions of parents, teachers and other colleagues it can be a valuable aid in understanding the child.

4

The Habitat of the Child

The child we are studying does not exist in a vacuum, nor is he simply and solely a 'school child'. He lives in an environment which is continually affecting him, which may extend geographically far beyond the neighbourhood of the school, almost certainly extends sociologically to scores of individuals outside the school and psychologically takes into account his own special way of viewing the world. It is our understanding, however imperfect, of this unique world which each child inhabits that enables us to make sense of our observations of the child's behaviour. Studying behaviour within its natural habit is called ecology and, when children are studied systematically in their environment of school, home and neighbourhood we have an ecological study of behaviour. Such a study produced *Midwest* (Barker and Wright, 1955), one important source of information about children's behaviour, and, similarly, whenever we are interested in studying an individual child, we must take time to try to understand his habitat.

Some of this habitat should already be known. The school is a familiar part of the teacher's habitat but, perhaps because of its very familiarity, needs to be studied afresh and looked at from the child's point of view. Nowhere is this done more effectively than in Elizabeth Richardson's *The Environment of Learning* (1967). In this book the effects of relationships, groupings, success and failure, emotional expression, leadership and control as well as the physical setting of the school itself upon school children are discussed. It is in this sense that the term 'psychological habitat' is used, since what is most important in a child study is not a description of the geography of the environment but some attempt to convey the way in which the child perceives this environment. It is impossible for us to get a true 'child's eye view of the world', our years of experience prevent us from seeing it this way again. Only in complete empathy with the child as he struggles to express his feelings about his world can we come close to this understanding, although it is true that literature can sometimes succeed in giving us entry into the child's world. Books like *Catcher in the Rye*, *Greengage Summer*, *Bevis*, *Kes* and many other novels feel like authentic windows into the psychological habitat of the child or the adolescent.

Through a process of sensitisation gained by reading literature of this kind, through our moments of empathy with a child, through our careful observation of the effects of the environment upon those whom we are studying we can come close to understanding their psychological habitat. Wright (1967) discusses the use of a literary form for conceptualising this habitat, 'bridging the gap between behaviour and non-psychological habitat with the wisdom of commonsense and art in the manner of the novelist or the biographer' (p. 31), and decides that, while subjective, this method is no more misleading than reporting so-called objective conditions like social class, race or climate which mean different things to different children. Statements of conditions in the child's habitat like 'loneliness', 'over-indulgence', 'boredom' should be conceptualised 'with enough precision that they can be related to behaviour in an orderly way' (p. 31). In other words our descriptions of the child's life space should not be limited to checkable facts like name of district, number of bedrooms in house, employment of father, but should contain estimates of family climate, character of the neighbourhood and the child's view of both. Such details should be capable of verification in that the evidence for them is contained within our observation.

Having said this it is necessary to look at the environmental conditions which affect the behaviour of the child. There are numerous studies of environmental influences on development but the one which seems to be most relevant to the purpose, concerned, as it is, with school-age children in England and Wales in the last decade, is *Born and Bred Unequal* (Taylor and Ayres, 1969). This survey, described as educational ecology, looks at the educational opportunity available to children and shows the disparity which exists from one region to another. The authors list the main factors in Britain which affect educational opportunity:

1. The level of health, physical and mental, enjoyed by parents and children.
2. The standard of social services; included among these are housing, medical and welfare services.
3. The standard of local prosperity measured in terms of (*a*) personal incomes and (*b*) income available to the local authority.

4. Local opportunities for, and variety of, employment both for school leavers and adults.
5. Population dynamics, i.e., increase or decrease in population, migration, density of population, social class structure and fertility.
6. The prevailing level of literacy among parents, relatives, employees and local leaders. (Taylor and Ayres, 1969, pp. 3, 4.)

These six points make a useful check-list for considering the effect of the environment upon local educational opportunities. They can help in drawing up a comprehensive inventory of the environmental factors operating on the individual child. These factors I have listed in the order in which they affect the child (see Figure 3) and I have dealt with them in more detail in the following pages:

The home
Even for the adolescent the home remains the most significant part of his habitat, for the young child it is all important. We should

FIGURE 3. THE EXPANDING HABITAT OF THE CHILD

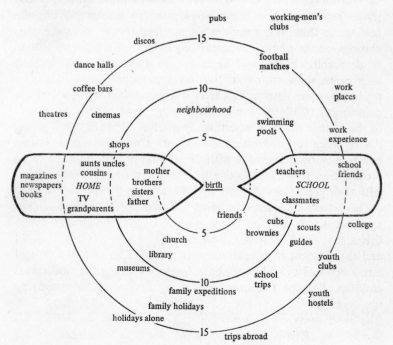

know what kind of a dwelling he lives in – a flat, a semi-detached or a terraced house for example, what kind of condition it is in – dilapidated, neglected or cared for. We should know what facilities exist in the house; how many bedrooms, whether the subject has to share, what opportunities for homework exist, what bathing and washing facilities exist (in England and Wales in 1961 15 per cent of homes were without a fixed bath and 16 per cent had no inside lavatory). We should know what play space there is, what books, TV, radio, musical instruments are available. We should have some idea of the food habits in the house, nutrition level, times of meals. Most of all we need to know something of the atmosphere of the household. How do the parents feel towards each other and their children? How much love, protection, security, for example, do the children receive? What approach do the parents have towards bringing up children? We know, for example, that democratic, rejecting and indulgent parents tend to have children with different behaviour characteristics (Baldwin, Kalhorn and Breeze, 1945). Baldwin and his associates compared nursery school behaviour with the observed behaviour of parents at home. In another study by Watson (1957, see Jersild, 1969) children from strict homes and those from permissive homes were rated by teachers. While the findings in these two enquiries do not lead to any sweeping conclusions, on the whole it appears likely that children from permissive or democratic homes will be more active in their relations with their peers, show more initiative, produce more creative ideas and tend to be more enterprising, freer to express their feelings and less conforming. Children subjected to more rigid control are likely to be restricted into asserting themselves through playfulness, disobedience or aggressive behaviour. Children whose homes combine warm acceptance with democratic procedures tend to be most active, free and effective in asserting themselves in relations with their peers (Jersild, 1969, pp. 229–30).

One interesting research studied 'a day at home', asking children such questions as 'Who is the one who cooks breakfast?' 'Who drives the car?' This gave the researcher a picture of the household and the different roles each member played. This is, however, still a research tool and it has not been developed for studying individual children. Perhaps the most interesting instrument for studying family relationships is the Bene-Anthony Family Relations Test. The child posts cards describing various relationships within his family (like 'This is the person in the family father makes too big

THE FAMILY RELATIONS TEST

a fuss about') into a number of cardboard figures representing 'Mum', 'Dad', 'Our Bill', etc. (see plate 1 on p. 54 f). The results are summarised into these categories:

Outgoing positive mild responses ⎫
Outgoing positive strong responses ⎪
Outgoing negative mild responses ⎪
Outgoing negative strong responses ⎬ for each member of the
Incoming positive mild responses ⎪ family.
Incoming positive strong responses ⎪
Incoming negative mild responses ⎪
Incoming negative strong responses ⎭

This test is often used by educational psychologists and the results can give us insight into a child's feelings about his family; it is not a suitable test for use outside a clinic, however (Bene and Anthony, 1957).

Information about the home circumstances must be extended backwards to discover occasions when the child has been deprived of care. A wealth of evidence points to the effect of maternal deprivation on future behaviour and the development of personality and it is crucial to know of times, particularly in the first three or four years of a child's life, when the mother or the child have been hospitalised, or otherwise separated, if we are to understand the child. Rejection or neglect which may produce similar effects are less easy to discover. Paternal separation, whether complete as in fatherless families, or partial as when father is frequently away, is more equivocal in its effects but should be documented. Information about the family should include the number of siblings, their birth order, their sex and age and the attitudes which exist between them, the other people living in the family home and their relationship to each other.

The school
The school occupies the second most important place in the child's habitat. It might seem unnecessary for teachers to be reminded of this or to suggest that they need to study that part of the child's environment which they know so well. It is probably for this reason of familiarity, however, that it is necessary for teachers to study 'the environment of learning', to look at the school as a psychological habitat. To do this it is necessary to see as far as is possible what goes on in school through the eyes of a child. Research into

the sociology of the school can help to alert us to those educational variables which are most crucial; thorough analysis of the school as an organisation, e.g., 'a systems approach', can give us new insight into the way in which the society of the school functions, but these approaches can only supplement and not completely replace a sensitive attempt to put oneself into the place of the child.

The buildings of the school and their lay-out, its approaches and its appearance inside all affect the pupils' feelings about it and his adjustment to it. His reception when he first arrives at the school from nursery school, infant school or primary school, and the extent to which he is made to feel comfortable and 'at home' is likely to have a lasting effect upon his attitudes. This transition continues to be important even when it is transition from school to university and at one school I know into which pupils enter at 14+ it was found that difficulties of transition from the Junior High School were so great as to seriously affect the school progress of a substantial number of the pupils. Now they have taken steps, including the use of sociometric tests, for class placement, to reduce the sense of loneliness and strangeness experienced by the new pupils.

It is not only the transition from one school to another that is important to children but transition from class to class and even their daily transition from home to school. Some schools make this difficult for pupils with red tape, formality and ceremony to start the day; others begin gently with form groups and a period of preparation and calm.

School is essentially a series of group experiences for children and, of all the skills needed by teachers, skill at handling groups, is the most necessary. This book is not the place to teach such skills but some of the characteristics of groups can be pointed out so that the implications of school groupings can be considered in a child study. One of the most important features of a group is its self-image. A group functions according to the expectations it has of itself – anyone who has taken part in encounter or sensitivity groups is aware of this – and a group will establish these expectations from all kinds of cues which it receives from its environment. Expectations for streamed classes are clearly set out in academic terms and for the bottom stream there is little that the school appears to have to offer them. The result, as Hargreaves (1967) has pointed out, is that children in bottom streams may develop a negative self-image and then a 'delinquescent sub-group' forms.

Even where the boundary lines between groups are blurred, the children in the groups can pick up from their teachers or from other children feed-back about what is expected of them and they will function according to these expectations. It is not even necessary for these expectations to be consciously expressed. I received a dramatic demonstration of this in a new comprehensive school in which I was school counsellor. All the classes were purposely made up in such a way that each one was as nearly identical to the other in the ratio of sex, age, distribution of intelligence and distribution through feeder schools as I could make it. They differed in only one important respect – they were numbered from 1–6. This was sufficient, however, and Form Six soon established itself as the most troublesome and the least co-operative. The selective school they would normally have gone to before the opening of the comprehensive school was streamed and Form Six in that school would have been the bottom form. Our Form Six were reacting, not to our expectations, but their own expectations of what was implied by the label they were given. We had to carry out a big rehabilitation job on Form Six before it saw itself as equal to Forms One to Five. Experimental studies have demonstrated the effect of teacher expectations on pupil performances (Rosenthal and Jacobson, 1968; Martin, 1973) so that my experience was not an isolated one.

This is just one way in which school organisation can affect the individual child. Others that need to be studied will be considered more briefly.

The general and specific aims of the school

Schools very rarely state their aims in any systematic way or consider them very carefully, and when such aims are stated they are usually in terms which defy evaluation. There is no doubt about it, however, that the way in which a school sees its objectives is going to affect the school as a psychological habitat and, when making a child study, some attempt should be made to ascertain these objectives. Objectives may be made explicit or they may remain implicit. The headmaster may state the aims publicly on Speech Night or they may be implied by the organisation of the school. One head may see his school as a 'guidance community' (Rowe, 1971), another as a machine for producing university scholarships. Someone making a child study cannot set about the kind of thorough investigation into the general and specific aims of a school which a full understanding demands but, by directing his attention to other aspects of the school, he may arrive at an answer to this question too.

The quality of pastoral care within the school

Schools vary considerably in the importance they give to their caring role and in the ways in which they institutionalise it. At one extreme are those schools where every pupil belongs to a tutorial group with a tutor who understands and accepts his responsibilities to them. In one such school tutorial groups are themselves grouped into houses with a housemaster who sees his job essentially as a guidance one. Alongside this basic pastoral care organisation there is a headmaster and two deputies who are trained in guidance, a full-time trained counsellor and a careers teacher. Perhaps the attitude to pastoral care in this school is best summarised by the headmaster writing about the counsellor's job:

> He is fundamentally a living symbol and a practical demonstration of the school's continuing concern with every individual pupil as an individual. We all feel this concern, but the counsellor is unique in that his job involves giving it priority in every case. (Thompson, 1970, p. lxix).

At the other extreme are schools we all know where no one cares except for examination results or schools like those described by Clegg and Megson (1968, p. 50).

> An insensitive school is amongst other things one in which those who are undistinguished intellectually count for little, those who are weak are not helped over their weaknesses, and those who make trouble are kept down by superior force and little is done to find the root cause of their troublesomeness.

Under this heading we should consider not only the attitude of teachers towards children, but their attitude towards each other, the extent to which they co-operate and support each other, the stability of staffing and the extent to which teachers live locally. Another consideration is the school's attitude towards parents. The importance of parent-school co-operation has been stressed many times (e.g., Jackson and Marsden, 1962; Young and McGeeney, 1965; McGeeney, 1969) and schools cover the spectrum from 'Parents keep out' to 'Parents are welcome'. Where parent-teacher co-operation is good, attitudes towards school and work are likely to be good. Where there is little or no liaison with parents, the school is likely to be seen as an alien place, one to be resisted. It is also necessary to understand the extent to which the school has gone into the community in other ways, through community action, local studies, co-operation with the youth service. The extent to which the school has useful liaison with other helping agencies, educational welfare, child guidance, social services and the youth employment service should be noted as another indication of its concern for child welfare.

Approach to curriculum and teaching method

Another variable to be taken into account when considering the school as a psychological habitat for a child is the kind of learning environment it provides. Approaches to curriculum and methods of teaching can vary from extremely traditional to extremely progressive. The effects of teaching procedure upon the current attitudes and future personality of pupils is insufficiently documented but it is clearly germane to the understanding of the child's habitat that the methods used in a particular school should be studied. Again there is need here to look at such aspects of the school as its emphasis upon games and physical education, the types of extracurricular activities it encourages and the number and variety of school trips and expeditions.

Expansion of the child's environment

The home and the school dominate the young child's environment but it gradually expands with the child's increasing mobility. The environment for some children is very restricted. Slum children may have the run of their local streets but never go to the city centre or out into the country. Country children, on the other hand, may know their local fields and woods but never go alone into the town. Some children may travel widely with their parents but have no independence. Others seem to want to restrict their habitat to the home, the TV set, their books and toys, the garden. For most adolescents there is a great expansion of their environment at sixteen or thereabouts. They begin to use the local community for their leisure and move out of the youth clubs – a logical extension of school – into discothèques, dance halls, concert halls and cinemas, coffee-bars and pubs. They begin to move about the countryside, to away matches and pop concerts, in search of summer jobs or visiting friends, on camping and hostelling trips.

It is important to discover the extent of a subject's habitat and the confidence with which he moves about that habitat. It is also important to understand something of the attitudes and values of the people in this wider environment. Each local district has its own special view of life and the individual cannot help but be influenced by this. So the neighbourhood needs to be studied from a sociological and a social psychological point of view. What are the social class groupings in the district, the political, economic and religious attitudes? What kind of a community is it, warm and friendly, cool and reserved or embittered and angry? For the extreme effect of a community on children look at what is happening to the children of Northern Ireland.

The resources of the community as they contribute to the child's habitat are also important for our understanding. Medical and social services vary considerably from district to district, as do libraries and museums, swimming pools and sports facilities. Some children live in a cultural and social vacuum; others live in exciting and interesting places. In general the wealth that a community has to spend upon its needs decreases as we move northwards and westwards up the country and, as income decreases, so need for expenditure increases.

To study the habitat of our child in the detail I have described must seem an impossible task. In fact, much of the factual material will already be known and can be compressed into a very brief summary. What are more important and what takes longer to document than facts are the kinds of descriptions which breathe life into these facts and help us to see the habitat as it affects the child we are studying.

5

Anecdotal Records

In a previous chapter we surveyed the whole field of observation and measurement. Informal observation was seen to be the basis of all other more sophisticated techniques and to have great value in itself. In fact all teachers are using informal observation continuously. They are observing the children in their classes, their school work, their behaviour with their class-mates and their changes in moods, their gestures and their facial expressions. They make observations of the pupil's attainment such as:

'How well Jane read that page.'
'Jim made six mistakes in his arithmetic today.'
'Mary's spelling is still very weak.'
'Tom answered that question well.'

They will observe the child's day-by-day behaviour, his interactions with other pupils, his reaction to the teacher and other members of staff in such terms as:

'John fidgets continually.'
'Brenda is always late.'
'Bob has been in a fight again.'
'Brian looks unhappy.'
'Sally was cheeky to the canteen lady again.'

The observant teacher will seek to see in the child's posture, gait, gestures and other non-verbal behaviour as well as in his words, indications of his personality. Very often these observations will not be verbalised but, if they were, they would take such form as:

'Fiona still hasn't any friends.'
'Bill is scowling again.'
'Frank is full of beans today.'
'Mary is still making catty remarks.'

This kind of observation is usually unsystematic. The teacher does not plan it in any particular way and does not record it. Frequently he is not really aware of having made the observation although it may affect his future behaviour or his attitude towards a particular child. Sometimes the teacher will carry out deliberate observations making some remark to himself as, 'I must look out for John's reaction next time I read poetry. He seemed to be in a trance last time.' Sometimes he will make records of a child's behaviour although usually this will be in the form of test results or remarks on report forms.

There is a need, as I see it, for this type of informal everyday observation to be refined in such a way as to make it both more reliable and more productive. This means that the teacher has to be helped to observe in a way which avoids observer bias and to record these observations systematically. The method to be described in this chapter is the keeping of anecdotal records. This is a way in which the teacher can put down observations made in the classroom, playground or canteen in a way which enables the records to be used subsequently to check hypotheses made about the children concerned.

The point needs to be made that such informal observation is valuable. Children are giving clues continually to their inner life in their everyday behaviour. Jane will say pettishly, 'I don't want to be in the play.' By itself this remark is not very informative about Jane. Taken in conjunction with a series of observations of Jane it may help to confirm or disprove the picture of Jane as a person which the teacher is gaining. If the teacher is looking for an explanation of some particular problem behaviour this remark may help him with a solution. It does not have to be written down to have this effect, informally observed by the teacher it may still help him to understand Jane's problem but the recording of incidents in the classroom will enable the recollection of these incidents away from the heat of the moment. Comparisons can be made with other records and balanced conclusions reached.

Study of children in their natural settings is most valuable. It has already been stressed that observation without control of the situation, although posing problems of objectivity and reliability, does not so alter the behaviour in the process of observation as to render it inapplicable to practical situations. This, of course, is the drawback to observation in which the situation is controlled. Herbert Wright discussing the observation of children in the American town of Midwest makes the point that most research findings we have on children's behaviour come from laboratory settings:

Psychologists have not often ventured as scientists into naturally occurring environments. They have not often sought to record and examine the characteristics and the behavioural effects of exterior conditions that nature and society create. In short . . . psychology lacks a developed ecology of human behaviour. (Wright, 1967, p. 2.)

We have already gone into the question of how to describe the social environment in which the child is behaving; we now need to be able to look at that behaviour. The methods which were used by Wright and his colleagues to describe the children of Midwest have been used by teachers in the classroom to improve their understanding of children in general and of individual children with problems. At the Institute for Child Study of the University of Maryland, children were studied by their own teachers who kept records of their behaviour and discussed it with colleagues in case conferences. One of the principal sources of case material was the anecdotal record. Strang and Morris (1964) say that anecdotal records, which they define as 'descriptive, dated accounts of pupils' behaviour', have several values:

They centre a teacher's attention on individual pupils. They also give him insight into an individual's attitudes and behaviour, reveal patterns or trends and call attention to needs. Interestingly enough, when teachers become involved in this process they derive more personal satisfaction from their teaching. (pp. 31–2).

No special equipment or training is needed for teachers to write anecdotal records although discussion of the results with interested colleagues helps to improve the quality. All that is needed is that the teacher takes the time and trouble to write down records of children's behaviour observed around the school.

A loose-leaf notebook is recommended so that the records can build up into a cumulative chronicle of the child or children being studied. Each anecdote should give full identification details so that the teacher looking back on the record will know the condition under which the observation took place. These details will include the time, day and date of the incident, the place in which it was recorded and the situation in which it took place. This means that all those significantly present need to be noted or in other words a record should be kept of all those who participate actively in the incident.

An example of the identification details of a typical record would be:

10.15. Wed. 27 June. corridor outside form-room.
Jane is talking loudly to Christine and Carol, the rest of the form are already seated in the form room. . . .

It is important to record the time since the behaviour recorded may be affected by the time of day, e.g., a child on a treatment of drugs will behave differently at different times, changes in metabolism may occur before and after meals, closeness in time to home may affect behaviour and the time will be a clue to other circumstances. It is important to record the date for the same kind of considerations and it is inconvenient to have to look back to a calendar to find the day on which the behaviour took place. The location must be noted because it is important to have a clear idea of the setting and the 'significant others' in the incident need to be established.

Having set the scene it is important for the observer to record the incident as fully and clearly as possible. It may be practicable for the teacher to make some brief notes as the incident is taking place or soon after. For this reason the notebook needs to be kept in a convenient place. Mostly it will be necessary to write up anecdotes as they are recollected after the lesson or even at the end of the day. This means that some rules must be followed if the records are going to have the qualities of objectivity and reliability which are necessary for them to be generally useful. The first rule for recording is that the record should be complete, i.e., it should describe 'the actions of the child, the reactions of the other people involved, and the response of the child to these reactions.' (Prescott, 1957, p. 153).

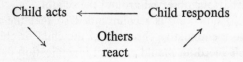

A circular process is involved since the child's actions are a response to the reaction of others to his actions. In order to understand those actions it is necessary to record other people's responses. This entails a suspension of judgment since the teacher needs to record without making any immediate interpretation of the behaviour. This is not an easy skill for teachers to develop. Traditionally the teacher's task in the classroom has been seen as a matter of evaluating the child's behaviour immediately and then taking action in order to control it. The teaching situation seems to demand this kind of reaction – when teachers see a child making a mistake in his work they correct it immediately. The same sort of rapid evaluation and immediate correction characterises their manner of dealing with social or emotional behaviour.

'Stop talking to your neighbour and get on with your work.'
'Don't pull faces as you work.'
'There's no need to bite your nails all the time.'
'You're squinting at the blackboard – come nearer to the front.'

In child study there is a need to record the behaviour observed without making inferences about its wider significance. This is not to suggest that the teacher-observer can never become involved in behaviour in the classroom – this would defeat the object of naturalistic observation – but it is to ask the teacher to separate out the interpretation from the recording.

Prescott says emphatically that the anecdote should not contain interpretations but Wright more carefully distinguishes the level of interpretation. If all inferential material was excluded, he suggests, the function of the observer as a sort of psychological camera would be lost. How could one estimate the meaning of 'John throwing a ball towards him' unless the observer records the inference he made at the time that the ball was thrown *to* him and not *at* him? What is necessary is to draw a line between the immediate inferences made about observed behaviour and the interpretation or theorising which follows.

The immediate inferences should be included in the record along with as many of the cues which led to those inferences as the observer can remember. On the other hand interpretation should be excluded or written up separately. The recording of cues or 'mood-cues' as Prescott calls them, is essential if the observer is to become aware of the basis of his inferences.

Let us continue with the anecdotal record begun above:

Jane, tossing her head, 'You had a party and you didn't ask me. That's what it boils down to.' She was shaking with anger. The other two looked at each other for support. 'We didn't think you would be able to come,' said Carol apologetically. 'You could have asked me,' said Jane, 'but you didn't. You were

C

sneaky and secretive.' Her voice was very loud. Christine was red in the face and rather inarticulate. 'You always make such a fuss. That's why we didn't ask.' 'Fuss, now she talks about a fuss. Just now you thought I wouldn't be able to come.' They became aware of my presence. Jane tossed her head again. Christine moved up to her and put her hand on Jane's shoulder. She pushed it aside and walked with back held straight and lips together into the classroom. Carol and Christine followed sheepishly behind as I closed the door.

There are numerous mood cues here and several inferences. Let us list the mood cues:

Tossing her head	red in the face	pushed it aside
shaking *with anger*	rather inarticulate	back held straight
for support	tossed her head	lips together
apologetically	put her hand on	*sheepishly*
very loud	Jane's shoulder	
	tossed her head	

These are words or phrases which describe behaviour, mostly non-verbal behaviour, which give clues to the mood of the subject. Inferences made about the mood which are themselves based on verbal or non-verbal cues are *in italics*. An adverb like 'sheepishly' is an inference made about the mood of Carol and Christine. The behaviour which led to this inference could not be recorded by the teacher because it was made up of 'subliminal' cues. These are perceived below the level of conscious awareness – the posture of the girls, the way in which they looked at their class-mates, their manner of walking. Again the phrase 'with anger' is an inference made about Jane's emotional state, an inference which is based on a number of cues including the one stated here, 'shaking'. Others might have been the tone of Jane's voice, her posture, her facial expression.

The anecdote written above is not intended as a literary effort but indicated the teacher's observation and the inferences which she drew at that time about the behaviour of the three girls. There is nothing to stop the teacher adding an interpretation of this incident based on wider knowledge of those involved, for example she could have concluded:

This outburst by Jane is typical of her present attitude towards her friends. She is very touchy and quickly becomes abusive.

It would be clear however that this was her own interpretation based on observation of previous incidents. On the other hand the detail recorded was such as to make alternative interpretation possible if later evidence should be gathered.

What is important then is that the observer learns to recognise the cues which lead to the inferences he draws about a child's behaviour. When he has recorded these cues, he has some check on the accuracy of his observation and upon the inferences he has drawn. Mood-cues are words and phrases which describe in objective terms the outward manifestation of the emotional states of of those observed. As I have suggested in addition to those cues of which the observer is aware there are many others which are below the threshold of his conscious awareness but which, none the less, have influenced the observer in his judgments. If we describe a child's behaviour as 'sulky' we usually have good reason for it, but we may not be able to distinguish the information which has led us to this description. The expression on the child's face, his posture, his gestures as well as the words he spoke all help us to decide what kind of behaviour we are observing. The teacher making anecdotal records will note down those gestures and facial expressions which he recognises as significant and by re-reading his notes and discussing them with colleagues will evaluate his own perception and sharpen it in future observations.

Wherever possible the actual words used by the children involved should be quoted. Direct speech is more objective than reported speech because it avoids some of the intermediary process of interpretation. It is, however, often difficult to recall the actual words used and our perception of what we have heard may distort our recollection. In other words what we think we have heard is often what fits in with our interpretation of the whole incident. This qualification must be kept in mind when assessing the objectivity of direct quotations in an anecdotal record. On the other hand recalling the actual words spoken becomes easier with practice and the record itself is more valuable for containing direct quotations even if some of them should be somewhat distorted. The degree of distortion is likely to be smaller than in reported speech.

The words spoken by other people in the incident should also be reported when this is practicable. They are often important in gaining a full picture of the subject; for example in the anecdote we have just reported, Christine says, 'You always make such a fuss'. It would have been quite easy to have left this remark out of our record. We could have reported that Jane had a quarrel with Carol and Christine because they had not invited her to their party without quoting the words used in the argument. This in itself would have been a valuable record but it would have omitted many useful observations such as the one just mentioned. Christine gives as a reason for not inviting Jane that she always makes a fuss. We have observed her actually making a fuss so that we have recorded two correlating pieces of evidence. Future observations whether in the form of anecdotal records or test results may confirm or disprove our view of Jane.

Let me summarise what is involved in writing an anecdotal record:

1. An incident in which the child being studied is involved is observed in the classroom or elsewhere in the school.
2. At the earliest opportunity the teacher writes down a description of the incident in a systematic way.
3. The record begins with identification details which should include a description of the setting, i.e. the time, date, place and situation in which the action occurred. The significant participants in the incident should also be made clear.
4. The observer records the incident in full, following it through to a point which forms a natural ending.
5. The observer describes the actions of the child and the reactions of others to these actions. Then the response of the child to the reactions of others is reported.
6. Conversation is reported wherever possible in direct speech.
7. The observer uses mood-cues, i.e., words describing the posture, gestures and facial expressions of those observed which give clues to the emotions of the participants.

Anecdotal records vary greatly in length and in the time taken in writing them. Prescott (1957) reports that at the Institute for Child Study the average time taken over an anecdote was eight minutes. Few took as long as fifteen minutes. This means that most anecdotes will need to be written up after school although notes can be taken more immediately. Four or five anecdotes a week are suggested as the basis of an intensive study of one child. When these are analysed and evaluated in a study group the observer develops skill in this method of child study.

Although the classroom provides the most useful situation in which to observe and record anecdotes the teacher-observer will find opportunities in the hall, corridor, canteen, cloakroom, as well as during specialist activities in gym and workshop and on trips and school visits.

The question of what anecdotes to write up is often a bothering one. If the child being observed is an extrovert, involving himself continuously with his class-mates, then it will not be difficult to find dramatic incidents to describe. If the child is an introvert, with little social interaction, then the teacher may report, 'I cannot write up an anecdotal record because he never does anything.' The best thing to do in these circumstances is to determine to write a record of the child's behaviour at a certain time. This crude sort of time-sampling will ensure that the child's characteristic behaviour is reported and will show that in fact the child is 'doing something' all the time. It is important that the teacher writing up anecdotal records does not restrict himself to dramatic events but does try to make his records over a cross-section of the child's day. In this way the teacher will avoid building up for himself a distorted picture of the child.

The anecdotal record is a relatively simple and easily organised technique of observation, but it has many advantages over the more formal methods. It is important to have a description of the child's life style, that is the characteristic way in which he behaves. The anecdotal record with its emphasis on day by day behaviour is more likely to give this kind of information than other methods of child study. In studying disturbed or maladjusted children in particular, the anecdotal record provides an antidote to other reports and measures which emphasise the child's abnormality and thus helps to give a balanced picture. The anecdotal record also helps us to see the behaviour of children through their own eyes. The direct quotations in particular help us to put ourselves in the position of the child and to see the incident through his eyes. The report of mood-cues is a valuable step in the direction of the empathy necessary if we are to be of help to the child.

The accumulation of anecdotal records and the evidence of recurring patterns of behaviour help us to identify the developmental tasks which face the child at the time of study. Jane's tendency to 'make a fuss', if confirmed by further study, might indicate that she is having difficulty in mastering the vital developmental tasks of controlling emotional reaction (she is tending to over-react) and of coping with peer group relations. If this is confirmed then Jane may need help with these tasks. Counselling may prove to be the most appropriate help for her since it will help her to identify her problem for herself and to expose alternative ways of coping with the situations in which she finds herself.

Another important outcome of the keeping of anecdotal records is the insight it can give the teacher into his own handling of the child. By re-reading the records he has kept, and noting his own reaction to the child's behaviour, his intervention into the class-room situation can be evaluated in a way that is rarely possible otherwise. In this way the teacher is helped to gain a correct pers-pective not only of the child's behaviour but also of the part that he himself plays in this behaviour.

Strang and Morris report also that anecdotal records can be useful in parent-teacher contacts, when, for example, the teacher is trying to explain the child's behaviour to his parents: 'Detailed descriptions add concreteness to the points the teacher wants to make.' (Strang and Morris, 1964, p. 33)

Anecdotal records can be a very useful form of child study. Keep-ing such records can be recommended particularly to the following:

1. students writing up a child study.
2. teachers anxious about the progress of a particular child, an under-achiever, for example, a withdrawn child or an over-aggressive one.
3. teachers of special classes wishing to understand more fully the problems of the children they are teaching.
4. teachers working in close collaboration with a counsellor/ educational psychologist who wish to observe a problem child in particular detail.

In order to help teachers to keep good anecdotal records and to evaluate the ones they write, some examples of good anecdotes follow. You will note that literary ability is less important than objectivity and completeness.

Anecdotal records

Elizabeth
Grammar school 6th former, born March 1956; Mary born January 1953.

1. 4.30 p.m. Saturday, 25th November 1972.
Scene: Elizabeth's home. (I had arranged to go there to give her some tests).

Elizabeth's sister Mary and Mary's boy friend John let me in. Elizabeth was sitting on floor of lounge apparently absorbed in a Spirograph. Looked up and said 'Hello' in a friendly way, then went back to her Spirograph.

Mary said, 'Would anyone like a cup of tea?' Elizabeth said enthusiastically, 'I would.' Mary and John, after switching on TV and reminding Elizabeth that they wanted football results, went to make tea. Elizabeth demonstrated Spirograph (Mary's), said she wasn't very good at it, but that John had done some – also, with every appearance of sisterly pride (smiling, talking quickly and enthusiastically, eagerly pointing out one example after another), showed me some complicated patterns once done by Mary.

Sports programme began. Elizabeth shouted 'Football results'. Mary and John came in and for next ten minutes all drank tea and watched sports programme. All three exclaimed with surprise, delight or disappointment at various results. During excerpts from a Rugby match, John sat absorbed, Mary exchanged one comment with him and Elizabeth asked about half-a-dozen technical questions on rules and the finer points of the game (to which John replied politely without taking his eyes from the set). Elizabeth also uttered excited little squeals from time to time.

When this part of the programme was over, I suggested that we had better go and do the tests. Elizabeth got up very promptly and we went into the dining-room.

2. 5.45 p.m. Saturday, 25th November 1972.

Scene: Elizabeth's home (an hour or so after anecdotal record no. 1.)

When Elizabeth had finished the tests mentioned in anecdotal record no. 1. she showed no inclination to go back to join Mary and John in watching TV, so we just sat and chatted. We heard the front door open and she said in a cheerful voice 'That's my Mummy!' Her father put his head round the door and she said, 'No, it isn't. It's my Daddy!' and got up to give him a hug. Her father asked if she had told me about 'Freddie' (her flute). She said, 'I've got to give up Freddie. Miss Brown says there are lots of young ones coming up and not enough flutes, so she says I've got to let this girl in the first form have it in the week and then have it back for orchestra, but she's got another think coming. I don't want to play somebody else's flute and I don't suppose she wants to play mine. The others don't practise either, but I'm the only one who's honest.' When she began this speech she seemed quite cheerful and calm, but as she went on she spoke more and more emphatically (the last clause was spoken with very great emphasis) and also with some signs of emotion – her head was lowered, but when she did look up there were tears in her eyes, in spite of her attempt to sound flippant and insouciant.

3. 9.00 a.m. Monday, 18th December 1972.
Scene: 6th Form Common Room at Elizabeth's school.
About six or eight girls from the Lower Sixth were sitting in two rows of armchairs (one row facing the other) at the far end of the room. They seemed to form one group, but most of the interaction was between pairs. Elizabeth was in an end chair and was listening to what her immediate neighbours were saying. Occasionally she made a quiet comment. When the Assembly bell rang most of the group made no immediate move, but Elizabeth got up quietly and went out of the room.

4. 10.45 a.m. Thursday, 28th December 1972.
Scene: Elizabeth's home.
Mary is brushing Christmas tree needles out of Elizabeth's hair. When she had finished, Elizabeth just sat there looking peaceful and contented while Mary picked up the needles which were all over the carpet, and then smiled at her and said 'Thanks Mary'. Their mother came in and (as usual) had an amusing anecdote to relate. During this account Elizabeth and Mary sat impassively on the floor. Elizabeth had a dreamy look and didn't seem to be paying any attention to what her mother was saying, but she and Mary interrupted at one point to correct some minor detail.

Just as the anecdote was finishing, father came in and sat down. Mother went out to prepare drinks. Elizabeth got up, went nearer to her father and became much more animated. Father began to recount an anecdote and Elizabeth joined in. They kept smiling at each other while they were telling the story.

Mother came in with drinks. She began to tell another story. At first Elizabeth and Mary sat impassively as before, but when father joined in they too joined in. They all talked animatedly and then began to tell me about a Morecambe and Wise record which Elizabeth and Mary had bought for their parents. Mary, with what seemed to be a slightly exaggerated look of disgust, said one of the songs was 'filthy'. Elizabeth had her back to Mary and therefore could not see the expression on her face. She apparently took the comment seriously, and protested 'No – it's not really all that bad!'

They began to tell me about the Morecambe and Wise show on TV on Christmas Day. Elizabeth stood up to demonstrate the scene with Glenda Jackson as Queen Victoria. She threw herself into the part quite uninhibitedly – no trace of self-consciousness – and seemed quite absorbed in what she was doing. Very graceful movements. She kept trying to tell me that she knew some disaster would befall 'Queen Victoria' at the end and her father agreed that she had indeed predicted correctly. She also claimed that she was the first to penetrate Morecambe and Wise's disguise in an earlier item. Mary muttered, 'John said "It's Morecambe and Wise",' but Elizabeth continued to insist that she noticed first.

They put on a record and Elizabeth and her father began to dance up and down the room – again she showed no sign of embarrassment or self-consciousness, but a few minutes later, when we were preparing to make some tape-recordings of Elizabeth's singing, she blushed and said in a 'little girl' voice that she wanted Mary to sing with her.

Mary said she couldn't sing but her father said, 'Come on, don't be silly' and they sang a duet to Mary's guitar, after a few murmurs of 'I can't' from Mary. Then they played a recorder duet and both burst out laughing when Elizabeth made a mistake and it had to be re-recorded. When mother joined with the others in singing 'Bring me sunshine' she made one or two mistakes and Elizabeth began to giggle and stopped singing. At the end, mother exploded with laughter and the others joined in. When Elizabeth sang a solo both parents tried to persuade her to sing louder, but she wouldn't. Mother said 'false modesty'. Elizabeth said 'just modesty'.

6

The Use of Tests in Child Study

Measurement has long been an essential part of education and teachers are inveterate measurers. Children are measured for height, weight, time taken to run a distance, number of laps they swim, number of runs they score, number of sums done correctly, number of spelling mistakes made. Measurements are made of capacity, achievement, temperament and attitude.

Sometimes this need for quantification serves no obviously useful purpose. Routine school examinations and classroom tests frequently fall into this category. At other times potentially useful measurements like those of intelligence, for example, are misused or neglected. Yet measurement, carried out accurately and interpreted sensibly, is an invaluable aid to child study.

Measurement was described previously as 'observation with control of the situation'. This was explained as meaning that specific measurements carried out on children almost inevitably affect the behaviour of those being measured. In other words when we carry out, for example, a test of any kind on a child we interact with him to some degree and this interaction effectively alters his behaviour. This is in contrast to more naturalistic observation such as anecdotal records. Altering behaviour in this way is clearly a disadvantage; what corresponding advantages can be attributed to observation of the controlled type? Let us take a simple example: we measure a child's height. When we do so he straightens his shoulders, pushes back his knees and generally stands up several inches taller than he normally does. We have altered his behaviour and his measured height does not correspond closely with his everyday height. On the other hand, if all the other children in the class are made to stand up straight in the same way then we are able to compare the height of one child with that of another. This is one advantage that we can gain from measurement over less formal observation – comparability. Again if we had tried to estimate a child's height without using strict measurement, our judgment is likely to have been affected by many factors – our opinion of the worth of the children we are observing, their relative fatness or thinness, their posture. Our estimate is likely to be different from that of another observer; it would remain subjective. So, by following a standardised method of measurement, we are able to reduce bias brought about by the reaction of the children being measured and to reduce observer bias. This would make comparison possible not only between the children measured by the first observer but with children measured by other observers.

Measuring height is a relatively straightforward procedure and it is easy to make a case for its being objective and standardised. There are of course many other aspects of classroom behaviour for which we need measurement procedures. We may wish to measure educational outcomes in order to evaluate the effectiveness of teaching or the usefulness of a particular teaching method. We may wish to measure the achievement of the pupils we teach for purposes of selection, classification or individual study. We may wish to measure the ability of a pupil or his aptitude for specific skills in order to decide his fitness for a particular course, to decide the extent to which his attainment matches his aptitude or simply to understand him more thoroughly as an individual. In order to carry out these kinds of measurements many tests have been devised. It is these particular tests, which we call psychometric tests, or at least those of them which are suitable for, and available to, the classroom teacher, which we are most concerned about in this chapter.

Psychometric is a term used to describe tests which measure mental rather than physical aspects and which are standardised. Standardisation refers to the process by which tests are constructed so that comparisons can be made between different people taking the test at different times. This is brought about in the same way as the teacher standardising the measurement of his pupils' height. The conditions under which the testing takes place, instructions, timing and test material, are kept constant and *norms*, or standards, are established so that an individual's performance may be compared with a representative group of his peers. School examinations and teacher-made tests are rarely standardised and some kinds of psychological tests (e.g. projective tests and check lists) are not standardised and are not, therefore, properly speaking, psychometric tests.

There are two other main ways in which tests can be classified. The first classification concerns the method of administration of the test. Group tests can be administered to a large number of

subjects at one time, an obvious saving in time and expense. Individual tests can only be given to one person at a time, but, though
time-consuming, give opportunities for motivating the subject and
for observing his reactions and general performance which are
valuable to those studying children. Group tests can usually be given
individually without loss of comparability and when given in this
way can give some extra information of this kind although they are
unlikely to be as productive as tests specially constructed for individual administration. Individual tests, however, are rarely
suitable for group administration. The second classification is
whether the test is verbal, non-verbal or performance. This is not a
straightforward distinction. In group tests the term *verbal* refers to
the questions being written in the form of words; *non-verbal* refers
to the question being in the form of numbers or, more often, in
diagrams. The important distinction is that verbal tests assume
a high standard of reading, non-verbal tests do not. On individual
tests *verbal* refers to tasks involving words, i.e., oral tasks, while
the term *performance* is used for tasks which involve physical
action, a movement response rather than a spoken response. Reading
ability is rarely crucial in individual tests.

Having made these distinctions about tests we can go on to look
at the criteria which a teacher should adopt when using tests in
child study.

The teacher should be sure that:

1. Testing is the most appropriate way of meeting his purpose.
2. A test is chosen which suits this purpose.
3. The test is given under standardised conditions.
4. The scoring of the test is accurate.
5. The interpretation of the test is justifiable.
6. The results of the test are used in a worthwhile way.

Some of these points need to be taken up in more detail.

*1. The teacher should be sure that testing is the most appropriate
way of meeting his purpose.*
It is assumed that, except when completing a Child Study for training purposes, the ultimate purpose for a teacher of using a test is
that a child should be better understood and, through understanding, helped. The teacher's role is that of helper rather than
observer, subjective rather than objective. His relationship with the
child should be one of I-thou rather than I-it. Testing can help him

to a better understanding of the pupil, can enhance the I-thou relationship by greater insight but, used clumsily or inappropriately, it can destroy this relationship. Testing, particularly individual testing, is a seductive occupation. Most children enjoy being tested and most teachers enjoy testing them. It is good to work with children in this interesting way, discovering both the uniqueness of the individual and his consistency to normal patterns and the child can come closer to the teacher as a result and most teachers who have learned about tests feel impelled to practise their new expertise. However, testing is essentially an evaluative, judgmental process and potentially destructive of empathy. For this reason the teacher should always ask himself, 'Is testing necessary? Is there a less obtrusive form of observation, a less judgmental situation which would provide the same understanding?' If the answer is that a test is not necessary, if the information is already on record, can be discovered by indirect observation or can be discovered in a non-directive interview then he should not use a test. If the answer is that testing is the most appropriate way of studying the individual, then he should be certain that he uses the right test.

2. The teacher should be sure that a test is chosen which suits this purpose.

There are thousands of tests to choose from and they vary greatly in their suitability for child study purposes. The biggest supplier of tests in this country is the National Foundation for Educational Research (NFER) (see Appendix D), which acts as an agent for overseas tests too. They will send their catalogue on request. Many tests are available only to those who have special qualifications and to make this clear tests are graded into six levels (see Figure 4). Teachers can purchase and use tests of Grade A; those who have attended special courses can use some tests in grade P and Q. Other publishing houses also restrict the sale of tests but they are usually less systematic about it than the NFER. Information about tests and reviews of their usefulness are given in the *Mental Measurements Year Book* (Buros, 1965) which should be available in a good reference library. A useful little book is *A Teacher's Guide to Tests and Testing* (Jackson, 1971). This will help teachers to choose and evaluate the test they wish to use. Having decided what kind of a test they want and whether it should be group or individual, what sort of questions should they ask about tests and what sort of answers should they expect?

FIGURE 4. NFER CATEGORIES OF TESTS

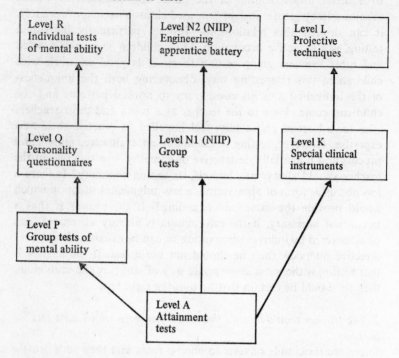

Level A (Attainment Tests)
Easily and simply administered, objectively scored attainment tests and inventories requiring the minimum amount of technical knowledge for their administration and interpretation. These will be available to responsible people who have had some experience of testing.

Level P (Group Tests of Ability)
Apart from those with higher qualifications, these tests can be used only by a person qualified by successful attendance at a course of training in test administration and interpretation which is approved by the British Psychological Society, or by a person who can produce evidence of experience in the use of tests (under the guidance of someone qualified by training), which the British Psychological Society and the company recognise as equivalent.

Level Q (Personality Questionnaires)
Tests which require a thorough knowledge of the principles underlying testing and which presuppose fairly wide practical experience in addition to specific training in the type of test ordered.

Level R (Individual Tests of Ability)
Tests which require a high degree of professional skill and experience for their proper administration and interpretation and which generally call for special post-graduate training. Psychologists wishing to use such tests must be Associate

How valid is the test? A test should measure what it sets out to measure and the teacher using the test should be able to estimate how far it does so or at least what evidence is offered that it does. The validity of a test can be estimated in several ways and evidence of validity can be highly technical but it is useful to ask, in the first instance, what is the aim of this particular test? In the case of an intelligence test our answer may be that the aim of the test is to predict future performance. The evidence ideally should be of predictive validity; that is, the test results should be compared with a later criterion of performance, e.g. IQ at 11 + should be compared with performance at GCE. It is unlikely, however, that such a procedure has been adopted. The test constructor is more likely to have compared his test results with those of another more established test for which predictive validity has been proved. Comparison of two tests given at roughly the same time is known as *concurrent validity* and it is more appropriate where the aim of the test is to indicate present performance, such as in a reading test. In this case we might also like to check the *content validity*. If our test purports to test 'reading' does it sample a range of reading skills or is it

-----

Members of the British Psychological Society or of equivalent training and experience.

Level K (Special Clinical Instruments)
In their application, clinical instruments are usually dependent upon a clinical judgement by the user, who would normally be a qualified clinical psychologist or psychiatrist, rather than upon the interpretation of objective scores. Level K instruments are issued only to persons who have had specific training in the use and application of the instruments ordered.

Level L (Projective Techniques)
Tests and instruments used for clinical and diagnostic work, which require a high degree of professional skill and experience for their proper administration and interpretation and which generally call for special post-graduate training. Psychologists wishing to use such tests must be Associate Members of the British Psychological Society or of equivalent training and experience. Normally, a background of clinical training would be required.

(T)
(T) usually after the category P, indicates that the test is also suitable for and available to teachers in Schools, Colleges of Further Education or Technical Colleges, for selection and guidance. The psychological qualifications needed to administer, score and interpret these tests are minimal.

(Reprinted from *Qualifications of Test Users* with permission of NFER)

restricted to one, e.g., word recognition? Are the items themselves appropriate for the age level and the type of material which the child will have experienced? A reading test constructed twenty years ago will have a vastly different vocabulary from that experienced by children today. It would hardly be valid to test the reading of modern children on such a test. Yet this is frequently done.

Validity is usually represented by a correlation coefficient, that is a figure from -1 to $+1$ which indicates the degree of association between two sets of scores. A close association, e.g., similar results on two tests, say, given to the same class of children, would be represented by a high positive correlation coefficient ($+0.07$ to $+0.09$). A moderate association, e.g., the same class's results on two dissimilar tests, would be represented by a low positive correlation ($-0.02-0.05$). A negative relationship, e.g., between age and intelligence scores, would be represented by a negative correlation ($-0.02-0.05$). Concurrent validity should be indicated by a correlation coefficient of about $+0.80$. Predictive validity would necessarily be lower, probably in the range $+0.50-0.80$.

Validity figures can only be interpreted in terms of the number of children involved in the validation study, i.e., the size of the sample. The larger the sample the more trustworthy the results. The sample should be representative of the population (age, sex, scholastic standard, geographical location, social class). The same remarks apply to the standardisation sample. One of the most pertinent questions that can be asked about a test is, 'Are the norms calculated on a sample which is appropriate to my use?' If the standardisation sample consists of grammar school pupils in Gloucestershire and you teach in a London comprehensive, you might well be sceptical about the relevance of the norms to your use.

Another question that needs to be answered is, *'How reliable is the test?'* A measurement needs to be accurate and consistent. If you use the test again on the same subject one should hope that the discrepancy between the two scores would not be too large. The reliability of a test is measured in several ways. One way is to use the test twice on the same sample; this is known as the test-retest method. The split-half method compares one half of the test against the other (all the odd questions against all the evens for example). The results are expressed as a correlation coefficient and should be above $+0.80$ to be acceptable.

The answers to these questions should be found in the test manual along with instructions for administering the test and marking and interpreting the results together with full tables of norms. Other information about the construction of the test and its use and references to other articles about it should also appear in the manual. Often, however, the manual is very inadequate and it is surprising how test constructors reduce the value of very useful tests by giving little information about them. It is always useful to look at the reviews of the test in the *Mental Measurements Year Book* to get a second or third opinion. The final question, *'How useful is this test going to be to me?'* is perhaps the most important one for teachers. The kind of information that is needed for this answer is essentially practical:

    cost of material
    method of scoring (hand, template, machine)
    time involved (and whether stop-watch is needed)
    type of normative score (IQ, percentile, letter, grade, etc.)
    form of test including whether separate answer sheets
    difficulty of administration
    attitude of testees to test

These questions cannot always be answered in advance and teachers considering any test are advised to buy a specimen set from the test agency or publisher. This gives the opportunity to study the manual, examine the test forms and even try out the test.

3. The teacher should ensure that the test is given under standardised conditions.
The importance of giving the test under exactly the same conditions as those which applied during its standardisation has been stressed before. Unless this is done the normative data no longer apply. This means that the teacher has to keep very carefully to the instructions in the manual. More than that the standardisation of conditions includes the standardisation of motivation. The assumption behind tests of capacity is that the subject is trying as hard as he can. Generally speaking most children in our culture do try their best when put into test situations. This does not apply necessarily to children from other cultures. Gipsy children, for example, do not co-operate easily in formal situations and to some immigrant children the whole idea is incomprehensible. This has implications, of course, for the validity of intelligence and attainment tests on immigrant children. It also implies that one important condition which must remain standardised is that of rapport. The tester must

ensure that the subject is relaxed and at ease, encourage him to feel that the test is worth doing and maintain this interest throughout the test. This is a straightforward, although skilled, task in individual testing but in group testing it is less straightforward. Rapport is more difficult to maintain with a whole group and the larger the group the larger the number of children likely not to perform at their best.

4. The teacher must ensure that the scoring of the test is accurate.
This is too obvious for much comment. Just one word of warning. Make sure, where 'parallel' forms are available, that answer sheets are paired with the correct question paper and that the correct template is used with the answer sheet. Tests are very confusing and publishers get confused as well as testers so you may not get a matching set in your order.

5. The teacher must ensure that his interpretation of the test is justifiable.
Interpretation is really the most difficult aspect of testing. It is easy to jump to the wrong conclusions about our results and, for example, generalise a single score on an intelligence test into a statement about the whole personality of the subject. The only general advice that I care to give at this point is to urge modesty in the claims made. If a test is one of word recognition, then we should not claim that it tests reading; if a score is in the normal range, then it should be described in this way and not as above or below average; if there are sub-tests, it should not be assumed that they are reliable measures on their own. The question of interpretation will come up again when we look more closely at different aspects of development and specific tests are described.

6. The teacher should ensure that the results of the test are used in a worthwhile way.
Having interpreted the test sensibly it is necessary to use it sensibly. Here we come back to the whole question of why we are using tests at all. To use a group test on a whole year level in a school presupposes that we are going to be able to use the information we have gathered. If we enter the data on record cards and then forget about it, the test results are not being used sensibly. If we use a single intelligence test score as the basis of a selection decision which is going to affect the child for the rest of his life this is hardly a

sensible use of test results. If we use a profile from a vocational test as a firm recommendation of the type of career a boy should take up rather than as the basis of discussion, we are not being sensible in our use of test results. The principles of test usage should be, therefore, that we do not use tests unnecessarily and that we are restrained in the claims we make for our test results and the decisions we make as a result of them.

The plan I shall follow in the rest of this book will be to introduce tests in the context of a child's development. Different aspects of the developmental process will be described and tests will be suggested where they are felt to be appropriate.

7

Studying Physical Development

Ever since early Christian times there has been an uneasy split in our culture between body and mind. In successive attempts to stress spirituality or intellectualism the importance of the body has been underrated; it has been relegated to a subsidiary position. Nowhere is this truer than in our schools, where the claims of the body to recognition as the basis of all human behaviour are reduced to a few slots in the timetable. Physical education and games take care of the body, the remainder of school time is given over to the dominion of the mind. Even within the physical education programme the kind of treatment the body receives is designed on the whole to reduce physical awareness rather than extend it, to concentrate upon a relatively few specialised skills rather than an understanding of the individual body as a whole. These remarks are intended to emphasise the concern that all teachers should have in the physical development of the children they teach, not as an unwelcome intrusion into the job of transmitting knowledge or teaching intellectual skills, but as an essential priority in the business of achieving the 'all-round development of the individual'.

The child's genetic inheritance
Physical factors begin to be important in the child's development long before he is born. The physical characteristics of his parents, as laid down in their genes, begin to operate upon him from the moment of conception to influence the kind of person he is going to become. More and more is being learned about genetic transmission and it is now possible to link many specific innate characteristics to specific parental genes. This raises the possibility of 'genetic counselling' in the avoidance of congenital handicaps. It is also helpful in our understanding of children's behaviour to know what conditions are genetically determined.

Some of the conditions most clearly linked to specific genes are listed below:

cleft palate
phenylketonuria
gargoylism
spina bifida
colour blindness
haemophilia

The child's genetic inheritance, of course, does not only affect him in specific ways like those above. It sets the limits to the rate and extent of his physical growth, for instance, his general fitness and his muscular strength but these factors are modified by the environment to a much greater extent than the monogenetic conditions listed above.

As soon as the baby is conceived the embryo is influenced by the environment of its mother's womb. The gene products interact with the mother's own cells so that, at birth, inheritance has already been modified by environment. The baby in the womb can be affected by the health and nutrition of the mother, by radiation from outside her body, by drugs that she takes and even, in subtle ways, by her mental state. One example of an environmental influence on the unborn child is rubella or German measles. If the mother contracts this infection during pregnancy her baby is likely to be affected. The way in which the baby is affected will depend upon the stage of pregnancy in which the infection is contracted. The tragic effects of the drug Thalidomide on unborn children is only too evident. Then there is the Rhesus Negative effect. If the mother's blood should differ from her husband's in the rhesus factor, then there is a 50/50 chance that her child's blood will differ similarly. If this happens then, during pregnancy, her blood-stream will grow anti-bodies to protect itself from the alien blood. This is unlikely to affect the first baby but, if subsequent babies are conceived with incompatible blood, then the anti-bodies are likely to attack the baby's blood. This may necessitate a massive blood transfusion immediately after birth if the baby is not to be permanently damaged.

The actual birth process itself may be a crucial factor in the baby's development. If a baby is born prematurely it will need intensive care to develop normally. If the birth process is protracted the baby may suffer damage from the pressures of labour, from the instruments used in delivery or from having too much or too little oxygen. This latter, known as annoxia, is one of the commonest causes of brain damage at birth, the damage varying from gross, leading to various kinds of cerebral palsy, to minimal brain damage. This term, minimal brain damage or minimal cerebral dysfunction is used when there is no measurable damage but its presence is inferred from various symptoms of perceptual-motor deficiency.

The child's physical development
After birth the child's development is still governed by physical factors such as nutrition, infection, exercise and accident. There is a subtle interaction between physical and emotional needs and physical and emotional development. A young child deprived of maternal love and care or adequate substitute will suffer physically as well as emotionally. It is important, therefore, when making a case study of a child to take account, not only of his health history, but also of periods of hospitalisation and other separations from his mother. The main items of information to be sought on the child's physical development are summarised in an observation schedule (p. 87).

Many of these items are concerned with very personal details and the observer must use careful judgment about whether to seek some of the information at all and if so how best to do it. Mothers may, if they are sympathetic to the study, be helpful with details about the child's earliest history. They are less likely to understand the point of a quiz on their family health. Some of the more pertinent information is likely to be summarised on the child's health card or the health visitor's card which preceded it. If it is not available on such records it is probably wiser not to seek it, unless the rapport between observer and child's mother is very close.

The section on General Fitness contains several points which need further explanation. The idea of 'developmental age' is discussed by Tanner (1961). He suggests many criteria of developmental age: height, weight, dentition, skeletal maturity, but feels that 'carpal age' (the maturity of the wrist bones as revealed by X-ray) is the simplest and most reliable, although beyond the resources of the teacher in an ordinary school. Tanner feels that developmental age is the most important single piece of information to know about a child since so much evidence points to the correlation of developmental maturity and success at school and he suggests that, 'Within a flexible and continuous system, early and late developers would be better able to avoid the present Procrustean Bed, and develop their talents at a tempo, and in an environment suited to their individuality' (Tanner, 1961, p. 53). More recently, however, Douglas has pointed out that maturity itself correlates highly with family size. 'The early maturing boys and girls make higher scores in the attainment tests at eight years as well as later,

FIGURE 5. AN OBSERVATION SCHEDULE IN PHYSICAL DEVELOPMENT

Family Health History
   Handicaps in members of the family ....
   Chronic illness in members of the family ....
   Acute illness in members of the family ....
   General family health ....

Birth History
   Mother's health (including emotional state) during pregnancy.
   Birth details: full-term or premature, easy birth or complicated; induced or natural, instruments or anaesthetics used; complications (including anoxia).
   Weight at birth .... any unusual features ....

Health History
   Unusual features of early childhood:
   Milestones: age of walking ...., feeding ...., teeth ....
   Hospitalisations or other absence of child from mother or mother from child
   ....
   Illnesses: *Injuries:*

General Fitness
   Height for age ...., weight for age ....
   (developmental age estimate ....)
   indications of puberty: ....
   tempo or energy level (very energetic .... listless)
   physical efficiency gross motor movements, fine motor movements
   (well co-ordinated .... badly co-ordinated)
   laterality: handedness .... eyedness ....
   sensory acuity: vision .... hearing ....
   speech defects:......................................
   robustness: (very robust .... frail)
   general health: (very healthy .... very sickly)
   eating and sleeping habits: ....
   posture: (erect .... stooped)
   body build: (endomorphic, mesomorphic, ectomorphic)
   mannerisms: ....
   general appearance (tidiness, style of clothing, facial characteristics, colour of hair, skin, eyes)

N.B. Read p. 86 on need for caution in making these observations.

get better 'O' levels and stay on longer at school, than the late maturers. Their advantage however appears to be largely explained by the fact that proportionately more children from small families come into puberty early. It seems that stage of puberty need not be taken into account when selecting or allocating pupils to streams or schools' (Douglas, 1971, p. 200). It would seem therefore that family size might give a more reliable forecast of school ability than developmental age. Maturity level is so crucial to social and emotional development, however, particularly at puberty that it is essential for teachers to make observations of it. From age nine in girls, and in boys age ten onward, children begin to vary more and more from one another in physical maturity as they enter puberty at different times. One boy may begin the physical changes of puberty at ten while another, equally normal, may not begin until $15\frac{1}{2}$. Then again one boy may experience rapid pubertal change (growth spurt, development of genitals, development of secondary sexual characteristics) while another may take four years to complete the change. This means that young people of similar chronological age can vary in physical maturity level by as much as six years. The implications of this for social and emotional development and adjustment should not need to be spelled out. It is important therefore to observe the level of maturity of the children we are studying and, while precise measurement is not possible, the kind of judgments summarised on the schedule plus observation of social maturity can help to give a general estimate of developmental age (size, weight, co-ordination, changes in voice, development of independence, leadership, emotional control).

Tempo, or general energy level, is not only a physical matter, it is also an important aspect of temperament for it describes the manner of our whole approach to living:

Some people are presto, some andante, some largo. Some are staccato, some legato. Some babies drain their bottle in a single rush, others remain unhurried and even indifferent during a feeding. Some babies can hardly wait to become mobile, others seem content to stay comfortably in one place. Even though there is probably an hereditary basis for tempo, parents and their children do not always move at the same pace, any more than they necessarily match in other hereditary traits.
(Stone and Church, 1957, p. 61).

In order to estimate the tempo at which a child lives his life it is necessary to make observations of:

pace:	the rate at which he moves about fast – moderate – fluctuating – slow
movement:	the way in which he uses his body *legs*, style of walking and running *hands and arms*, expansiveness, gestures *games*, approach to play, energetic or lethargic
voice:	loud or soft, fast or slow, hesitant or assured
work relevant behaviour:	perseverance (high or low) distractability (high or low) concentration (high or low)

Physical efficiency

This is an important concept in physical education and many measurements have been used in its estimation. Typical measures are those of grasp, leg strength, pushing and pulling, jumping, running and throwing. A similar kind of approach, but one more concerned with sensory-motor development, is described by Kephart (1960). This test is considered more fully on p. 96 where other perceptual and motor tests are described. For general observation of physical efficiency the teacher needs to rate the child being studied according to degree of co-ordination in (a) gross motor-movement as observed in games, PE, play and general movement around the school and in (b) fine motor-movement, for example, in writing and drawing, using scissors, needle and thread and tools. The subject can be rated on a scale from very nimble to very clumsy or extremely well co-ordinated to extremely badly co-ordinated.

Body build

Matters of general health and robustness need to be considered alongside posture and body build. Posture is obviously very much related to body build and so, in a rather more indirect way, is robustness. The general picture or stereotype of a sturdy muscularly built person of erect posture can be set against that of a frail, thin and long person of stooping posture. We assume that the more heavily built of the two is also the more robust even though experience tells us that the skinny ('wiry') are often the toughest. Observation of an individual's general healthiness needs to take account of stereotypes such as those illustrated above. The fine, well-built boy is not necessarily healthier than the pale, undersized one and, in estimating a child's general health, we should be less influenced by his appearance than by our records of his attendance at school, the kind of absence notes we receive from his parents, and the remarks made by the doctor at the child's medical inspection and recorded on his medical card.

As we have seen, our observations of body build affect our judgment of a person's general health and robustness. It goes further than this, however, for we also make judgments on temperament based on observation of body build. Many attempts have been made to investigate the relationship between body build and temperament, of which the most successful was carried out by Sheldon (1942). He distinguished three main dimensions of body build which he linked with temperamental characteristics:

Endomorphy	*Mesomorphy*	*Ectomorphy*
Emphasis on *roundness* fatty tissue, softness	Emphasis on *square-ness* muscle tissue, hardness	Emphasis on *linearity* bony tissue, fragility
Viscerotonia emphasis on comfort, sociability generally relaxed *extravert*	*Somatotonia* emphasis on bodily activity vigorous, assertive *extravert*	*Cerebrotonia* emphasis on restraint inhibited, unsociable *introvert*

Individuals have varying proportions of these characteristics. Sheldon used a seven-point scale to summarise these characterics so that an extreme endomorph, a round, fat person, would have a rating of 7–1–1. Most people, of course, do not have such an extreme physique and in some the proportions would be equally balanced, 4–4–4. Sheldon reported a correlation between physique and temperament of 0.80 but his results have been criticised in that the observers making the temperament ratings were obviously affected by the physical characteristics of those they were rating. In child study the value of the 'somatotyping' is further reduced by the difficulty of relating childish physique to adult physique (e.g., puppy fat). The approach does provide us with a way of summarising a child's physique, however, and we can speak of a child as 'predominantly mesomorphic' and know what this implies about body build without necessarily accepting that he has a temperament to match.

Laterality

The term 'laterality' has been included on the schedule under physical efficiency because this seems the most appropriate place to include it. The term is used to describe the achievement of dominance in hand and eye and the consistency with which this is maintained. A child may be left-handed but right-eyed and this condition, known as cross-laterality, has been considered to bear a close relationship with reading difficulties. Again a child may have weak dominance, shifting his hand and eye preference according to the task he is doing. The National Survey reported that 7 per cent of boys and 5 per cent of girls in their sample consistently used their left hand while a further 10 per cent of boys and girls were inconsistent in their preferences (Douglas, Ross and Simpson, 1971). There was no evidence from the survey of differences in attainment between the right-, the left- and the inconsistently-handed. This finding is confirmed by the Isle of Wight survey (Rutter, Tizard and Whitmore, 1970). Again there appeared to be little evidence of persisting behaviour disturbance in the left-handed, the cross-lateral or the inconsistently-handed. Even so it is still worthwhile observing the pattern of dominance in an individual child although no clear-cut conclusions may be drawn from the findings. It is an abiding personal characteristic which, at a relatively unimportant level, enters into almost everything a person does. Some simple tests of hand preference are:

hand used when – writing, drawing, tapping, throwing, brushing hair, cleaning teeth, hammering, pointing, etc.
eye used when – sighting a 'gun', looking through a telescope (a roll of paper).

With young children this can be done in the form of a game, e.g., 'Pretend that you are throwing a ball'. With older children the purpose of the exercise will need to be explained. A test which can be used for testing dominance is The Harris Test of Lateral Dominance (Harris, 1958) which is useful from 7 years onwards.

Sensory acuity

A child's hearing and eyesight are, after his height and weight, the most often tested aspects of his physical development. The results of this testing are usually noted on his medical record form (Form 10M). Vision is recorded as a fraction in which the top figure indicates the distance (usually in metres) between eye and chart.

The bottom figure indicates the size of print that can be read at that distance with either eye. $\frac{6}{6}$ $\frac{6}{6}$ indicates perfect vision in both eyes. The bigger the denominator, the poorer the vision $\frac{6}{66}$ $\frac{6}{66}$ would indicate that only the very largest point on the Snellen card would be visible. A suitable vision test for use with infants is the Stycar (NFER, 1968). Hearing acuity is often recorded as an audiogram based on response to pure tone signals on an audiometer. The example shows such an audiogram for both ears and records the point at which the signal was inaudible.

FIGURE 6. EXAMPLE OF AN AUDIOGRAM

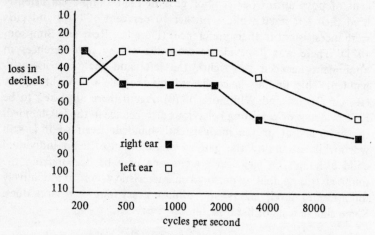

It would perhaps seem in these circumstances that any observation of visual or auditory acuity is best left to the experts. This would be quite untrue. Even in the secondary school, perceptive teachers can spot children with undiagnosed defective eyesight or hearing. These may be conditions which have developed since medical inspection or conditions which were not picked up by standard screening tests. There are a wide range of sensory defects and some of them are too subtle to be picked up in a standard test. In 1967 half a million school children in England and Wales suffered from visual defects (DES, 1969) and these varied in type and seriousness. 'In a class of forty children probably six or seven should be wearing glasses. If they are boys at least one will be colour blind. Another will have a squint. Two more will have eye strain from one cause or another, and more rarely somebody will have a visual defect or nystagmus. The entire class, of course, will be subject to epidemics of conjunctivitis, or the common childhood illnesses that may cause irritable or sore eyes' (Smith and James, 1968, p. 63). Visual difficulties can occur at different distances, at different angles and in different kinds of lighting. Sometimes subtle defects can only be observed in the first instance by those who are in close personal contact with children. A teacher having observed what appear to be visual difficulties should go on to report the need for careful specialist examination. Visual handicaps can be identified by the teacher by observation of one or more of the following behaviour characteristics:

1. frowning, rubbing eyes, blinking, tensing of body when looking intently
2. shuts one eye or covers it up when observing
3. tilts his head at an angle or pushes it forward when examining something
4. seems sensitive to light, has watery or red eyes, complains of aching or burning eyes
5. red-rimmed encrusted eyes, sties
6. dizziness, headaches, nausea, double vision
7. clumsiness, trips easily, stumbles
8. holds objects close to eyes
9. difficulty in catching or following a ball
10. lack of interest in visual media, e.g., films
11. confusion with colours
12. recurring writing defects, e.g., O into Q, C into G (indicating astigmatism)
13. uses half the paper, copies half a picture (indicating field defect)
14. mirror-writing, reversals (possible visual-spatial defect)

As Smith and James (1968) say, 'Close and accurate observation is still, so far as the eyes are concerned, the most effective way of suspecting that something is wrong' (p. 65).

The same might be said of the ears too. Hearing loss is not straight-forward. It is not simply a lack of sensitivity to noise. Sometimes the loss occurs at some frequencies and not at others and lack of sensitivity to the higher frequencies can be a particularly puzzling condition. A child with high-tone hearing loss will hear all sounds except those at the highest frequency, sibilants for instance. This usually leads to language retardation since the language the child hears others around him uttering is very different from what they hear. Signs of this kind of hearing loss may only be found in speech defects, lack of comprehension or reading difficulties and may well be confused with intellectual retardation.

Signs of the presence of a hearing handicap which the teacher may observe are:

1. consistent inattention
2. failure to respond to questions, asks them to be repeated or says 'What?' frequently
3. frequently cannot hear in a group, cannot tell who is speaking
4. frowns, tenses body, leans forward when spoken to, puts head on one side or turns ear
5. change in behaviour following illness
6. omits sounds or substitutes sounds, mispronounces common words
7. has an unusual voice – too loud, too quiet or oddly pitched
8. complains of noise, ringing in the ears
9. swelling about the ears, discharge, earache
10. withdraws from other children, has little interest in things around him.

Some tests of hearing which may be of use to teachers are: The Picture Screening Test of Hearing (Reed, 1960), The Auditory Discrimination Test (Wepman, 1958).

Speech defects

Speech is one of the first and most important developmental tasks faced by a child and failure or partial failure in the task will mean continuous difficulties in both learning situations and social situations. Speech troubles can indicate hearing difficulties or emotional difficulties and it is important to keep a record of any defects observed in the classroom. One large-scale survey of speech disorders carried out in USA discriminated a number of different conditions and the percentage observed in the sample.

Articulation	2.5%
Voice	0.1%
Stuttering	0.7%
Cleft palate	0.05%
Delayed speech development	0.05%
Cerebral palsy and other types of neuromuscular impairment	0.05%
Miscellaneous fluency and rate problems	0.05%
	3.5%

(Johnson, 1959)

In Britain, 2.7 per cent of 5-year-olds in Leicester schools were observed to have speech defects (DES, 1966).

When the teacher is satisfied that a speech problem exists referral to a speech therapist should take place as quickly as possible. The child may need the teacher's support and help since speech defects often lead to teasing and rejection. There may be study problems which need sorting out but most of all the child will need his self-confidence restored.

Some general remarks on the child's appearance are useful when rounding off a child study. This will give a picture of the child to those who read the study but it will also help the observer to crystallise his impressions of the child, his facial characteristics, the colour of his hair, his eyes, his skin, his standard of tidiness, his style of dressing and any special feature which can be observed.

The medical record card

School medical officers examine school children on school premises and keep records of these examinations. The type and timing of these examinations is changing and becoming more flexible:

> The trend – still far too slow – is away from the routine examination of all children in a number of age groups to a more selective system that enables school doctors to spend more time with children (and with their parents and teachers) whose development and education are, or may be, affected by disabilities and handicaps, including those which may arise from divided, broken, or socially deprived homes. (DES, 1969, p. 5).

It is still generally agreed, however, that the initial examination at school entrance is essential for all children. School doctors make this worthwhile by circulating questionnaires to parents which saves time by alerting the doctors to areas of special concern. The findings of the examination are entered upon a medical record card (Form 10M) which covers not only physical matters but psychological and social information too. School doctors are advised to maintain good communication with teachers and this is seen as a two-way process.

The sharing of observations about children in this way may be as valuable as the exchange of information. A school doctor cannot afford to dispense with the observations of, or discussions with, teachers about children who for one reason or another do not conform to rule (DES, 1969, p. 28).

My experience is that this two-way process works well in the infant school, rather less well in the primary school and hardly at all in many secondary schools. Liaison in the early stages is maintained by the school nurse who is often also the health visitor and knows the family background of the children. In the secondary school with its wider catchment area this tends to break down and it is essential that communication is preserved via the record cards. In many schools a good relationship exists between SMO and headmaster so that access to medical cards is available to anyone with legitimate reasons, e.g., educational psychologists, speech therapist, school counsellor, class teacher or form tutor. When this happens the medical card provides a wealth of valuable information which can be used to help the child. Sometimes the cards are considered as confidential medical documents and are kept locked up in County Hall. Provision has been made for this by means of a supplementary (or subsidiary) medical card (Form 10bM) to be kept in the school. While not as full as Form 10M, the subsidiary medical card can be an important source of information about the more serious aspects of a child's medical history. Unfortunately not all local education authorities keep these cards since they are not mandatory. This means that some schools do not have access to any medical information other than what can be gleaned from the school nurse or doctor when they call. This is not good enough and headteachers, in fact all teachers, should urge the completion of Form 10bM, at least for all children with medical problems.

Students completing confidential child studies should ask to see the child's medical record card. It will be at the discretion of the head (provided that he has access to the cards) whether he gives them this privilege but it is reasonable that confidential records should be available for professional purposes and training is such a professional purpose.

Tests of co-ordination and perceptual motor development
Tests coming into this category may be interpreted as being concerned with intellectual development or physical development. Many intelligence tests have items in them which test visual perception through spatial discrimination or visual-motor skills through

items such as jigsaw puzzles. Some few tests concentrate upon motor-co-ordination tasks which are less dependent on intelligence, e.g., the Lincoln-Oseretsky Motor Development Scale. These tests usually involve elaborate equipment and are unsuitable for use in schools. One test which is relatively simple to administer and which is related to a remedial programme is a non-standardised test of motor-co-ordination devised by Kephart (1960). This is only useful with children of infant school age, and educationally subnormal children of primary school age. Beyond these limits it ceases to discriminate. An adaptation of this test is shown in Appendix E. Kephart recommends a remedial programme which children deficient in any particular skill may follow. For example, children who do badly on the Test 3, 'Identification of Body Parts', could be given remedial practice with such games as 'Simon Says'. The tests themselves suggest the kinds of activities which would help children with perceptual/motor deficiencies.

D

8

Studying Intellectual Development

We are concerned here with the development by the individual of mastery over his own body and over his environment. Although the growth of intelligence depends upon and keeps pace with the growth of the brain, we can only infer the growth of intelligence from our observation of intelligent behaviour, that is from the ways in which the child interacts with his environment in a purposeful way. When the child is young it is relatively easy to observe a representative range of intelligent behaviour, since the child's repertoire of responses is limited. As he gets older, however, this becomes increasingly difficult and it is more and more necessary to use samples of his total behaviour. Intelligence enters into almost every aspect of human behaviour but it becomes most crucial when we are involved in learning new skills or applying previously learned skills in new situations.

Intelligent behaviour may be summarised under these headings:

Perceptual-motor behaviour: perceiving the world in an orderly way and co-ordinating the motor-system with these perceptions.

Symbolic learning: using symbols, oral and written, verbal and numerical, in the formation of concepts.

Memory: retaining skills and symbolic learning and retrieving this learning in a purposeful way.

Operational thinking and creative activity: solving problems, producing responses of a convergent or divergent nature.

Young babies begin to demonstrate a degree of mastery over their environment from a very early stage. They can learn, at two or three months, to manipulate a switch by sucking in order to switch a light on or off or to focus a picture. They can learn to manipulate their mother so that she gives them food or comfort when they want it and to manipulate the rest of the family to retrieve toys or to provide entertainment. They learn to control their own bodies and develop a range of skills; they learn to symbolise, to use words and numbers, to retain information and recall it at request, to solve problems and produce results. All this is relatively

easy to observe and, from such observations, developed the early
Binet tests (Binet and Simon, 1906). In its latest form (Terman
and Merrill, 1960) the first three-year levels set the following tasks:

YEAR II (2 yrs on)
1. Replace three geometric shapes in a form-board.
2. Remember where a model cat has been hidden.
3. Name the parts of the body on a drawing of a boy.
4. Build a tower of three bricks from a heap of twelve.
5. Name 3 common objects from 18 line drawings in a booklet
   (picture vocabulary).
6. Note the child's spontaneous word combinations during the
   interview. 2 combinations of at least two words score.

YEAR III (3 yrs 0 mths)
1. Thread 4 beads on a string.
2. Name 10 objects in picture-form (picture vocabulary).
3. Build 3 blocks into a bridge.
4. Find 3 drawings of animals on one page from many drawings
   on the next page.
5. Copy a circle.
6. Copy a vertical line.

YEAR IV (4 yrs 0 mths)
1. Name 14 common objects from pictures (picture vocabulary).
2. Recall which of three objects has been hidden from view.
3. Succeed with 2 out of five opposite analogies (e.g., a brother is
   a boy, a sister is a . . .).
4. Recognise the drawings of a number of common objects from
   verbal descriptions, e.g., 'Show me what we cook on'.
5. Find a geometric shape from a number of designs on a card,
   when shown a duplicate shape.
6. Answer two social comprehension questions.

These examples give an idea of the kind of intelligent behaviour
which is sampled at this early age level. As children grow up it
becomes increasingly difficult to find tasks like these and intelligence tests tend to rely very much on verbal tasks.

Intelligence develops as a result of growth processes within the
child (maturation) and his continual interaction with the environment. Bruner has suggested (1966) that a child forms a model of
the world from his experience with it and that he translates this
experience into a model by representing the world to himself in
three distinct ways. The first is in the enactive mode, that is in direct
motor action through the muscular and skeletal systems. The

second is the iconic mode, by sensory impression and 'summarising images', through the autonomic and central nervous systems. Finally there is the symbolic mode in which reality is represented in symbols, words and numbers principally, and this involves the higher processes of the central nervous system. Piaget has described the process by which sensory impressions are converted into concepts as one of assimilation and accommodation. New information from the environment is changed to fit into the existing mental structure and changes that structure as it itself is changed. Piaget has given us a description of the developing child as he passes from sensory-motor intelligence, where he is firmly in the 'here and now' and concepts as such do not exist, to the stage of concrete operations when he is capable of using and manipulating concepts so long as he is able to operate directly on the environment. Finally he is capable of formal operations when thought is freed from the concrete and can be carried out entirely in symbols.

The important periods here are the transitional ones, from sensory-motor to concrete operations (about age 5–7) when the child is struggling with concepts of reversibility and conservation and from concrete operations to formal operations during which he becomes more and more capable of abstract thought. It is useful when assessing intellectual development to observe the quality of the concepts which the child is using and his progress through the various stages described by Piaget.

It would be easy to spend a long time on the subject of intellectual development. So much has been written about intelligence; so many intelligence tests have been constructed; so greatly is education controlled by current notions of intellectual development. It is for this reason that I wish to restrict my treatment of this particular aspect of development. For I believe that education is preoccupied by the concept of intelligence. Lip service is often paid to notions of the 'all-round individual', to 'a healthy mind in a healthy body' but such ideas have not moved very far from the simple character-training of earlier days. A real appreciation of the development of the whole child, taking account of his emotional as well as his physical and intellectual development is still a long way off.

Even where the importance of human relationships in education is being stressed, it is justified by the effect it has upon the pupil's school progress. It is as if to say that teachers should be nice to the children they teach and take time to understand them, so that they will do better in their examinations. Stated in this way it seems rather cynical but it is certainly true that the commonest criterion of a school's success is its academic results and that the most frequently referred to indicator of a child in trouble is his failure to learn. There is a widespread belief, as a teacher blurted out in public discussion, that all that a teacher needs to know about a child is, 'whether he is dull or whether he is bright'!

Education's preoccupation with intellectual outcomes and psychology's preoccupation with the concept of intelligence are closely bound together. Psychology, at least in Britain, has tended to concentrate upon a search for general ability or 'g'. It has been felt that all intelligent behaviour, using words or manipulating jigsaws, surviving in the jungle or writing a computer programme, is determined by the degree of 'innate general cognitive ability' (Burt, 1955) possessed by the individual. In addition this innate ability was seen largely to determine what special abilities the individual is demonstrating although these special abilities were also said to be influenced to varying degrees by learning experiences. It follows then that, if we wish to measure intelligence, the best way to do so would be to measure 'g'. This would give an index of innate potential and, from this, we should be able to predict future performance on a wide range of intellectual activities. Experience with tests seemed to suggest that certain tasks, for example, recognition of spatial relationships and other non-verbal reasoning tasks, were less influenced by learning than other tasks, such as vocabulary or verbal reasoning and, therefore, non-verbal tasks were the best tests of 'g'. The search was on for a test of 'pure g'. Perhaps the most successful test to be developed from this search was the Progressive Matrices Test (Raven, 1956). This consists of a series of plates which depict patterns with sections missing; the testee has to choose a section to fit the one which is missing. It is a well constructed test and has proved to be very useful particularly in research. It does, however, highlight a number of difficulties encountered in developing and using tests described like this one as 'highly saturated with g'. For example the items in the test resemble each other very closely. This means that we have taken a very limited sample from the total field of intellectual behaviour. Alice Heim contrasts 'the healthy variety of the individual test and the ingrowing narrowness of the group intelligence test' (Heim, 1970). A result of both this narrowness and the intended freedom from the effects of experience is that such tests are less useful as predictors of academic success than highly verbal tests. The best criterion of future attainment is present attainment and verbal reasoning tests are mainly tests of attainment in vocabulary. Another difficulty which has become apparent is that even perceptual motor tasks are learned. Vernon (1969) has demonstrated that greater cultural differences exist between performance on a Block Design test than on a verbal test. His subjects included West Indians, West Africans and Eskimos. It is clear from perceptual tests and from cross-cultural studies like these that we learn how to perceive our environment in very much the same way as we learn language or social custom.

In order to get away from this dilemma of learned and unlearned intelligence Hebb (1957) suggested looking at intelligence from two points of view. He talked of Intelligence A, or innate general potential, and Intelligence B, intelligent behaviour or 'all-round mental efficiency', which is the result of experience. Our standard tests of 'g' are in fact measuring Intelligence B rather than Intelligence A (Vernon, 1964). Cattell (1957) speaks of 'fluid' intelligence, which is innate potential, and 'crystallised' intelligence, which is the result of the moulding of experience. Although descriptions of this kind are useful in conceptualising intelligence they are all over-simplifications of one of the richest and most varied aspects of human behaviour. In practice all intelligence tests are merely very limited samples of intelligent behaviour and reflect the test constructor's view of what intelligence is all about. What is even more unfortunate is that at the end of it all the individual's intelligence is represented by an intelligence quotient (IQ). A single figure represents the complexity of an individual's past cognitive growth, present activity and future performance, or as Torrance puts it, 'We have tried to make one metric, the IQ or a score on some scholastic aptitude test, represent the sum total of man's mental functioning' (1962, p. 20). The very audacity of being able to represent such an important aspect of personality by a number has led to the widespread popularity of the IQ. In education this notion of the IQ has largely been identified with a concept of educability and, fitting as it did current views of the scope of education, it was embraced with enthusiasm. Again summarising intelligence in a single figure in this way has led to its being seen as a single, relatively unchanging, entity. It has led to a view of intelligence as growing like a potato. I am not suggesting here that we abandon the use of intelligence tests altogether, since they can be very useful tools in understanding children, but that we use them with more care and sensitivity and that, at least, we abandon the IQ in favour of a reporting method which implies less easily that intelligence is a static condition.

There has been much debate about the relative importance of heredity and environment upon the development of intelligence. This can lead to very academic arguments which do not concern us here. It is enough to say that it would be strange if genetic factors did not produce differences in mental characteristics just as they do in physical characteristics. We can accept inherited differences in stature, for instance, whether individual, familial or racial. We should be prepared to accept similar inherited differences in cognition. We are also prepared to accept that environmental influences can greatly affect physical characteristics, e.g., the great increase in the stature of young Japanese as a result of dietary changes, and we should equally be prepared to accept that environmental factors greatly influence intellectual characteristics. Heredity in fact does no more than suggest an individual growth programme; environment determines the extent to which this programme is kept. The Plowden Report states the whole matter succinctly in a section on 'The Interaction of Heredity and Environment' (pp. 13–14): 'hereditability is not a quantity that belongs to a characteristic but to a population in its environment. The more uniform the environment, the greater the proportion of variability due to genotype. In England, for example, the differences in height between adults are largely due to hereditary causes, for most children have had enough to eat. But in many underdeveloped countries, where starvation and disease are rife, more of the adult variation will be environmental in origin and a smaller proportion genetic.'

The conclusion must be, as the Report draws it, that all characteristics develop as a result of the interaction of a complex organism with a complex environment, none is inherited directly.

On the other hand why should the suggestion that there is an hereditary component in social or racial differences in intelligence be so emotionally charged? The reason is that 'intelligence' has become a value loaded term. When it is said, for example, that black Americans have lower IQs than white Americans it is taken as meaning that blacks are inferior to whites, less able to 'adjust to the environment', to use one definition of intelligence. This brings us back to the point made before about the concept of intelligence. The intelligence test has become an example of the tail wagging the dog. A sample of certain kinds of behaviour has been chosen by test constructors to represent all intelligent behaviour. These particular kinds of behaviour have been sampled because they are simple to represent in a test, simple to score and because they appear to be representative of the concept of intelligence held by the test constructor. They work because they are made to work. Intelligence tests are artifacts and, like many well-used artifacts, they are gradually incorporated into the myths of society. Our society has adopted a myth about the potency of 'intelligence' and is trying to transfer that myth to other races and to other societies. Intelligence, however, is *not* what intelligence tests measure, and to suggest that any race is less *intelligent* than any other is both patronising and stupid. All we can say is that races may be different in the ways in which they adjust to the environment and that may mean that a particular race will score lower on the particular sample of intelligence that is currently being used.

The unfortunate fact is that, having devised tests which sample certain aspects of intelligence, we have made it very difficult for ourselves to see intelligence in any different way. Recent research on creativity has shown how we have emphasised convergent thinking at the expense of divergent. It is easy to see why this should be so – it is easier to measure a thinking process when its product is a single right answer than one in which the productions are, at least theoretically, unlimited. What applies to test construction may be applied also to educational practice which has tended to be based on the assumption that thinking is convergent. Most school activities are still convergent ones although many innovations may be observed, e.g., creative English and creative art and craft work are quite common, creative dance and music have been on the scene for some time and creative approaches to the humanities and social studies are being developed. In mathematics and science, however, the emphasis upon convergency appears to be so great that the divergers drop out and leave the convergers taking the subjects. All in all the general effect of education has beeen to discourage creativity. The change of direction which may be observed in education today is paralleled by an interest among psychologists in these whole fields of creativity. The new British Intelligence Scale will include a creativity scale among the six subtests so that, hopefully, a recognition of this further aspect of intelligence may be expected (see Jackson, 1971, p. 45).

Gardner Murphy (1958) has emphasised that if we are to realise humum potentially then we must build into our education the means of transcending our own cultural mould. Cattell's concept of 'fluid' intelligence (Cattell, 1967) seems a useful one here. If intelligence begins as fluid and infinitely shapeable, then it is important that the crystallisation process should not occur too early or be too absolute. A degree of fluidity, of creativity, a capacity for change, for transcending the 'cultural mould' would seem to be an essential characteristic of human intelligence.

I have spoken of intelligence as an aspect of personality and this is the most useful way of considering it. Cattell has included it among the basic personality factors (1962). Wechsler says, 'The theory underlying the Wechsler Intelligence Scale for Children is that intelligence cannot be separated from the rest of personality' (Wechsler, 1949, p. 5.). While Heim (1970) puts it even more strongly:

'The term "personality test" by tacit consent means a test which cuts out the cognitive elements (as though this were possible), this is an affront to psychology, to common sense and to semantics. It is an untenable distinction' (p. 19).

It is not just that intelligence is affected by personality, by level of anxiety or level of aspiration, for example, but that it is as much a part of the total person as emotions, attitudes or values. Thus intellectual functioning is completely tied up with general human functioning. In this way intelligence can be an index of the individual's general level of functioning, for anything which affects a person's emotional well-being will affect the way he thinks and his general level of intelligence. This has led to the useful notion of 'available intelligence'. At any time an individual has available only that degree of intelligence which he can spare from coping with immediate threats to his self. If the person is well adjusted and generally free from threat, most of his developed intelligence will be available for his use. If the person is anxious, frustrated or threatened then this is likely to be reflected in his intellectual performance and intelligence test score. Conversely a drop in IQ may indicate the presence of stress or a discrepancy between attainment and IQ may indicate either long-term emotional difficulty or environmental stress. This is one of the most useful diagnostic purposes of the intelligence and attainment tests which are available and which need to be described next.

Types of tests which measure intellectual development

It is necessary to distinguish between different kinds of 'intellectual' tests and to assign them to the categories in general use.

Tests of general ability
Usually called 'intelligence tests', these are measures of the attainment of various cognitive skills and attitudes which predict fairly accurately future performance on tasks demanding similar skills. They are therefore often taken to be tests of educability although this implies a prediction which in turn depends upon similar conditions being maintained during both administrations of the tests. Included among these conditions would be the maintenance of similar emotional states and similar motivation.

Tests of special aptitude
These are measures of the attainment of certain skills which predict fairly accurately future performance in skills, fields of study or occupations which have not previously been attempted. There are tests for aptitude in a wide range of skills from shorthand to mechanical efficiency and they are used for selecting for occupations or educational courses. Aptitude tests, in theory, should be indispensable in educational or vocational guidance; in practice their usefulness is limited. On the one hand, tests of general ability and present academic performance are usually just as accurate in predicting performance on a new skill. Then again the skills which are necessary in any particular occupation are difficult to isolate and are very specific. There is some point in those who are responsible for recruiting for particular employment, spending time and money identifying the particular skills needed for that job, and estimating which of potential recruits have those special skills, but this is not a task for teachers or counsellors.

Educational and vocational guidance is concerned less with trying to match talent to occupation and, much more, with helping the young person to sort out his interests and attitudes towards himself, his fellow-beings and his work. At the present time when job descriptions are changing almost as quickly as job opportunity, we should not fall into the trap of over-specific guidance.

Tests of attainment or achievement
These set out to measure the degree of competence in present skills or areas of knowledge. Attainment tests differ from school examinations or teacher-made tests in being standardised so that any individual's performance may be checked against norms or standards for his age. They are sometimes used to predict future performance, e.g., when used in 11 + selection but are more usually

taken as an indication of present needs, e.g., the need for remedial reading. Another form of attainment test stresses what the child cannot do rather than what he can do, e.g., what arithmetic calculation he makes errors in, what spellings he gets wrong, what words he cannot read. These mistakes are then used to suggest areas of difficulty and methods of help. These are called *diagnostic tests*.

Some useful tests in each category are described in Appendix D.

Using tests of intelligence and attainment in education

Tests of intellectual functioning such as those described previously may be used to satisfy a great number of educational needs. Their principal use with which we are concerned in this book is for general child study, that is, to find out more about an individual child who is being studied intensively. Other purposes, connected with selection and appraisal, involve the group administration of tests, e.g., selection at 11 +, the regular administration of standardised tests, reading surveys, and are not so relevant to our present purpose. I shall describe the use of these tests in child study in some detail and the other uses less fully and only as their use impinges in the understanding and welfare of the individual child.

Studying the individual child through tests of intelligence and attainment

These tests may, for example, be used in child study as another source of information about a child. Information about a child's cognitive life is as important as any other aspect. It, however, should not be limited to an IQ score – a quantitative estimate – although such an estimate is useful. What is more important is that we try to understand the way in which our child thinks, the standard of conceptual development he has reached and the strategies he uses in solving problems. In doing this we need to adopt an interview technique such as that made familiar by Piaget. This would consist of:

1. a demonstration of some learning task such as the relationship between physical objects, e.g., weights on a balance, or beakers of water;
2. questioning children individually about what they think will happen; and
3. exploring their answers with them, asking them why and how.

This technique may be used with any learning task which is appropriate to the age of the child. With pre-school or infant school children the way in which the child plays with building bricks and verbalises about what he creates can be investigated. An older child can be interviewed about which objects will float or sink, can be asked to classify the objects in this way and then can be asked his reasons for making these classifications. Another situation would be to ask the child about the surface level of liquids which have been poured from lemonade bottles into different shaped vessels or to ask him about the quantity of plasticine squeezed into various shapes. These are all experiments carried out by Piaget to enquire into the development of concepts, in these examples, the concept of conservation. This type of technique can be applied to any school subject, at any age level. I once made an interesting investigation into concept development with a group of 18-year-old students. They were asked to draw a diagram of an island on a sheet of paper on which two lines, one representing the surface of the sea and the other the bed of the sea, were already drawn. The results showed a widespread lack of understanding which further questioning established as of two kinds, either poor conceptualisation of 'island' or poor understanding of cross-sectional drawings (see Figure 7).

In another investigation the same students placed significant historical events, e.g., the building of the pyramids, the birth of Christ, on to a time line. This again revealed wide variations in the understanding of historical perspective.

Goldman (1963, and also in Gordon, 1966) has shown how historical and biblical material can be analysed along Piagetian lines. Gordon gives an example of a story used by Lodwick (1957) and of the kinds of answers that are given by children to questions:

King Alfred was an English king who lived long ago. In his time the Danes came from across the sea and tried to take the land from the English. King Alfred fought against them; and at first, they beat him and he had to change his clothes and hide himself.

One story says that he came one day to a hut where a woman was baking cakes on the hearth. She let him sit by the fire to warm himself, but asked him to see that the cakes did not burn while she was busy.

He said he would, but began to think about the Danes, and so

FIGURE 7. DIAGRAMMATIC REPRESENTATIONS OF AN ISLAND, AS COMPLETED BY SOME 18-YEAR-OLD STUDENTS

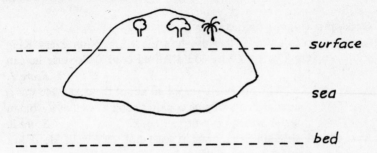

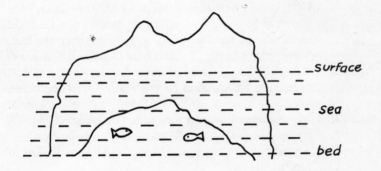

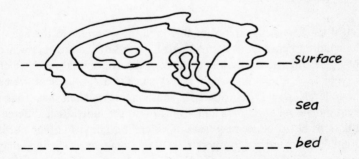

forgot all about the cakes. When the woman came back the cakes
were burnt. So she scolded him, not knowing that he was the King.

Question: Could Alfred cook?
Answer: Yes (Why?). Because he's the King. (Can every King
           cook?) No. (Why could Alfred cook?) Because he can
           fight.   *Score 1.*
Answer: No (Why not?). He forgot all about the cakes. He was a
           man and that's why he couldn't cook as well as a woman
           does. A woman is a proper cook.   *Score 2.*
Answer: I shouldn't think so, at least not very well. He didn't
           pay attention to the cakes. If he had been a cook he
           might have known they'd been done.   *Score 3.*
Answer: I don't think so, because if he could have cooked he'd
           have known how long it takes for them to bake. (Are
           you sure he couldn't cook?) I've never heard he could
           cook. Kings are supposed to have servants for that.
           You couldn't be sure. I wasn't born in his time.   *Score 4.*
Answer: I do not know because if anyone could cook and had
           something on his mind he might still forget the cakes.
                                                         Score 5.
Score 1.   *pre-operational:* answer limited to one aspect
      2.   *pre-operational:* but crude attempts at classification
      3.   *concrete operations:* inductive/deductive logic limited to
           perceptual clues
      4.   *concrete/formal operational:* moving towards abstraction
      5.   *formal operational:* can start with a theory and work
           back.
(Lodwick, 1957).

If a teacher uses material of this kind, appropriate to the age of
the children being taught, and keeps a record of the answers which
they give, then it is possible to discern the conceptual level which
they have reached. Although Piaget suggested the ages at which
these levels could be expected, subsequent research has found
great individual variations and, even within the individual, different
situations can produce responses of different quality. In other words
a child may normally operate at the concrete level but may
be occasionally inspired to think abstractedly or sometimes regress
to pre-operational thought. A representative sample of the
responses which individual children make to challenging material

will give valuable information about both the development of their thinking and the adequacy of their concepts.

In addition to this kind of information it is useful to have some knowledge of the cognitive style of the children being studied. By this is meant the general approach which they have to solving problems and the strategies which they adopt. Kagan, Moss and Sigel (1963) have indicated two main cognitive styles: analytic and non-analytic.

Children who think analytically tend to group stimuli into categories according to the characteristics of the stimuli. They tend, that is, to take an objective view, to separate relevant cues from irrelevant, to base their judgment on what they perceive in the environment. Non-analytic thinkers, on the other hand, tend to respond according to their own reaction to the stimuli. They make a subjective response in terms of their own likes or dislikes, or the emotions that are aroused by the stimuli. Now it is obvious that all people respond in this way at certain times or to a certain degree and that ability to think analytically increases as children grow older. On the other hand, research indicates that children differ in the style they adopt and this can be observed in their day-to-day response to learning tasks. More particularly certain methods of tackling intellectual problems may be adopted. Bruner has defined four such methods or strategies (Bruner, Goodnow and Austin, 1956) which he called: simultaneous scanning, successive scanning, conservative focusing and focus gambling. These strategies are described in technical terms and no firm criteria in their observation have been laid down. It would be sufficient for our purposes if the teacher studying the child took note of the way in which he tackles a problem, whether he tries to get an overall picture before beginning or takes a piecemeal approach, whether he learns quickly by trial and error or persists in his errors, whether he is generally persistent or gives up easily, whether he needs frequent reinforcement from teacher or examiner or whether he will delay such gratification, whether he uses verbal cueing, that is tells himself what to do next, or works silently. It may not be easy to gain information as specific as this from observation of individuals as they solve a task but it is certainly worth trying.

Another aspect of intelligent behaviour which has already been mentioned is the dimension of divergent/convergent thinking. Guilford (1959) included these two types of thinking with cognition, memory and evaluation as 'products', one of the 'three faces of intellect'. Since then it has been considered as an aspect of creativity and tests of divergent thinking have been developed (e.g., Torrance, 1962) in a search for a measurement of creativity. Conventional tests of intelligence, on the other hand, would seem to be tests of convergent thinking since they require only one correct answer. A conceptualisation of the creative process which explains the relevance of the divergent thinking stage has been diagrammed by Fisher (1972) see Figure 8.

FIGURE 8. A MODEL OF CREATIVE THINKING

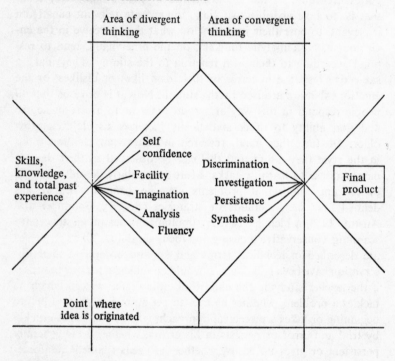

(From Fisher, 1972)

Looking at it this way divergent thinking is seen as a stage in every production, a mental activity employed by everyone at least on some occasions. It is possible, however, to distinguish between those who characteristically employ divergent thinking, the divergers, and those who characteristically think convergently. Highly creative individuals employ both modes of thinking, diverging widely before converging. Starting with an idea they diverge from it by a process of fluent association, until, having fully explored the possibilities of the idea or the medium, they begin a process of convergent thinking to achieve a final product. The convergent thinkers, however, follow a relatively straight line from stimulus idea to product. Since they are not included to deviate from a set task they tend to be more successful on conventional intelligence tests than those who are diverted by irrelevant associations. On the other hand, there can be divergers who, because they cannot use the convergent stage, never produce, and convergers who produce prolifically, if unoriginally. One can envisage a child, for example, who is unoriginal, who makes convergent responses but who is always painting pictures, writing stories or writing poems. Is such a child less creative than one whose responses are always divergent but who produces nothing? The truth is that creativity is as complicated a concept as intelligence and we should be very careful lest in trying to measure it we produce some new orthodoxy, perhaps even a CQ, a Creativity Quotient.

There is, however, in child study a need to take account of the degree of divergency in the child's thinking as well as his creative output. Fluency, for example, the speed and facility with which he associates new ideas, can be measured by some word association game such as: 'In one minute tell me as many things to eat as you can think of, . . . toys to play with as you can think of, . . . means of transport as you can think of.' Such a test can be given in oral or written form and some idea of how many responses can be taken as normal or abnormal can be gained from the responses of all the children in the class. Originality, another aspect of divergent thinking, can be derived from tests such as 'Unusual Uses' which would begin with instructions such as: 'Tell me all the unusual uses you can think of for the following objects: brick, straw, bottle, tin-can etc.' Again this may be given orally or in written form. Another test of this kind would be 'Consequences', with the instructions: 'What do you think would happen if everyone was invisible? If everyone was six inches tall? If everyone was a millionaire? If there was no night?'

It is necessary to evaluate responses on these tests from the point of view of unusualness (originality), fluency (no. of responses) and relevance. Ways of estimating creativity include the evaluation of imaginative stories. Children are asked to write a story about a character (animal or person) with divergent characteristics. Yamamoto (1961) and Torrence (1962) have developed methods of analysing such stories but these are very complicated and the teacher would be advised to mark them more simply from the point of view of originality and degree of interest. Some suggested titles (Torrance, 1962): 'The Lion That Won't Roar', 'The Flying Monkey', 'The Woman Who Won't Talk', 'The Man Who Cries'. It is useful also to take account of creative output, the end-product of the creativity process. One way of doing this is to use a check-list like the one shown in Appendix C3 (Torrance, 1962, p. 251). This can be checked by a child or for a child. It could also be used by the teacher to estimate the creative opportunities offered by a school.

It may not be easy to gain information as specific as this from observation of individuals as they solve a task but it is certainly worthwhile trying. What I am suggesting here is that, in order to understand how a person behaves intellectually, we take time to observe them with the following questions in mind:

(*a*) What level of conceptual development has been reached, pre-operational, concrete operational or formal operational? How firmly established at these levels and how firmly based is the understanding of concepts appropriate to age and standard of learning?

(*b*) What style of learning is adopted, analytic or non-analytic? What strategies are used in tackling a problem?

(c) What is the level of creativity studied under the headings of originality, fluency and productivity?

Tests may also be used to indicate general levels of competence
The need arises frequently to assess a pupil's intellectual level in order to decide upon his competence to undertake a particular course. Intelligence and attainment tests can provide objective information to help in such a decision. If we wish, for example, to know whether a child is ready to begin a course in a reading laboratory we should check his present reading attainment. This will indicate whether his reading is good enough for him to profit from the laboratory and at what level he should start. This illustrates how cognitive tests should be used – to help the individual pupil rather than attach arbitrary labels to him.

It is important, when estimating intellectual competence, to match the test to the purpose. A reading comprehension test would be appropriate for the purpose just described rather than a word recognition test. The latter would indicate the size of the child's reading vocabulary but not the use of which his reading can be put. Again an intelligence test which demands a high standard of reading will give an inaccurate indication of the intelligence of a poor reader.

Tests can also be used for screening for under-achievement

Under-achievement is a tricky concept. What we are saying, when we talk about under-achievement, is that performance is not matching promise. Performance is usually judged by attainment, assessed formally by attainment tests or informally by observation of general classroom achievement. Promise is less easy to estimate. It may be judged by previous performance, by performance in other activities (e.g., out of school activities, non-academic activities) or by intelligence tests. We may talk of under-achievement when a child's examination results do not match up to expectation based upon his general behaviour or when his reading quotient is found to be below his intelligence quotient. In each case we are making the assumption that performance should match promise, that a child's general ability, measured or inferred, should correlate with attainment in specific tasks. Of course this does not necessarily hold good. Whether we accept the idea of a hierarchical structure of abilities or prefer to think of intelligence as being made up of distinct factors, it is true that, even with group data, the correlations between general ability and special ability or between special abilities are rarely higher than about 0·8 (intercorrelation on the WISC at age $10\frac{1}{2}$ vary between 0·10 and 0·75 for sub-test scores, full-scale score correlates with verbal score 0·93 and performance score 0·90) so that we could expect variations in individual scores to be quite high. Wechsler warns against using variations in sub-test scores on the WISC as a diagnostic tool. How much more should we avoid using variations between different tests or between informal observation and examinations? Jackson (1971) says, 'One should regard with suspicion any figures that purport to show that a child is under-achieving or over-achieving unless they are accompanied by detailed information about the kind of tests used.' (p. 30).

This is not to suggest that it might not be useful to compare promise and performance. For instance, if we carry out a reading survey, we can compare reading age with chronological age and this gives us an indication of how far some individuals are performing below the norms for their age. Similarly a comparison of reading quotients $\left(\dfrac{\text{reading age}}{\text{chronological age}} \times 100 \right)$ with intelligence quotients can give some indication of how far the individual is performing in

116   *Child Study and Guidance in Schools*

reading below his own norm: a norm, that is, which has been established from his own performance on other tests. This means that when we find discrepancies in performance we take them as an indication of a need for further study rather than as necessarily an indication of under-achievement.

When screening children for remedial programmes, therefore, we should assemble information about attainment and ability and set it against other information which may be available. With all this information it should be possible to fit any child into a flexible reading programme that is one which takes account of the needs and capability of the individual as opposed to one which arbitrarily assigns a child to a group on the basis of test scores.

9

Studying Social Development

Social development is the reverse side of the coin of personality from emotional development. The way a person feels about others and the way that they feel about him are as important to his personality as the way he feels about himself. His emotional reactions, his attitudes, ideas and values and even his self-concept develop in a social milieu. 'No man is an Island' said John Donne and perhaps human personality does not exist except in human company. Can Robinson Crusoe remain a man without his Man Friday? Certainly 'wolf children' and others deprived of social intercourse appear to grow up without human intelligence or human emotions. Describing two children who, on two separate occasions, had been confined in upstairs rooms, merely being kept alive with the minimum of food, Sprott says: 'It is quite clear that when these children were found at the age of six, they could not be described as "normal children" or even as human at all, save in bodily form' (Sprott, 1958, p. 27). In fact, one of the children, Anna, did not learn more than a few words before her death at the age of ten. The other girl, Isabelle, was eventually able to go to school as a normal child, but, then, she had not really been shut up alone but had been confined in the dark with her deaf and dumb mother. As Mead says: 'The self, as that which can be object to itself, is essentially a social structure, and it arises in social experience' (Mead, 1934).

In any discussion of personality it is, therefore, necessary to interweave both emotional and social factors and it would be wrong to attempt an artificial separation. On the other hand, there are certain social factors which may profitably be separated from individual factors and it is these we shall look at now. They include:

1. the way in which the child develops as a member of society;
2. concepts of social maturity and social adjustment;
3. the groups to which a child belongs and, in particular, his peer group, the child society; and
4. the ways in which a child relates within a group: role, status, belongingness.

Social development

Each child brings to the society into which he is born his own innate potentialities so that, no matter how uniformly he may be treated in that society, he cannot but develop as a unique individual. The first primary group which he enters into is that of the family and it is here that most of his social learning takes place. From his mother he learns to love and to be loved. From her he receives the close human contact which he requires for all his growth needs and which will determine that quality of response to others which will be the basis of his social behaviour. In the family he will learn language, both a code which is restricted to this group and eventually an elaborated code which will enable him to communicate more widely. He will learn to play roles and will see others playing roles: the roles of mother, father, brother and sister, the roles of adult and child, boy and girl. In the home, too, he will learn a style of social behaviour. As his own basic needs are satisfied or thwarted by his parents in the earliest months and years of his life so he will retain or develop needs which will set the style of his approach to others. For example, from the basic need for close human contact on a physical level will develop a need for other kinds of human contact, for recognition, acceptance, prestige. Eric Berne (1966) describing the development of 'recognition hunger' says it originates in the stroking of a child by its mother. The need for this stroking continues through life and persists as a need for close human contact. Lack of satisfying human relationships, of 'human nourishment' as an American counsellor (Carkhuff, 1967) calls it, can account for many childhood emotional disorders and much adult mental ill-health. It accounts also for the need for counselling, for a warm, understanding professional relationship when we are in mental or emotional distress.

Play provides the main opportunity for social learning and, with pre-school children, a means of studying their social development. Susan Isaacs charted the development of play through the stages of solitary play to parallel play, associative play and finally to co-operative play. Children who have the opportunity of playing together, in nursery school, for example, move quickly through these stages and, in co-operative play, learn to give and take, to share and take turns and to form concepts of justice and co-operation. Piaget has placed the learning of these concepts later in the child's development, suggesting that the child proceeds in middle childhood from a morality of constraint, in which adult commands form sacred absolutes to a morality of co-operation in which free association with peers produces a morality based on reciprocity. At this time, he suggests, ideas of fairness are internalised to take into account questions of motivation. It seems to me, however, that children in the play situation have already learned to co-operate, to take turns, to share, even at the pre-school stage, although they may not have learned the language to explain what they are doing. The description given by Bull (1969) of the pattern of moral development takes such early learning into account. He considers that there are four overlapping levels of moral development:

   (a) anomy (pre-morality; behaviour modified through pain or pleasure);
   (b) heteronomy (external morality; behaviour by rules imposed by others);
   (c) socionomy (external–internal morality; behaviour modified by social considerations); and
   (d) autonomy (internal morality; behaviour modified by inner ideals of conduct).

Children pass through these levels in a definite sequence so that the levels may be considered to be developmental stages. The levels overlap, however, and any individual is likely to operate at any level at different times. For example, a driver may act out of self-preservation, fear of the law, social conscience and altruism during one short drive.

Although the home remains the most important single influence on moral development, the school is also influential both in formal and informal ways. The kind of learning involved in moral development demands social interaction and it is when schools give opportunities for such interaction that social learning can most easily take place. Interaction can take place in teacher-controlled groups or in peer groups. In teacher-controlled groups the personality of the teacher and his style of approach is a crucial factor, particularly with younger children. In one investigation teachers were tested on their mental health judged by their responses on personality tests. They were also asked to give their opinion as to the seriousness of one hundred items of 'objectionable pupil behaviour'. The least mentally healthy teachers were found to be least tolerant of relatively harmless misbehaviour, such as inattentiveness, while the most mentally healthy teachers were least tolerant of more serious, socially harmful behaviour like bullying (Clarke, 1951). Other studies have shown that the teacher's style of approach to a group, whether authoritarian, democratic or *laissez-faire*, produced significant changes in group behaviour (Lippitt and White, 1952). If these two pieces of information are put together they suggest that children's social behaviour is influenced by both the personality and mental adjustment of their teachers and by the manner in which they are taught. While teachers are usually very aware of the ways in which they themselves can influence children's behaviour, they are perhaps less aware of the influence on social development of the children's own groups. This influence becomes particularly crucial after puberty but in most children there is a gradual increase in the influence of the peer group from pre-school days.

When we consider the social interaction of very young children, what is most striking is the extreme individual variation. In fact there are greater differences between individuals of the same age than there are between the average behaviour of children of two and children of five. There are differences in such behaviour as co-operation, aggressiveness, forthcomingness and sociability. As Jersild (1954) describing a study of the conflicts of two- to five-year-olds, says: 'At one extreme was a child who engaged in 141 conflicts during the course of the observations, while at the other extreme was a child who took part in only 17.' Differences as great as these at such early ages are difficult to account for solely in terms of differences in upbringing. They must at least partly be the result of temperamental factors, such as the degree of extraversion or introversion which Eysenck (e.g., 1965, ch. 2) suggests is largely constitutional in origin. Such individual differences in social behaviour tend to persist throughout life, although they are never so startlingly obvious as in the pre-school days. After that time individual differences in social response become overlaid by social learning so that they are more difficult to observe.

Beginning school represents a problem of transition to many children, a problem which is often alleviated by attendance at pre-school or by a gradual familiarisation process within the infant school (see the Plowden Report). In one study some 39 per cent of children were reported as having been reluctant to go to school on some days at the beginning of their school life and this was most often the result of peer group troubles (Stendler and Young, 1950). The playground and the school lavatories are often the places the child fears most because when there he can feel most clearly the impact of the other children and it is then that teachers who are sensitive to children's needs can help to make school a happier experience.

Children in general settle into school quite quickly, adjusting to teachers and lessons more easily than they adjust to other children and to playtime. Even so, by the time the junior school is entered most children are living a highly active social life. Some of the more timid children and, in particular timid boys, are frightened by boisterous games and become onlookers. An individual's isolation from his peers should be noted by his teachers so that he can be helped to join in and become an active member of the group. Some teachers object to this, saying that children's need for privacy should be respected, but it is very rare for a child to be a happy outsider. Even when he seems content in his isolation there is likely to be some disturbance in the social dynamics of the class and this needs investigation by the teacher. At 9 or 10 children tend to be members of gangs (one study suggested that four-fifths of boys and two-fifths of girls are gang members at some time during childhood) and much of this gang behaviour in boys and a fair amount in girls seems to be socially disapproved (Crane, 1952). The setting of this gang behaviour is important in just how socially disapproved it is. Suburban or country children can behave in ways which would be unacceptable to city children. A number of slum children whom I taught were brought before the court charged with trespass and wilful damage. They had been playing Cowboys and Indians in a local timber-yard when their camp-fire went out of control. This was classified as delinquent behaviour. When this normal gang activity takes place in a background deprived of other sources of gratification, a background, for instance, of loveless homes and purposeless schools, then the gang becomes more than a stage of normal social development. It becomes a substitute for living. Anti-social behaviour then becomes the norm, a norm which is confirmed by the expectations of authority, the police, for instance, or perhaps the teachers. The street-corner gang, the delinquent gang is, in this way, perpetuated. (For a description of a Glasgow street gang see Patrick, 1973.)

Not all the children find in their peer groups a substitute for their lack of recognition elsewhere but, for most adolescents, their age-mates increasingly help them to become independent. Relations between the sexes become complicated in middle childhood when there is some antagonism between boys and girls. Although as a group boys and girls have little to do with each other during this period, except in teasing relationships, individual boys and girls often form close relationships and sometimes even fall in love before the onset of puberty. The sex groups gradually come together again in the mid-teens, particularly with middle-class boys and girls, and the mixed groups formed at this time provide the jumping-off point for 'pair-bondings', courtship and marriage.

Social maturity

When the process of social development is described in this way, the assumption is being made that children grow up in a relatively predictable way and that norms of social development apply in the same way as norms of physical development. Social maturity scales (of which Shakespeare's Seven Ages of Man is one of the earliest) are based on this assumption and also on the assumption that observed behaviour can be taken as an indication of maturational gain.

> It is possible to observe certain behavioural complexes as specially significant in those aspects of growth and development which effect an increasing identification of the individual with his social environment. (Doll, 1953, p. 16)

The Vineland Social Maturity Scale was constructed as a measure of the social competence of mentally retarded children. It is still most widely used for this purpose. Intelligence tests do not discriminate very effectively with the severely retarded and the Social Maturity Scale is very useful in deciding a child's readiness for particular educational experiences or his suitability for a particular group. The Scale is constructed on the same principles as the Stanford-Binet Intelligence Scale, that is, according to age levels. A Social Age is calculated from the successful performance of a number of social tasks under the headings:

Self-Help General
Self-Help Eating
Self-Help Dressing
Locomotion
Occupation
Communication
Self-Direction
Socialisation

Unlike the Stanford-Binet, however, this scale does not require the child to perform any tasks; the items are scored from information given in an interview by an adult who knows the child well. This means that the scale is suitable for use with very young or very retarded children. It is not restricted to the young or the retarded, however. The scale may be used to give valuable information about any child of school age. On the other hand, the older the child, the more likely it is that cultural differences will distort the results. For example, young people in Britain have less access to the telephone and the car than American adolescents. It is for this reason that the Manchester Scales of Social Adaptation were developed from the Vineland. The Scales are divided into two sections. The first, social perspective, includes such general matters as sport and current affairs, while the second, self-direction, is concerned with matters of mobility, play, self-help etc. These scales have been standardised on children aged 6–15 in the Manchester area.

While both these scales are designed for use with third-party informants they can be administered directly to older children. In an interview situation the adolescent can be a reliable informant of his own social achievements and the experience of the interview itself can be an interesting one for him and the interviewer. It must be emphasised here that to do justice to these scales the tester needs to take care to master the techniques.

Another useful measure of social development is the Gunzburg PAC. The Progress Assessment Charts of Social Development, to give them their full title, are meant to control and structure the observation of teachers and parents of the mentally handicapped (see Figure 9). Gunzburg describes them as 'systematised report forms' which 'should be used by teachers even if not specially qualified in educational and psychological assessment methods' (Gunzburg – note on SEFA). The PAC is published at three levels:

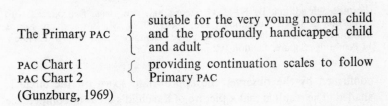

The Primary PAC	{ suitable for the very young normal child and the profoundly handicapped child and adult
PAC Chart 1	{ providing continuation scales to follow
PAC Chart 2	Primary PAC
(Gunzburg, 1969)	

The Scales provide a visual check on four main areas of social development: self-help, communication, socialisation and occupation. This visual check is given by the diagram which appears on all of the forms. All items are numbered and the level of the activity is specified on the report sheet by a letter (A–Z) which determines its position on the diagram. As a particular social competence is

FIGURE 9. PROGRESS ASSESSMENT CHART OF SOCIAL DEVELOPMENT (FOR THE MENTALLY HANDICAPPED)

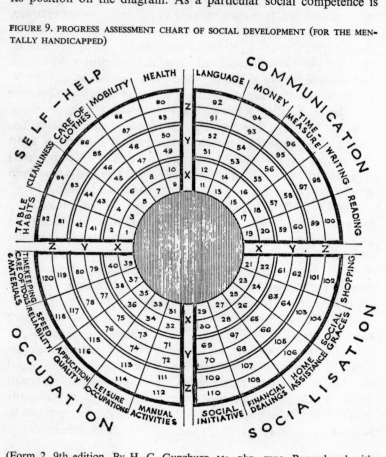

(Form 2, 9th edition. By H. C. Gunzburg, MA, PhD, FBPS. Reproduced with permission of SEFA (Publications) Ltd, 240 Holliday St, Birmingham. PAC is distributed by The National Society for Mentally Handicapped Children, 17 Pembridge Square, London W2.

confirmed by the observer the appropriate space on the circle is shaded. The result is that a picture of the child's areas of competence and levels of competence may be gained quickly and easily. There is a social education programme which is dovetailed to the PAC assessment and ensures that an educational programme may be given to a mentally handicapped person which is determined by his individual needs. The Progress Assessment Charts are designed specifically for the mentally handicapped but they may be very useful with normal children in the infant school, particularly when the teacher is in doubt about the child's level of social development. The visual presentation of an individual's social development provided by the Chart and its diagnostic extension is a valuable contribution to the concept of social development. When a teacher or student is completing a child study one of these scales can be invaluable in gaining an all-round view of the child in a range of social situations.

Another useful concept in the measurement of social development is that of social adjustment. In fact in the Bristol Social Adjustment Guides (Stott, 1971) what is being measured is maladjustment rather than adjustment and for this reason it has been considered in Chapter 10 under 'Personality Development'.

The child society
Child studies often concentrate upon the child as an individual, describing the ways in which he compares with or differs from other children. Usually his family relationships are taken into consideration and sometimes his peer group relationships, but it is rare to find a thorough consideration of the society which is all important to him, the child society. It is very difficult to study this society because its boundaries are so unclear. The child belongs to a number of overlapping groups each of which has its own structure and its own dynamics. The classroom group is the most accessible and easy to study, the street corner gang the most difficult. Both have received some study, although, compared with nomothetic studies, descriptions of particular child societies are rare (but see Hargreaves, 1967 and 1972; Richardson, 1967; the Opies, 1959 and 1969; and in fiction, Hines, 1969, Braithwaite, 1959).

The child society of the classroom in spite of its accessibility, has received little attention. Sociological studies of the classroom have tended to consider it as an aspect of the school as a whole. Thus it has been scrutinised to see the effect of the goals of the school and the attitude of the teachers upon the children within the class. At other times the social relationships of the children have been observed but again without taking sufficiently into account that these relationships exist within a society, a society which has its own culture (see for example the Opies), its own norms, its own patterns of association in which roles are assigned and status accorded beyond and apart from those of the school.

Anyone who wishes to understand the meaning of a child's behaviour must understand the social background against which it occurs. To understand why a particular child persists in apparently unprofitable behaviour, we must know what kind of behaviour is accorded status by his peers, what kinds of group loyalties exist, what ways the pupils have for controlling each other.

Many classes in school are primary groups, that is groups in which there is complete participation, in which each member relates to each other. This is particularly true of groups in many junior schools, where the children stay together, moving up together each year, having all their lessons together and having enough free activity for interaction to take place. Some secondary schools, by their organisation, give few opportunities for primary groups to develop. Setting and banding often mean continual change of class and the pupils have to relate, not only to different teachers but also to different children every forty minutes or so. In this kind of a situation primary groupings will most often consist of cliques from outside school rather than whole class groupings. Membership of primary groups is important for human development and we should be aware of those who are not admitted to membership of the existing primary groups. Such groups among children tend to be based on age-mates. There is usually little tolerance for children younger than the group although occasionally it may open its ranks. For example, one of my sons at primary school was accepted into the top class science club in his primary school because of his knowledge of natural history even though he was still in an infant class. At each age level there are different norms: of play, of humour, of attitude towards teachers and of attitude to work. Status within the child society depends among other things upon understanding these norms and living up to them so that, in a class of boys who value football prowess above everything else, low status will be given to those whose skills and interests lie elsewhere. On the other hand, status does not persist beyond each age-stage and a child of low status during one year because of lack of sporting prowess may have high status the following year because of success with the opposite sex.

Ritual and social tradition are part of the normative life of the primary group. These include initiation rites of one kind or another. With boys, fighting, bullying and teasing may provide means of initiation. Other traditions may lie in games, e.g., seasonal games, in clothes, in hair styles, and in taboos. Group loyalties are strong and often run counter to the rules of the school and the influence of the teacher. Many teachers have collided with group loyalties, faced with blank looks when demanding the culprit, with hostile looks when a group leader is criticised or amused looks when a group secret is trespassed upon. Within the groups there is the opportunity to escape from the rules and conventions which adults impose. Students, reporting on their gang membership as children, recalled many anti-social acts and yet these students represent the more law-abiding section of youth. (Crane, 1952).

Group relationships

It is impossible to understand the child society without taking into account the roles which children play. The concept of social role is a central one to the study of personality. In fact personality has been defined as the sum and organisation of all the roles one plays in all the groups to which one belongs. Besides the obvious roles of son (or daughter) and pupil, the child at school plays roles in the child society to which he belongs. Leader, trusted follower, clown, bully, scapegoat are roles which we can all remember from our childhood days. These roles are maintained in the classroom, although often they go underground. The leader must adapt his leadership in the face of the teacher's superior power. The clown must modify his fooling, the bully restrain his aggression. Often a child finds himself playing a role that he does not like but one that has been chosen for him by the child society. Since, by playing this role in the way that his peers demand, he receives status in the group he will go on playing it as long as they require it.

What kinds of roles do children play in the child society of the classroom? The Opies in their study of the language and lore of children (1959) identified the following roles recognised by the children themselves:

 spoil-sports, clever dicks, dafties
 copy cats, swank-pots, cry-babies
 stare-cats, cowards, nosy-parkers
 sneaks, crawlers, bullies

The names given for these roles are those used by the children themselves although different names are used in different parts of the country. These are all negative roles and some of the names

describe transitory behaviour (e.g., stare-cats) rather than persisting roles. Figure 10 shows some of the roles which I feel a
knowledgeable teacher may observe children playing in the classroom.
The list is adapted from a very much longer list of group membership roles given by Lifton (1966) in his book *Working with Groups*.
He has distinguished these roles in discussion groups with adults
and, while it is likely that children take on much the same parts

FIGURE 10. MEMBER ROLES IN GROUPS

Initiator	:	starts things off; keeps things going; prods the group into action.
Information-seeker	:	wants more information and is prepared to seek it from other members of the group.
Information-giver	:	seems compelled to give information and to answer questions even when directed elsewhere.
Monitor	:	always prepared to perform routine tasks for the group.
Harmoniser	:	tries to patch up quarrels and to relieve tension.
Observer	:	tends to watch what is going on; does not participate but knows what is happening.
Follower	:	goes along passively, a friendly audience.
Aggressor	:	deflates the status of others; attacks the group or member in it; may joke aggressively.
Blocker	:	negative in his reactions; digs his heels in unreasonably.
Attention-seeker	:	tries to call attention to himself, boasts, calls out, struggles to prevent himself being put in an inferior position.
Clown	:	avoids involvement; fools around; jokes unaggressively.
Dominator	:	tries to manipulate the group by flattery, guile, assertion of superior status or interruptions.
Sympathy-seeker	:	tries to obtain help and sympathy from the group through expression of helplessness, insecurity or misfortune.
Scapegoat	:	accepts a part as the butt of the group or takes on the blame as scapegoat.

(Adapted from Lifton, 1966)

in similar kinds of situations, it is difficult to differentiate one from
another, particularly as the classroom situation is so much more
diverse. The teacher can observe children playing these roles and
keep anecdotal records, can learn what roles are assigned to what
children in interviews with pupils or in their autobiographies and
can survey them in sociometric techniques.

Sociometric techniques

These are often called 'sociometric tests' although they are not properly tests in the sense that the term has been used previously. The technique is not standardised in any way, but even so, as Northway (1952) says, 'as well as being highly accurate, it has the added values of simplicity in use and speed in administration'.

Developed originally by the sociologist Moreno (1934), the sociometric technique has been used extensively in social psychology, sociology and education. It is a particularly useful technique in the classroom since the classroom group is one with closed boundaries, a relatively permanent group in which there is time for relationships to develop. To administer, the teacher has simply to ask each member of the class to state his friendship preferences within the group. The results are then tabulated to give a score of sociometric status or are arranged into a sociogram. It is important for the teacher to choose suitable 'criteria of association', as the questions on the pupil's friendships are called, if the sociometric test is to give useful information. Real opportunities for association should be chosen and these should be phrased in conditional form. For a class of juniors, for example, suitable criteria might be chosen from playtime, working groups, school trips or parties at home. An example of a sociometric test at this level is given in Figure 11.

FIGURE 11. A SOCIOMETRIC TEST

Name	Class

You are going to the High School in September. It would be helpful for us in the High School to know who your friends are so that we may put you into a Form Group which you like. Please answer the questions below so that we can know your friends and companions.

A. Whom do you like best to sit beside you?
   Give three choices:
   1.
   2.
   3.

B. Whom do you like to work with best?
   Give three choices:
   1.
   2.
   3.

C. Whom do you like to play with best?
   Give three choices:
   1.
   2.
   3.

E

It is important that the sociometric survey should seem relevant to the children taking the test. It may be possible to explain the test to them in terms of the needs of child study:

> A teacher should know as much as possible about the pupils he teaches, including who their friends are, so that he can organise his teaching and arrange groups in the best possible way. And so I should like you all to answer a few questions on the names of those you like to play with and work with. . . .

It is usually better, however, to relate the survey to a real need as perceived by the children. For example, I carried out a sociometric survey in a school which was experimenting with group teaching methods. It was decided to seat all the children in social groups and it was easy to explain the purpose of the survey so that the pupils' enthusiastic co-operation was assured. At other times forthcoming school trips, changes in school or changes in school organisation can become the justification for asking for such information. For example, children moving from primary to secondary school may be asked to co-operate in a sociometric survey so that their own friendship choices may be taken into account when forming new classes. It goes without saying, of course, that their friendship choices when given should be used for the purpose for which they were requested. Again, if confidentiality of results has been promised then confidentiality must be maintained. Absentees must be taken into account in the survey. A list of all the children in the class could be given to each child before they complete their choices or the names of absentees could be written upon the blackboard. If these children return to school within a week or so they should be given the test to complete. Even so absentees may receive fewer choices than they would have done if they were present and this should be kept in mind when evaluating the results. Each child should be urged to fill in all the choices although he should not be forced to do so.

When the results are obtained they need to be tabulated. The best way is to prepare a large summary sheet (see Figure 12). Unless there are many cross-sex choices (and this is unlikely) separate summary sheets for boys and girls may be used. The names are arranged in alphabetical order, across the page and down the left-hand column. The answer sheets are put into alphabetical order and choices are recorded in the row allocated to the chooser and the column allocated to the chosen. Alan has chosen David, John

FIGURE 12. SOCIOMETRIC SUMMARY SHEET

Choosers (Chosen →)	Alan	Bob	Brian	Charles	David	Gary	Hugh	John	Kevin	Martin	Neil	Robert	Sean	Vic	Intensity Store
Alan	\	0110			1011			1101	1110		0001				5
Bob	0111	\			1111			1110			1001				4
Brian			\	1111	1111	1111									3
Charles	0010	0010	1101	\	0011	0100		0100	1000		0001		1000		9
David	1111	1101	0110	0011	\			0100		1111				0110	5
Gary			1011		1111	\		1111							5
Hugh							\								3
John	1111	1101		1111	1101	1111		\			1010	1000	0001	0010	6
Kevin	1100	0010		0101	1001				\			1001			4
Martin	1111	0110		1111		0100		1010		\	0111	0111			5
Neil	1000	1101		1010	1111			1011		0010	\	1111			5
Robert	1111			0010				1110			0101	\		0001	4
Sean	1111					1111		1101					\	1001	5
Vic											0001				4
Girls choosing Boys — Ellen															2
Girls choosing Boys — Joan					1101										1
Choices received per question	7776	3543	2222	4465	8669	3533	0000	7654	2110	1121	2226	3223	1001	1122	
Total number of choices	27	15	8	19	29	14	0	22	4	5	12	10	2	6	
Total number choosing	9	7	3	7	9	5	0	9	2	2	7	4	2	4	

FIGURE 13. INDIVIDUAL SOCIOGRAMS

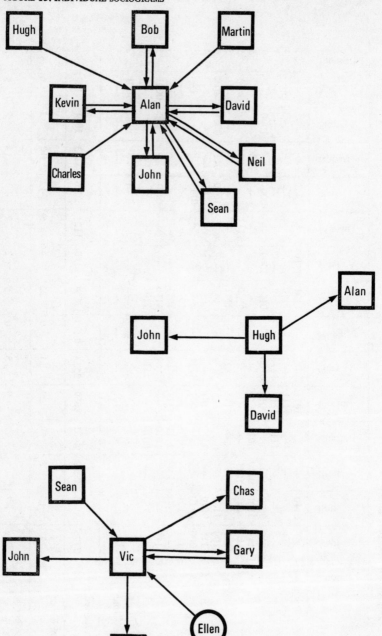

Alan: 'Star'

Hugh: an isolate, chosen by no one

Vic: low-status in the group but an interesting cross-sex choice

and Kevin on the first question and a check mark is put in each of their columns. On the second question Alan has chosen Bob, John and Kevin. Bob is marked 01, to show that he was not chosen on the first question but on the second; John and Kevin are given another 1 and David is given 0 to follow his first 1 in order to show that he was not chosen on the second question. At the end of the tallying the scores can be totalled across to give a 'social intensity' score for each child, that is the number of friends each one chooses. This (on our survey with four criteria) can vary between 3 and 12. The child who chooses the same three children each time would appear to have a more intense relationship with them than one who chooses a different child each time. By totalling down the column we can find the number of times a child is chosen, this is called the 'socio-metric status score'. A child who is chosen a large number of times is very popular while a child who receives few choices may be isolated or rejected. Spaces can be left on the summary sheet to write in the names of girls who are chosen by boys and the names of boys who are chosen by girls. If there are a large number of such choices then boys and girls need to be put on the same sheet. In our example Hugh is the only real isolate. He was chosen by none of his class-mates and he chose three of the most popular boys in the class to give his choice to since he recognised their status in the class. Further observation would be needed to ascertain whether Hugh is a tolerated 'hanger on' to the fringes of the high status group or is totally rejected by the class, making his choices only because he has been asked to by the teacher. The two stars are Alan and David, with David receiving choices from a girl, Joan, to swell his total. It would seem likely that David is rather more mature than the rest of the group and has established a boy–girl relationship. The other cross-sex choice has been given to Vic who is not highly chosen by the other boys so that Ellen's choice is particularly interesting.

We can draw sociograms to illustrate the social relationships in the class which have been revealed by our survey. These sociograms may be *individual*, i.e., show the choices of one child and those who chose him. They may be *group sociograms*, i.e., show all the choices made by a group of children. They may be *target socio-grams*, showing the whole class, all the boys or all the girls in the class or major groups in the class.

Sociograms are helpful in explaining the meaning of your socio-metric survey. They can demonstrate the kinds of relationships which exist in the classroom but they can never explain why these relationships exist. You can only find answers to questions such as, 'Why is Vic chosen by a girl?' by observing the children and talking to them. (See Figure 13).

Sociometric techniques give useful information in child study, information which it is very difficult to obtain in any other way. For example we can learn in a counselling interview the details of a young person's interpersonal relations but we cannot relate this readily, without a sociogram, to the pattern of interpersonal relationships within the class. On the other hand, the arrows of a sociogram mean very little without the flesh and blood detail provided by formal and informal observation of young people relating to each other in the classroom. Sociometrics, however, are useful in practical tasks such as determining the structure of groups and arranging classes. They have been used, for example, to smooth the transition from primary school to secondary school by ensuring that friends stay together. They are also very useful in distinguishing isolated and rejected children who need extra support from the school. In the past sociometric surveys included negative criteria such as: 'Whom would you least like to sit beside?' but these are felt to be harmful to social relationships, and are not advised for the classroom.

10

Studying Personality Development

All our study of children is aimed at understanding them as individuals, that is, we wish to know what distinguishes them one from another, what makes them unique. We call this distinguishing characteristic of the individual his personality and it is the development of the personality and the way in which this development may be studied that is the subject of this chapter. Physical, intellectual and social development all contribute to the development of personality, and we have stressed in earlier chapters the development of individual differences. The individual, however, cannot be understood solely from a consideration of the ways in which he differs from other people. If he is to be understood we must take into account how each one of his characteristics interacts with all his other characteristics. For example, we can only make predictions about a child's success in school if we know his cognitive ability and his motivation and how these two factors interact with other factors such as health, interests and values. A young person with high IQ and an extreme need for success may still fail to achieve in school because his need for success is diverted towards succeeding with girls or because of fluctuations in either his intellectual output or his motivation. I am not suggesting that personality study can make these kinds of predictions with a high degree of accuracy but I feel it should strive to make these predictions.

The unique characteristics of the individual begin at conception when one of 300,000,000 spermatozoa fertilises a random egg cell with a random selection of genes. The chances of any two individuals (other than identical twins) having identical genotypes are unimaginably remote since the number of possible gene combinations has been calculated as 'vastly greater than the number of atoms in the entire universe' (Dobzhansky, 1956). Even with identical twins two unique personalities develop as a result of the unique environments in which they grow up (see Allport, 1963, p. 5). This unique environment begins in the mother's womb where each of the twin foetuses occupies a different position, receives a different blood supply and is born under different conditions. With children who are not twins vastly different environments are experienced. Within a family, for instance, two brothers are likely to find the world a very different place according to their position in the family, the age and experience of their parents, the attitude of siblings to them and their attitude towards each other.

Early learning experiences are perhaps the most potent influences in the shaping of personality. Since habits acquired in the first twelve months of a child's life cannot be expressed verbally they remain unconscious, stable and very difficult to change. Freud was the first person to emphasise the importance of early childhood experiences in forming enduring personality characteristics. He described the effect of such common experiences as feeding and toilet training upon the developing personality to produce recognisable types such as the oral and anal erotics. Research has failed to demonstrate any firm connection between methods of child feeding (breast or bottle, early or late weaning) or toilet training and adult personality and it is now felt generally that it is the attitude of the mother as she feeds her child and trains her child, rather than the method she employs, which forms his personality. The mother, the father and other significant people in the child's environment 'communicate approval or disapproval, express their tendency to be prudish, anxious, harsh, perfectionistic, and impatient, or kindly accepting, and willing to let the child be himself and develop in his own good time'. (Jersild in Carmichael, 1954, p. 844). This emphasises the reciprocal relationship between parents and child. Even from the first moment that the child is placed in his mother's arms, her feelings of disappointment or tenderness, apprehension or elation are communicated to the child through posture and gesture. Individual differences in the parents are just about as important as those in the child.

It has been suggested that the inherited personality characteristics of the child (his temperament) are modified, first of all in the uterine environment and then in the home environment, by various influences (nutrition and disease for example) and experiences (such as parental attitudes and frustration). It is easier to understand how nutrition, by acting upon the body chemistry, can modify behaviour than parental attitudes. We talk of this modification of behaviour through experience as *learning*. We *acquire* temperamental traits and primary motives; we *learn* attitudes, ideas, values, roles, secondary motives and concepts particularly the all important self-concept as we call our own feelings of individuality and identity.

Eysenck's theory

Eysenck has suggested one explanation of the way in which innate traits, through learning experiences, become complex behavioural patterns. He begins with an inherited constitutional factor which he theorises as being at the basis of all human personalities. It is not possible to observe this factor but only to deduce its presence from various observable phenomena. The factor which he postulates is inherited human variability in the degree to which the body can be excited, or aroused to action, and inhibited, or satiated with action. The child, born with this tendency, encounters a particular type of environment and the interaction between his genotype or constitutional personality and his environment helps to produce in him a degree of extraversion or introversion and a set of accompanying traits such as sociability, impulsivity and activity. With these kinds of traits, and as a result of further environmental influences such as education, these primary traits develop into attitudes or thought

FIGURE 14. THE INFLUENCE OF HEREDITY AND ENVIRONMENT ON PERSONALITY

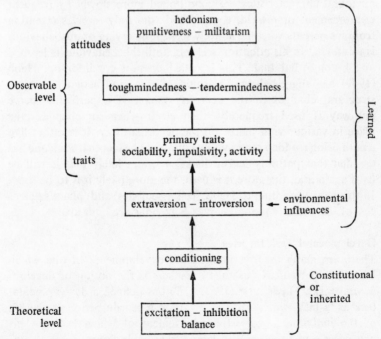

(Adapted and simplified from Eysenck, 1965, p. 79)

habits, on the dimension of tender-minded/tough-minded, such as punitiveness, militarism or hedonism.

This is simply a model of the development of some traits and attitudes from one theoretically deduced constitutional basis. It still does not explain how a constitutional tendency develops into an attitude towards life. The missing link is the word 'conditioning' in Eysenck's diagram. He has made the observation that there is a considerable difference in the ease with which those who are high on excitation condition (that is, learning to respond to stimuli), compared with those who are high on inhibition.

Learning theory

Attitudes, values and, to a lesser extent, traits are learned in very much the same way as language, reading and writing are learned. Some emotions and behavioural responses are conditioned by association with particularly vivid stimuli, e.g., fear of water or fear of dogs. This is called classical or Pavlovian conditioning and it appears to operate via the autonomic nervous system. Other behavioural characteristics are conditioned more slowly by frequent reinforcement or reward, e.g., a child who only receives attention from his parents when he actively seeks it by crying or misbehaviour is reinforced in his attention-seeking, until this behaviour is learned and becomes habitual. This is called operant conditioning. Hebb (1949) has suggested that learning of this kind actually involves structural changes in the nervous system. If a particular nerve pathway is used frequently, then electro-chemical changes take place in various vital places on the nerve pathway. It is rather like a path being trodden out in virgin country. The fact that someone has trodden that pathway before makes it more likely that it will be used again and, the more it is used, the more likely it is to be used. In this way, according to Hebb, 'cell assemblies' and 'phase sequences' of increasingly more complex behaviour are built up.

Developmental Task theories

There are many theories about child development but one which I think is particularly useful to teachers is the notion of developmental tasks. Havighurst (1953, p. 7) has defined a developmental task as 'a task which arises at or about a certain period in the life of the individual, successful achievement of which leads to his happiness and to success in later tasks, while failure leads to unhappiness in the individual, disapproval by the society and difficulty with later tasks'. The idea of sequence in development is not new. Freud described a series of stages through which every child has necessarily to pass. Gesell's observations led him to postulate a spiralling development in which the child passes through alternating periods of equilibrium and disequilibrium, while Piaget has described sequential stages in both intellectual and moral development. Earlier still there had been the biological idea of critical or sensitive periods in growth during which the organism is particularly ripe for certain kinds of development and after which it is very difficult for development to catch up. This notion came originally from observing plants and then was confirmed by ethologists studying animals. Its relevance to human development has received some support from the evidence of damage done to unborn children by rubella or German measles and the difficulties experienced by adults following the removal of congenital cataracts in developing sight. It is certainly true that some aspects of development occur most favourably at certain times in the child's life and that, if a child fails to accomplish the necessary growth or learning involved at this time, then he is handicapped as he grows older.

The concept of developmental tasks takes into account both the maturational factor described above and also the control exerted by society on the form and timing of these tasks. Consider the important developmental task of learning to read. In Britain society places the age at which children face this task at 5+ yet it has been demonstrated that children can learn to read at as early an age as $2\frac{1}{2}$ (Doman 1965). In USA reading is begun at $6\frac{1}{2}$ and in other countries later still. The age at which the developmental task of learning to read falls depends, therefore, less upon the readiness of individual children to learn to read than upon the age at which society expects formal schooling to begin. This societal factor influences the timing of all the developmental tasks which face children as well as the nature of the tasks themselves.

Havighurst has drawn up a comprehensive list of the developmental tasks of childhood and has shown their implications for teachers. The tasks he describes are straightforward and relatively unsophisticated, e.g.;

Learning physical skills necessary for ordinary games.
Building wholesome attitudes towards oneself as an organism.
Learning to get along with age-mates.

They provide, however, a useful basis for conceptualising the aims of the school in specific terms appropriate to different age levels. They are less useful in the conceptualisation of the individual child. Erikson (1950) offers a much more imaginative and broad-sweeping picture with his 'Eight Stages of Man':

Infancy: in which the chief task is the development of a basic sense of trust.
Early childhood: where the task is the development of a sense of autonomy.
Play age: which is concerned with the development of a sense of initiative.
School age: in which the chief tasks are the development of industry and competence.
Adolescence: where the chief concern is personal identity.
Young adult: in this stage the chief task is the development of intimacy.
Adulthood: where the main task is the development of generativity.
Mature age: where the tasks are the development of integrity and acceptance.

Blocher's theory

The statement of developmental tasks which I find most useful is a compromise one suggested by Blocher (1966). This takes into account both the simple social learning tasks of Havighurst and the more complex psychological processes of Erikson. Blocher describes first of all the social roles which are played at different ages and moves on to list the developmental tasks which need to be achieved if these roles are to be filled successfully. In achieving these tasks the individual acquires various coping mechanisms which help to deal with situations which arise in his encounters with his environment. If he has difficulty with his developmental tasks, then the mechanisms with which he tries to cope with his environment will be maladaptive; that is, while they satisfy immediate needs, they set up more disharmony which needs further adjustment. Children with severe coping difficulties are said to be maladjusted. Take, for instance, a child who has failed in the developmental task of learning to read. He will be thwarted in the development of several of the coping behaviours needed by children in his age group. Take, for example, those coping behaviours called 'mastery behaviour' by Blocher. He will be able to achieve fewer of the goals set by the school and receive less satisfaction than children who can read. This will mean that he is less likely to develop the same feelings of control and mastery over his environment.

'Value-relevant' behaviours will be lacking, particularly in the important area of self-valuation, while 'work-relevant' behaviours will be difficult for a child who is constantly failing in the work the school values most highly. Denied the achievement of these coping mechanisms the child is likely to develop behaviour which provides him in some degree with the recognition that is denied to him, for example, attention-seeking or power-seeking behaviour.

In Blocher's scheme, the earliest life stage through which a child passes is the Organisation Stage. For our consideration this may be sub-divided into three sub-stages related to the educational divisions used in Great Britain, that is: Pre-school (3–5 years), Childhood (5–11 years) and Early Adolescence (11–14 years). I shall describe the stages of Childhood and Early Adolescence in more detail.

The Childhood Stage (5–11 years)
The central developmental tasks of this stage are those which are concerned with the learning of initiative and industry. Children in school are faced with many different kinds of work some of which are self-imposed and some imposed by others. It is important that the proportion of self-imposed tasks should increase as children grow older so that there is plenty of opportunity for the practice of initiative. It is also important, particularly at this stage of schooling, that the level of work imposed or aimed at should be appropriate to the child's abilities and level of maturity. Too many children are placed in positions in school where failure is inevitable. When failure occurs too frequently, then the child develops a negative self-image. He expects to fail and he builds up a picture of himself which is consistent with this constant failure. Instead of initiative and industry he develops a sense of his own worthlessness. This lack of self-respect will stop him from trying a new task or persisting in an old one because he has no confidence of success in either. Besides the tasks of learning to read and to value himself other developmental tasks at this stage which are quoted by Blocher include:

Learning to defer immediate gratifications for the reaching of greater anticipated rewards.
Learning to control emotional reactions with greater flexibility.
Learning to deal with abstract concepts such as truth, beauty and justice.
Learning to give of himself to others.
Learning to formulate values and make value judgements. (p. 53)

Early Adolescence (11–14 years)

The physical and social changes which take place at puberty produce considerable disequilibrium. This has been called a period of 'storm and stress' and the developmental tasks which the adolescent faces reflect this turbulence. Erikson has stressed that the important developmental task of adolescence is the achievement of a sense of identity. In the earliest stage this involves the resolution of the conflict between dependence and independence. Children are completely dependent on their parents; adults should be independent. During early adolescence there is vacillation between these two extremes. Sexual identity also needs to be achieved at this time. As Blocher says, 'The adolescent must answer the question of "Who am I?" first within the context of masculinity–feminity and the roles and relationships that accompany sexual identifications in our culture.' Identity needs also to be achieved through occupational identification but this is denied to many adolescents who leave schools to go into unemployment or monotonous jobs. In fact it is often those adolescents who are least equipped to face the world who have to tackle this developmental task first while others delay occupational decision by staying in higher education. Other developmental tasks mentioned by Blocher include:

Learning to belong in various relationships.
Learning to control impulses.
Learning to be positive towards work and study.
Developing a relevant value hierarchy.

It is necessary to study a child's achievement of developmental tasks by observing him against the background of his peers.

Insufficient systematic research has been carried out upon the concept of developmental tasks so that normative data is not available except in well-trodden areas such as intelligence, attainment and social maturity. There are numerous measures of personality characteristics but these do not usually take account of the developmental dimension and so, while they can help to answer the question, 'How does A differ from B?', they are less suitable for answering the question, 'Has A achieved this quality which is shared by B and others of his age group?'

By using what suitable tests are available (e.g., verbal intelligence tests for measuring the attainment of the developmental tasks concerned with vocabulary attainment; reading tests for measuring the attainment of the developmental task, the development of communication skills in reading, writing and calculation; the various developmental scales [such as Gesell and Griffiths] for measuring the achievement of the tasks of early childhood; social maturity or social competence scales for measuring tasks such as the achievement of independence) and combining these with informal observations made against the background of the behaviour of peers, a teacher can estimate the progress of an individual child as he climbs up the ladder of developmental tasks.

Because of the paucity of specific tests geared to measuring the achievement of developmental tasks, it is more useful to look at personality study in terms of a model of personality rather than a model of personality development. The concept of developmental tasks is a model of personality development; while a model of personality which will fulfil our needs in child study is shown in Figure 15.

Figure 15 represents personality as a series of concentric circles with those aspects of the individual which are most accessible to observation as the outermost rings and the least accessible aspects as the innermost rings.

FIGURE 15. A SCHEMATIC REPRESENTATION OF PERSONALITY AND ITS STUDY

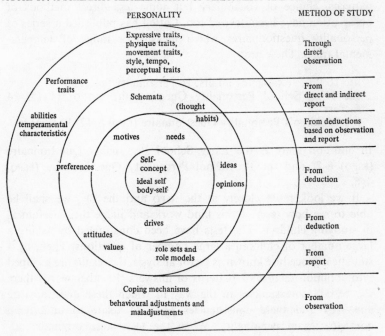

The outermost ring represents those aspects of personality which may be studied by direct observation. It includes traits (which may be defined as consistencies in observable behaviour) and coping mechanisms which are behavioural adjustments and maladjustments made to particular situations. There are two main classes of traits: expressive traits, which include all the characteristic reactions made by our bodies, and performance traits which McClelland (1951) defines as 'consistent modes of responding to problem situations'. The term 'expressive trait' covers many aspects of personality which have been discussed already, e.g., physical traits such as may be studied by Sheldon's somatotyping (see ch. 7), style and tempo (see ch. 7). Performance traits include abilities, aptitudes and attainments (the measurement of these characteristics was discussed in ch. 8. Included in the notion of traits, however, is temperament, or those characteristics constitutional in origin although affected by experience which are concerned with mood or emotional expression. These traits have been more thoroughly investigated than any aspect of personality other than ability. They can be studied by direct observation of behaviour, e.g., movements, gestures, posture, speed of response, expression of face, speech patterns, choice of vocabulary but some less direct methods of observation have been devised too. Cattell has published a series of personality questionnaires which measure a range of temperamental traits. These are:

the 16 P.F. suitable for adults, 16 personality factors
the High School Personality Questionnaire (HSPQ) 11–18, 14 factors
the Children's Personality Questionnaire (CPQ) 8–12, 12 factors

In addition there is the Early School Personality Questionnaire (ESPQ) 6–8, and the Pre-School Personality Questionnaire (PSPQ) 4–6.

If we look more closely at the HSPQ and the CPQ we shall be able to see how tests of this kind work and judge their usefulness in studying children. The tests have been constructed by asking a large number of children a large number of questions. Then, by a statistical procedure known as factor analysis, the results are grouped into common factors or patterns of answers. In other words there are certain consistencies in the way in which these questions are answered and these consistencies seem to relate to underlying consistencies in personality. When the tests were originally administered to adults, 16 such factors were derived, with adolescents 14, and with children 12. It is not always very clear what underlying trait has been identified by what cluster of scores. When it is clear, as for example in the factor of intelligence or the extraversion–introversion factor, then the factor is known by its commonly recognised name. At other times the factor is identified by a letter or an acronym. It is clear from this description that personality questionnaires beg a large number of questions and it is no wonder that some psychologists, Allport and McClelland for example, reject them. The latter says for instance, 'They [personality question-naires] involve a miscellany of correlated responses out of which it is nearly impossible to make any theoretical sense.' Or to use Allport's words, 'As the statistics grow better and better, the in-telligibility grows less and less.' The empirical nature of these tests, however, while making their contribution to personality theory doubtful, ensures that they possess some predictive power, and Maguire, in a recent study, found that both the HSPQ and the Minnesota Counseling Inventory could be used effectively in diag-nosing young people who need counselling help (Maguire, 1971).

The HSPQ consists of 142 questions printed in a booklet. The subject is required to answer yes, no or sometimes to such questions as 'Do you dislike going into enclosed places?' The answers are recorded on an expendable answer sheet. The test is a group test and the marking is simple. The results are recorded on a summary sheet in the form of a profile in which the score, expressed as a 'sten' or standardised score, is shown as a point on a continuum between the two extremes of the factor being measured, e.g.:

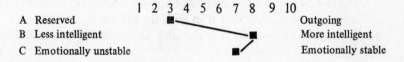

The test is untimed and takes about 50 minutes to complete. There are parallel forms A and B. It is graded as level Q (see Figure 4).

It is a lengthy and expensive test and teachers qualified to admini-ster this type of test will have to think hard before deciding to use it. Its main uses are:

1. As a screening test to identify children in need of special help. The snag in using the HSPQ in this way applies to all screening

devices. Having identified those children who need special help what special services are we to give them? Any large-scale screening process is likely to result in the identification of more children needing help than existing services can cope with. Only if a counsellor is able to take on more clients or if a group counselling venture can be begun is the process worth while.

2. As a way of helping a young person to learn more about himself. In this situation the test can be administered individually and the counsellor interprets the results to the pupil. When this is done sensitively it can be very helpful in the development of self-understanding.

3. In child study to help build up an all-round picture of the subject.

The CPQ, the ESPQ and the PSPQ are all similar in construction and administration although with younger children the test has to be administered orally and individually.

Another group of tests, used extensively in research but less often in child study, have been devised in Britain. They are the Eysenck Personality Inventory (EPI) (suitable for age 16 to adult), the Junior Eysenck Personality Inventory (JEPI) (7–16) and the New Junior Maudsley Inventory (NJMI) (9+ years). These tests are all similar to each other in measuring just two of the factors included by Cattell in the HSPQ as 'second-order factors'. These are extraversion–introversion and emotional stability–emotional instability (or neuroticism). The tests have been found to be very productive in research terms, discriminating among other things between neurotics and non-neurotics, delinquents and non-delinquents, tough-minded and tender-minded.

Eysenck has used the two dimensions of personality as a model of personality as a whole, tying it in with the ancient theory of temperaments (see below) and it is certainly an interesting and useful description of a complicated subject.

The difficulty comes when applying it to individuals. Most people fall in the middle, that is within the average range on both dimensions and when this happens there is little that the test can tell us.

The JEPI consists of 60 questions to be answered 'yes' or 'no' directly on to the question paper. Marking is simple when a stencil is used and the scores need to be compared with means and standard deviations for the child's age group. Any score which falls with the range Mean Score ± One Standard Deviation may be considered normal. It is a simple test to give and, where a child falls outside the normal range, it can give useful clues about his personality.

The Minnesota Counseling Inventory is another test of diagnostic significance, American in origin but demonstrated as useful in this country too (Maguire, 1971).

FIGURE 16. PERSONALITY AND THE THEORY OF TEMPERAMENTS

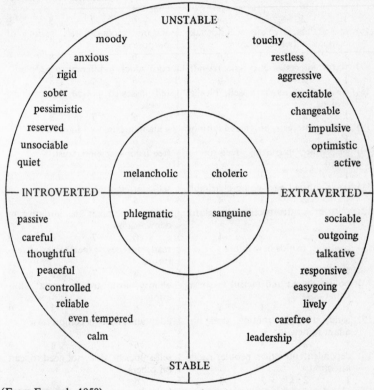

(From Eysenck, 1958)

In addition to questionnaires and inventories, temperamental traits can be measured more directly by rating scales in which the characteristic is described briefly and then the subject is rated by the observer along a points scale. Rating scales are often incorporated into school record cards and then they are often misused. The characteristic to be rated is usually too vague and the rater is too likely to be influenced by previous ratings also recorded on the card. One example of a rather more useful rating scale is shown

FIGURE 17. A PERSONALITY RATING SCALE

(1) has little understanding of another's feelings | able to put himself 'inside another's skin'

    1   2   3   4   5   6   7   8   9

(2) generally unco-operative and obstructive | co-operates readily

    1   2   3   4   5   6   7   8   9

(3) completely unpredictable in words and actions | always consistent in what he does and says

    1   2   3   4   5   6   7   8   9

(4) self-assertive, dominant, boastful | tends be submissive, modest, too unassertive

    1   2   3   4   5   6   7   8   9

(5) depressed, does not smile easily | generally optimistic, enthusiastic, cheerful

    1   2   3   4   5   6   7   8   9

(6) thoughtless, frivolous, will not take responsibilities seriously | accepts responsibilities, serious of purpose

    1   2   3   4   5   6   7   8   9

(7) warm, interested in people, friendly | cool, aloof, indifferent to people

    1   2   3   4   5   6   7   8   9

(8) easily upset, embarrassed, blushes easily | self-possessed, poised, retains composure

    1   2   3   4   5   6   7   8   9

(9) narrow interests, provincial outlook | wide interests, well informed

    1   2   3   4   5   6   7   8   9

(10) suspicious, untrusting, feels persecuted | free from suspicion, trustful

    1   2   3   4   5   6   7   8   9

(11) good-natured, easy-going, charitable | self-centred, selfish, egotistical

    1   2   3   4   5   6   7   8   9

(12) says little, introspective, thoughtful | talks a lot, takes the initiative in conversation

    1   2   3   4   5   6   7   8   9

(13) cautious, avoids new things | ready for new experiences, adventurous

    1   2   3   4   5   6   7   8   9

(14) polite, poised and tactful in social situations | clumsy, awkward in social situations

    1   2   3   4   5   6   7   8   9

(15) rigid, sticks to routine, does not adapt to new ideas | adaptable, accepts compromise

    1   2   3   4   5   6   7   8   9

(16) dependent on other people, needs attention | self-sufficient, does not need to lean on others

    1   2   3   4   5   6   7   8   9

(17) placid, calm, peaceful, serene | worrying, anxious, sensitive

    1   2   3   4   5   6   7   8   9

(18) conscientious, scrupulously honest | not very scrupulous, inclined to be slightly dishonest

    1   2   3   4   5   6   7   8   9

(19) has a rich and vivid imagination | lacks imagination, matter-of-fact

    1   2   3   4   5   6   7   8   9

(20) frank, open, expressive | secretive, reserved, keeps feelings to self

    1   2   3   4   5   6   7   8   9

(21) inclined to accept the opinion of others | independent-minded, makes up his own mind

    1   2   3   4   5   6   7   8   9

(22) apathetic, sluggish, unemotional | very excitable, over demonstrative

    1   2   3   4   5   6   7   8   9

(23) genuine, sincere | phony, insincere, putting on a show

    1   2   3   4   5   6   7   8   9

on the opposite page. It has been adapted from one used by Mc-
Clelland who himself adapted it from Fiske (see McClelland, 1951).
When the rating is complete – and it is useful to have the ratings of
several observers – those characteristics receiving high scores (7,
8 or 9) or low scores (1, 2 or 3) can be useful in helping to understand an individual. Broader descriptions of personality such as
'social adaptability' may be arrived at by looking at the pattern
of contributing trait ratings. This rating scale is more useful with
older adolescents than young children. A scale devised by Rutter
(1967) and used in the Isle of Wight survey is likely to be more
useful with primary school children. This is a simple and easily
administered scale and can be useful as a screening device for
behavioural disorders. This type of rating scale differs from the
first in being a record of direct observation of behaviour rather
than interpretation of behaviour. A similar but more elaborate
scale of this kind is the Bristol Social Adjustment Guide (BSAG).
Coping mechanisms appear on the outer ring of my representation
of personality along with Performance and Expressive Traits and
the BSAG is really a way of studying coping behaviour, adjustments
and maladjustments.

Another set of measures have been developed at the level of
schemata or thought patterns. These are tests of attitudes, interests
and values. There tends to be a group of attitude tests which have
been developed for research purposes. These are rarely used in
individual study. They include a test of social attitudes devised by
Eysenck (1958) using the dimensions radicalism/conservatism,
tough-minded/tender-minded. A more sophisticated and up-to-
date test is the Conservatism Scale (Wilson and Patterson, 1970).
This is designed to measure the general factor underlying those
social attitudes which are usually called 'authoritarianism' or
'dogmatism'. It is primarily designed for research work although the
catalogue suggests that 'it might also be used for individual assessment'. Another test in this group is the Bogardus Test of Social
Distance in which the testee is asked to say in which category he
would place people of different race, nationality (or social class),
see Figure 18.

A similar test is that of Social Stereotype (Katz and Braly, 1933)
where the testee is given a list of adjectives and is asked to select
those he can most appropriately apply to different races. These
are interesting tests from a research or teaching point of view but
they are not very suitable for individual study.

FIGURE 18. BOGARDUS TEST OF SOCIAL DISTANCE

Nationality	Accept as neighbour	as colleague or work-mate	as fellow-citizen	as member of family by marriage	as friend
English Irish Scottish Welsh					

The demands of 11 + selection have led to the construction of a couple of tests of children's attitudes which can help in a limited way towards their understanding. The Devon Interest Test (Wiseman and Fitzpatrick, 1955) was intended originally to give extra information to aid in the selection for a tri-partite system. It measures three areas of interest: practical, social and academic and can provide a useful area of discussion when commencing educational and vocational guidance. The Cotswold Personality Assessment (CPA) Test (Fleming, 1960) measures 'things', 'people' and 'ideas' which is substantially the same as the Devon. The latter has been standardised for ages 11–13 years while the CPA is suitable for 11–16 years.

The Allport-Vernon Study of Values is another test designed for investigation into this area. It is a multiple-choice, forced-choice test concerned with personal interests in six categories: Theoretical, Economic, Aesthetic, Social, Political and Religious and has been widely used in research. It is an interesting test to give and it produces some useful information. It is particularly appropriate for sixth formers or college students.

More widely used in schools are a group of tests designed for vocational guidance. The most popular are

the Rothwell-Miller Interest Blank (RMIB) (1968)
the APU Occupational Interests Guide (Closs, 1970)
the Connolly Occupational Interest Questionnaire (Connolly, 1967)
the Crowley Occupational Interest Blank (Crowley, 1970).

The RMIB is suitable from age 13 +. It consists of 9 lists of occupations which the subject is asked to rank in order of preference from 1–12. It is simple to score and the subject can be shown how to score his own blank. There is a very full manual which is helpful in deciding how to interpret and use the results.

The APU is similar in assessing the relative strength of interest in various vocational areas such as scientific, social service, practical etc. It works by asking the subject to indicate which one of a pair of statements he prefers. The results are marked by means of stencil.

The Connolly and Crowley have been devised for the Careers Research Advisory Centre (CRAC). The Connolly is more suitable for older pupils, particularly sixth formers. The Crowley is recommended for use with 'average or below average pupils' and is suitable in the fourth and fifth years. All four scales express their results according to interest areas, e.g., Active/Outdoor, Office, Social, Practical, Artistic (Crowley).

Tests of this type have been severely criticised for their use of forced-choice or other limited response questions, for their dubious use of familiar terms to cover empirically derived categories, e.g., 'political' in the Study of Values, 'practical' in the RMIB but, most of all, for their being 'ipsative' tests in which a high score in one category automatically means a low score in another (see Buros, 1965; Heim, 1970). I feel that interest tests can be useful in child study so long as the results are not taken too far. It is possible to say from the test for example that John is more interested in scientific occupations than aesthetic ones but not that John is more scientific in his interest than his friend James (for a discussion of the limitations of ipsative tests see the manual to the APU, Closs, 1970).

One way out of the ipsative test dilemma is a new technique devised by Alice Heim and her associates (Heim, Watts and Simmonds, 1970). It is called the Brook Reaction Test and consists of a tape-recorded word-association test. There are 80 stimulus words to which the subject responds by writing three associated words, e.g., DINNER: table, wood, tree, in 12 seconds. These are then sorted out into 22 interest categories. The authors claim that this is non-ipsative so that the relative strength of interests can be gauged. They also suggest that the test can be used as a clinical test of temperament. Some responses are classified as Q (questionable) and include words referring to death, illness, pain etc. These are put into one of twelve categories such as aggressive, emotion, physical illness. The test is still being developed but is proving itself both as a test of interest and as an index of some temperamental traits.

It is a very complex test to mark, however, and most teachers will feel that the information can be gained more simply by other methods. Tests of interests are most frequently used in vocational guidance when the results of the test are interpreted to a pupil in a one-to-one situation. It is on such occasions that I feel tests are least appropriate. The test is a formal situation and brings constraints into the I-thou relationship of the interview. Besides the test lends a somewhat spurious validity to what is after all a tentative procedure. The young person may end up with his interests not revealed by the tests but rather established by them. A further limitation in the use of tests is that we base our counselling on the end-product of a large number of decisions taken by the pupil but we have no information about how these decisions have been reached. We do not know for example why one particular occupation was chosen rather than another. A method which overcomes many of these disadvantages I have called the Keele Occupational Interest Sorting Kit (KOISK). KOISK consists of a number of cards printed on one side with the name of an occupation and on the other with a code letter indicating the area of interest. The pupil being interviewed is asked first to sort the cards into two piles: those jobs in which he is interested, those in which he is not. He is then asked what other jobs he has thought about and is given some blank cards on which to write these. Then he is asked to sort out the pile of 'interested in' cards into order of preference. This will give the counsellor or careers teacher the opportunity of observing the decisions made by the pupil and of asking him why he has made these decisions. At the end of the sorting process the code letter on the back of the card will help to give an index of vocational interests. The cards contributed by the pupil himself can be classified quite quickly by reference to an index of jobs. A sorting kit of this kind can be made by any teacher from a set of library cards and then be used without training (Bolger, 1973).

If we want further information about the schemata of an individual we need to look at that individual's own products. Poetry, free prose, paintings and drawings can be very revealing of thoughts, ideas, attitudes and values. I am not suggesting here a semantic analysis of a child's verse like an English Literature exercise on Donne's poetry but an impressionistic analysis of mood, theme and language. In the same way it is possible to read too much into a child's drawing but we are safe in drawing some conclusions about a child who never includes human figures into her drawing, another who always draws war and a third who always shows mother several times larger than father. Some of the most revealing and poignant pictures I have seen were drawn by an eleven-year-old aphasic boy who could not communicate verbally, scored highly on non-verbal intelligence tests and had spent much of his early life in institutions. His drawings were all remarkably detailed studies of prison-like walls with barred windows, downspouts and guttering and every chimney and tile drawn in – but no people.

More systematically we can study the attitudes and interests of the children we teach by asking them about themselves in several ways. Class discussions give endless opportunities of seeing how the children react to a wide range of situations both real and simulated. Attitudes towards work, towards the teacher and adults in general, towards fellow pupils and other children beyond the class, towards abstract ideas such as truth and justice will be revealed in any classroom which allows the children's voices to be heard. Some recent curriculum development goes further than this by putting the children into situations where they have to make decisions, sum up evidence and generally test their schemata against those of their peers. The use of simulation games and role-playing in moral and social education and in the teaching of the humanities is increasing and not only provides scope for interesting observation of children but, hopefully will help future children towards fuller personal development.

Written self-reports are another useful source of data about children. When children write their autobiographies a wealth of information is obtained about their personality as well as the physical and social conditions of their environment. Essays on personal topics like 'Dreams I have had', 'My Three Wishes', 'My favourite person', 'If I were Prime Minister', 'My greatest fear', and 'What makes me curious' will provide information about attitudes, values, opinions and also occasionally insights into the inner rings of the child's personality. The most useful way of asking children about their attitudes and interests is the interview and a whole chapter has been devoted to this subject.

The child's motivation, his needs and drives are much more difficult to observe. They have to be inferred from what he does and what he says. Since a person is usually unaware or at least only partially aware himself of these aspects of his personality he cannot report directly on his needs. Most investigations have tried to overcome this barrier to observation by using indirect approaches. They have asked their subjects to 'free associate', as in the Brook Reaction Test, to a range of stimulus words. They have asked them to react to ink-blots, ambiguous drawings, jokes, cartoons, stories, incomplete sentences. The most famous of these tests is the Rorschach

Ink Blot Test but this and the Children's Apperception Test (CAT) are clinical procedures and of little use to teachers. Some projective tests, however, may be adapted for child study. A teacher can collect some photographs from magazines and use these to stimulate the child into talking freely. The pictures chosen should be ambiguous, showing adult/adult, adult/child, child/child, child alone, child/animal in various situations. They can be analysed according to the evidence they contain of:

family dynamics
  attitudes to mother   positive – negative
           to father   positive – negative
           to siblings   positive – negative

peer relations
  attitudes to boys   positive – negative
           to girls   positive – negative
           to older children   positive – negative
           to younger children   positive – negative

needs
the need to dominate others
the need to achieve
the need to seek attention
the need for autonomy
the need to be defensive
the need to avoid harm
the need to be dominated
the need to be mothered
the need to be liked
the need to hurt or reject
the need to be hurt or rejected

(adapted from McClelland, 1951, p. 408)

Another way of arriving at the same kind of information is through a sentence completion test (see Figure 19). This can be given in a group situation and, since it is similar to familiar English tests, is acceptable to children.

This test may be analysed in the same way as the picture test; that is in terms of family, peer groups and the child's own needs. These do-it-yourself projective techniques have been suggested rather than one of the orthodox published ones like the CAT (Bellack, 1949) or the Rotter (1950) Incomplete Sentences Blank or Rohde (1957) Sentence Completions Test because these use complicated

methods of analysis demanding considerable theoretical understanding. As a result they are restricted in availability. Similar
techniques may be used by counsellors, teachers or student-teachers,
however, so long as they realise that the information obtained
must be treated tentatively as being just further observations of
behaviour, clues to understanding rather than evidence. Another

FIGURE 19. COMPLETE-A-SENTENCE TEST

Instructions:
  Complete the following sentences as quickly as you can. Try not to leave any
out.
  e.g., My dog .... is a friendly animal.

1. My house ....
2. My brother ....
3. My teachers ....
4. A happy thing ....
5. Bed ....
6. What frightens me ....
7. Holidays ....
8. God ....
9. My father ....
10. Boys ....
11. A sad thing ....
12. At parties ....
13. Teachers ....
14. My mother ....
15. Church ....
16. My schoolwork ....
17. Dreams ....
18. I am afraid of ....
19. My friends ....
20. Books ....
21. Death ....
22. What I want ....
23. Girls ....
24. School ....
25. Games ....
26. What I like best ....
27. My sister ....
28. I hate ....
29. My hero ....
30. What I like least ....
31. Friendship ....
32. Sickness ....
33. Ghosts and ....
34. I think animals ....
35. Little children ....

way in which these devices may be used is in promoting useful
discussion within an interview. Inarticulate, reluctant or naturally
taciturn children often find it easier to speak about themselves in a
counselling interview when they have some stimulus and their
responses on a 'projective device' can provide such a stimulus.
It is often helpful on occasions like this to get the client to draw a
picture or tell a story (see Figure 20). The Controlled Projection Test
(Raven, 1951) employs both these ideas but again is a restricted
test. An example of a story which may be used to investigate a
young child's feelings about himself and his family and promote
discussion about his inner life is shown opposite. The responses
may be analysed in a similar way to the completed sentences and
the reader can easily write other stories which will fulfil the same
purpose.
  Other means of obtaining information from which inferences may

be made about the child's perception of his world and his reactions to it have been described previously, e.g., the Family Relations Test (p. 54), sociometric devices (p. 129), and anecdotal records (p. 61 ff). The interview is described in Chapter 11.

FIGURE 20. TELL-A-STORY TEST

Instructions: Say 'Let us tell a story together. I shall start off and perhaps you'll help me by telling me what to say.'

Once upon a time there was a $\binom{boy}{girl}$ about (?) years old who went with $\binom{his}{her}$ parents on a holiday by the sea. The first morning the father said – 'Lets .... (what do you think the father suggested?) but the $\binom{boy}{girl}$ said 'I'd rather .... (what do you think the $\binom{boy}{girl}$ suggested?)'
Which of these did they decide to do?
The $\binom{boy's}{girl's}$ mother was very cross at this and she said, (what did she say?)
What did the $\binom{boy's}{girl's}$ father say to this?
How did the $\binom{boy}{girl}$ think about this?

Feeling rather fed up the $\binom{boy}{girl}$ went down to the beach and borrowed a boat. $\binom{He}{She}$ rowed out to sea. It was very enjoyable. The sun shone, the sea-gulls cried, and it was very peaceful.
(Did the $\binom{boy}{girl}$ like being on $\binom{her}{his}$ own? Why?)
Then the tide changed and the boat began to drift out to sea, the sky became dark and the wind began to blow. (How did the $\binom{boy}{girl}$ feel now? What did he/she do? What happened next?)

Finish the story off.

Did you like that story? Do you think the boy/girl was like you? (Why or why not?) Was the father like your father? (Why or why not?) Was the mother like your mother? (Why or why not?)

The innermost circle of personality which is inhabited by the self-concept is the most elusive of all to study. It is, in fact, misleading even to suggest that it is the inner core of a personality although that is true to an important degree. The self-concept is very much the integrating function of the personality, that is, it is that aspect of the individual which makes sense of the environment and the way he perceives it, on the one hand, and his own body and the way he perceives that, on the other. It should relate the two together in a satisfying way. Personality has been defined as the story of ourselves that we tell ourselves. While this story agrees with the evidence we receive through our senses then we can function adequately. When the story is no longer adequate, when external and internal evidence no longer agree, then 'mental disturbance' begins.

The best way to study the wholeness of personality is from the end point of an ideographic study of the kind we are advocating. Any one observation, any single test or measurement will give us a partial view only. A series of counselling interviews will bring us closest to understanding the child's own perception of the world. Add to this objective measures of traits and attitudes, observation of the child's behaviour in a variety of typical situations and some indication of the reaction of other people to the child and we come as close as we can in the present state of knowledge.

11

The Interview in Child Study and Guidance

One of the most neglected sources of information about children is the interview. Most books on child study describe techniques of observation, anecdotal records, tests and measurements. Most of them indicate how information can be gained from record cards, how reports can be obtained from other observers and how parents can be asked for information. What is rarely done is to suggest that if we want to know something, particularly if we wish to know the child we are studying, then we should ask the child himself. Sometimes it is the obvious which is most easily overlooked. Yet it is not just that books on child study are omitting to mention interviewing as being too obvious. It goes further than that. The fact is that teachers so often neglect to listen to children, at least, to individual children. Teaching is such a demanding job and the teacher is so concerned with dealing with groups that he finds it difficult, unless convinced of its value, to find time to talk to children alone. Yet it is remarkable how differently children behave when they have the undivided attention of an adult and how much can be learned which would remain otherwise undiscovered.

Although books on child study neglect interviewing this is not to say that it has not been studied. In fact many books have been written about the art of interviewing from the standpoint of the counsellor, the psychiatrist or the social worker (e.g., Rich 1968; Bessell, 1971).

I have been stressing the information-seeking function of the interview but, as these books show, this is only one of its two main functions. The other is the counselling interview. This is perhaps the most important and powerful means of helping others which the guidance worker possesses. In various forms counselling is used by psychotherapists, social workers, psychologists, marriage-guidance workers and careers officers as well as school counsellors. Teachers involved in pastoral care need consciously to develop their skill in one-to-one communication so that they can provide another source of help for the children they teach. It is impossible to learn from a book how to be a counsellor and certainly not from one concerned mainly with techniques of child study, but some guidelines can be suggested so that teachers will know which skills they need to develop and information will be given about the kinds of training courses which are available. But first let us consider the information-seeking interview.

The interview as a technique of child study
Interviews can be described in terms of the degree of structure they are given. At one end there is the individual test, a highly structured interview, at the other extreme would be the client-centred counselling interview which is very unstructured (see Figure 21). Information-seeking interviews are usually structured; that is they follow a pre-set plan or scheme. When administering a highly structured individual intelligence test the interviewer follows strict instructions and keeps rigidly to the wording and the timing laid down by the test constructor. When taking a social history the social worker knows beforehand what information he is seeking but gathers it in a relaxed and informal manner, and intends the interview to be a helpful experience. The vocational guidance interview is one in which both information is sought and information given by the interviewer. The degree of structure is likely to vary with the style of the interviewer who may see himself as having a fixed brief or an open-ended counselling role. In child study the teacher may need to interview the child or one or both of his parents to seek information. The nearest parallel to this would be the social case history interview although it is unlikely that as much detailed information would be needed by the teacher as the social worker nor would it be desirable for him to try to seek it. What is likely is that the teacher will either want to obtain some extra information about the child's attitudes and interests to complete his study of the child or he will want to talk to the child to get his point of view. Most likely he will have both of these aims in mind.

The orientation interview
An example of an information-seeking interview would be what many counsellors call an 'orientation interview'. This would be held with each new pupil soon after he entered the school. In this kind of an interview the counsellor has two main objectives: (1) to obtain background information about the pupil, (2) to introduce himself to the pupil and to begin a friendly relationship with him.

FIGURE 21. DIFFERENT KINDS OF INTERVIEWS (ARRANGED ACCORDING TO THE DEGREE OF STRUCTURE)

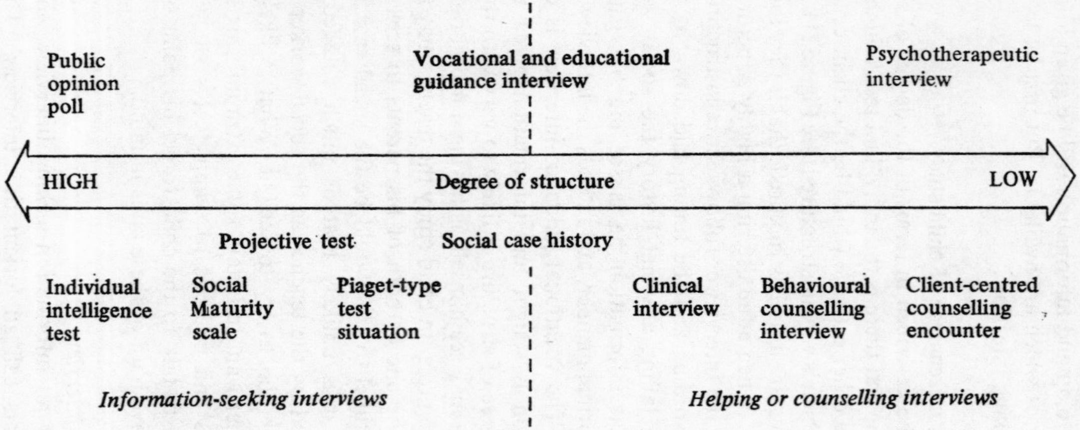

HIGH ←———————— Degree of structure ————————→ LOW

Individual intelligence test

Social Maturity scale

Projective test

Piaget-type test situation

Information-seeking interviews

Social case history

Clinical interview

Vocational and educational guidance interview

Behavioural counselling interview

Psychotherapeutic interview

Client-centred counselling encounter

Helping or counselling interviews

Public opinion poll

This will help to ensure that in the future the pupil will come to the counsellor if he has a problem or a difficulty and needs a sympathetic person to talk to.

The counsellor, in an orientation interview, will have some questions he wants answered. In order to keep the atmosphere friendly and to set the style for later counselling interviews, however, he will not pose these in a formal way. He will try to encourage the pupil to talk about himself and will ask as few direct questions as possible. The 'interrogation' style of interview is likely to impair any relationship so the counsellor will put general questions which will elicit a number of answers.

The term 'rapport' is used to refer to the relationship maintained in a structured interview between the interviewer and the one being interviewed. This relationship must be relaxed, warm, motivating.

Relaxed: There should be no tension in the interview. The interviewer must ensure that the pupil is quickly put at ease, that any worrying or disturbing element which creeps into the interview is reduced as quickly and as gently as possible, e.g., in an individual test situation the pupil may show alarm at being asked to do mathematical problems or unease when his father is mentioned. In these situations the interviewer hastens to reduce the tension in some appropriate way such as, by smiling, changing the subject, or by a humorous interjection. Notice that this is different from a counselling interview in which tension and the expression of emotion can be positive aids towards a deeper level of communication.

Warm: The relationship must be a warm and friendly one. The pupil must feel that the interviewer is friendly towards him and this feeling will only grow when, in fact, the interviewer does feel warm towards him. An artificial 'professional' warmth rarely deceives the child.

Motivating: This warm relaxed atmosphere should allow the pupil to perform well on an intelligence test or to talk freely about himself. If the interviewer can be not only warm and relaxed but stimulating too, then the pupil should respond in the interviewing situation with a liveliness and spontaneity which might be unusual. The pupil will feel motivated to do well in the test and will produce a wealth of interesting information about himself. This is especially important in those interviews which fall into the middle ground between the unstructured and the highly structured interview, e.g., the vocational guidance interview. On such occasions the careers teacher wishes to stimulate the pupil into thinking about himself in

F

an entirely new way and the degree of rapport he establishes will determine how far he achieves this aim.

The helping or counselling interview
When we get away from the highly structured interview, and most teachers and guidance workers will not wish to restrict themselves to formal situations of this kind, we enter into an interesting and exciting new world. Garry (1963) says:

> If you have ever stood knee-deep in the ocean surf, you have an impression of the dynamics of an interview. There are times when the ocean is almost still, the waves moving into the shore with barely a crest showing the movement of time; when the tide is running the force of the water as it pushes into the beach, or the undercurrent as the ebbing water cuts the sand from underfoot is keenly felt; and when a strong wind adds its force to the tide, the impact of the water as it hammers the shore is overpowering. Interviews range from the comparatively static and calm public opinion poll to the intense, at times overpowering, clinical interview. Calm or intense interviews are as dynamic as the ocean, with a constant interplay occurring between and within the participants as their attitudes, perceptions and feelings affect the course of the interview and determine its outcome. (p. 133)

This is a long way from the structured interview with its predetermined pattern, its fixed rules, its even calmness. To extend the analogy, if the clinical interview is a strong sea, then the structured interview is a placid canal. When we move on from the information-seeking interview to the helping interview we are moving into these less predictable waters. It is possible to train a good test administrator or a reliable public opinion pollster in a relatively short time and when trained these interviewers will be reasonably consistent. The outcome of a helping interview is much less predictable. There is considerable evidence, in fact, that any encounter of this kind can be either harmful or helpful and that the average effort over all helping encounters is a neutral 'no difference'. Commenting on this Truax and Carkhuff (1967) point out that some helpers are more effective than others and they have isolated the characteristics which make these counsellors more effective in their helping. Carkhuff (1971) has gone on to demonstrate the effectiveness of 'lay helpers', that is persons who have no formal training in counselling (see also Lawrence, 1972), and has produced in *The Development of Human Resources* a guide to their training. I have leaned heavily on his ideas in trying to draw up some useful suggestions for teachers who wish to act in a counselling role.

It has been found that helpful counselling experiences share three common characteristics. These characteristics are related to:

(a) the attitude of the counsellor towards his client, in this case the pupil in school
(*b*) the attitude of the counsellor towards himself as a person and
(*c*) the quality of communication maintained by the counsellor between his client and himself.

The attitude of the counsellor towards the pupil. The successful counsellor is characterised by the warmth and respect he shows towards the pupil he is counselling. Both of these qualities have been summarised under the terms 'acceptance' (Tyler, 1969) or 'unconditional positive regard' (Rogers, 1957). Warmth is not an easy emotion to learn. It comes from genuinely caring for the person we want to help but it also comes from being relaxed in other people's company, from being uninhibited about emotional expression, and from responding to the emotional cues which are given by other people. Many people I know who care deeply are hindered in their attempts to help others by apparent lack of warmth. What seems to happen is this, if a person responds appropriately to the tone of voice, the smiles, the eye contact, the gestures of others then he is seen to be warm. If he responds inappropriately, not looking at us, for example, or staring too hard or shifting eye contact rapidly, we feel he is rejecting our overtures of friendship and we perceive him as being cold. He will soon learn from us to perceive himself as cold. It is possible to learn to be more warm towards other people, close contact with a group who feel warm towards each other can teach one to pick up the cues and act appropriately, but this is not a quick or easy process.

Respect is equally important but somewhat easier to develop. It is important because only when a person feels self-respect can he begin to help himself and only when he feels that he is respected can he feel any self-respect. Many children in school have had no practice in self-respect. Failure in school, devaluing at home have left them with a negative self-image. The caring teacher, in a counselling interview, can help him to regain it. One example of what can be done by concentrating upon restoring self-respect is Lawrence's counselling experiment with remedial readers. Three groups of children, all backward in reading, were carefully matched. One group received a programme of remedial reading, another group received individual counselling, the third received counselling and remedial reading. It was the children who received counselling alone who made the best progress in reading. The explanation of this would seem to be that counselling increases self-respect, while reading, however skilfully taught, decreases the self-respect of backward readers since the children are being put again into a situation in which they have failed in the past. Hence the reading scores of those who received the least teaching in reading are the ones which go up most (Lawrence, 1971).

Examples of teachers talking to children with and without respect can be found in *Kestrel for a Knave* by Barry Hines.

The attitude of the counsellor towards himself. Carl Rogers says that the counsellor should be 'all of a piece', that he should have 'congruence'. Truax and Carkhuff describe the same characteristic as 'genuineness'. They are referring to the *sincerity* of the counsellor in the counselling situation. This is linked with the counsellor's own feelings of self-respect and the conviction of the value of what he is doing. As Carkhuff (1971) says, 'At first the emphasis is upon not being phony. Later the emphasis is upon the helper being as real as he can be. That is he is free to be himself' (p. 171). It is not easy for the teacher beginning counselling to sound sincere. He is too self-conscious, too concerned with technique. This is one reason why it is useful to begin counselling in a safe situation, in role-play, in counselling exercises, in routine interviews. After the teacher has had time to practise counselling skills with fellow-trainees without fear of hurting anyone he can move more quickly out of the self-conscious phony stage and into the stage when he is real and relaxed in the interview. Now it happens sometimes that there is a conflict, within the counsellor, between being warm and being sincere. Some clients are more difficult to warm to than others and if one simulates warmth then one is being insincere. Tyler says of this situation, 'In most instances the conflict is temporary. As the counsellor recognises and accepts the conflict in his own attitudes in the same way that he would accept it in a client, the negative reaction disappears' (1969, p. 58). This is why the term 'genuineness' is preferred by some to 'sincerity' since it implies that the counsellor must understand his own motives. Once he recognises the reasons why he is not feeling warm towards someone he is moving towards acceptance and eventual feelings of warmth. Sometimes it is necessary to recognise that our feelings towards the client are negative, not just lack of warmth but actual feelings of hostility. It may be necessary to discuss with the client the feelings that he is arousing: 'You know you make me feel angry when you talk about the boys in your class that way. I know they've done a lot for you and you just seem to me to be ungrateful.' A statement like this preserves the genuineness of the counselling encounter while perhaps endangering temporarily the warmth of the relationship. Most counsellors feel it is a risk worth taking. This kind of a conflict happens less often than one might suppose. It is the counsellor's constant aim to look at the world through the eyes of his client and it is difficult to do this and feel hostile. Besides, once a teacher has conducted a number of counselling interviews and these have been warm, rewarding experiences, his expectations are all positive and, just as the teacher can find himself liking even the most unlikable children if they are his special responsibility in the school, so he can find himself responding warmly in the interview even to an aggressive or cynical client.

The quality of the communication between counsellor and client. The counselling interview should be characterised by the depth of *understanding* and the *constructive* nature of the communication between counsellor and client. The term 'empathy' or 'empathic understanding' is often used to describe the first of these qualities since we are talking here about the ability to put ourselves inside the skin of another, to see the world as he sees it and experience it as he experiences it. The difficulty for adults of taking the child's point of view has been emphasised previously but it can be achieved both on a moment-to-moment basis and as a more general understanding of the pupil's point of view if we are prepared to listen totally to what he is saying. This means that we do not listen to him with 'half an ear', saving the other half for the more distant noises of the school or our own inner voices. This means that we listen not just to the words he uses but to the quality of his speech: 'loudness, pitch, speed, voice quality (such as breathiness or breaking to incipient tears and smoothness)', to use a list compiled by Argyle (1967). It means also that we listen, not just with our ears but with our eyes, so that we perceive facial expression, gestures, eye movements, posture:

If he leans forward or back, if he moves his chair nearer or farther from ours or turns it so that it is at an angle – these suggest approaches to or avoidance of the topic under discussion. Interviewers should take particular note of the feet, which he thinks are out of sight. The upper part of the body may appear quite at ease, but his tension and anxiety will be evident if he is curling his ankles around the leg of the desk. The small muscles of the fingers and jaw often give similar information. Tiny changes in the eyelids are invaluable clues – a slight widening when he is frightened and a slight closing when hostile or thoughtful. Skin changes should also be observed; these include slight flushing, pallor, and sweating. The eyes will turn towards or away from the interviewer much more rapidly than the whole body, thus indicating responses more immediately. (Rich, 1968, p. 61)

While catalogues of non-verbal responses like this can be useful in alerting us to the kinds of cues we can pick up, interpreting these cues is a more difficult and less satisfactory proposition. The meaning of particular gestures and mannerisms depends on the individual who is using them and the circumstances under which they are observed, e.g., pallor in the face can indicate fear but also tiredness, sickness or anger according to the person or the occasion so that we risk jumping to false conclusions but more than that, if the teacher is to achieve empathy with the children he interviews, he should observe without self-conscious interpretation or he will fall into the trap of objectifying his client and destroying the I-thou relationship.

What is being urged, therefore, is total listening, complete attention to the client. This in itself communicates so much to the pupil concerned. How often does anyone take the trouble to listen intently while he is talking? The fact that someone is attending to him communicates concern and respect. When that someone shows that he understands what is being said by responding in appropriate ways then some of the isolation, the sense of alienation from his fellows that so many people feel is diminished. He can feel that someone shares his problems and, once he feels this, his problems seem less important. Another result of the shared experience provided by empathy with a counsellor is that the person seeking help can begin to clear up distorted perceptions. Our view of the world can at times get out of focus. Relationships can seem twisted, problems can grow out of proportion, troubles seem giant-size. The only way to adjust the scale, to bring things back into focus is to compare our perception of the events with someone else who shares our viewpoint. Only in an empathic relationship with another person can this checking of perceptions take place.

The empathic understanding developed during the interview is the main therapeutic, or helping, agent in counselling. It is not quite enough, however. The interview must not just stand still. It must move forward into deeper levels of feeling, further shared insights and constructive forms of help. Various names have been given to this characteristic of the interview. The terms *concreteness* and *specificity* emphasise that the interview must not be woolly, that it should focus on the client's problems and that it should produce specific help. I have used the term *constructive* to describe it because I feel that the client should see the counsellor's intervention as constructive, useful, practical. It is this quality which raises the counselling interview into a purposeful therapeutic encounter.

The helping interview goes through three definite stages:

Stage One   :   exploring problems or possibilities
Stage Two   :   achieving understanding
Stage Three :   achieving action.

Stage One. The interview begins by exploring the client's problems, in a case which involves change, or his possibilities in a case which involves choice. A *change* case is one in which the client wishes to alter some aspect of his life, 'I'm lonely, help me to change', 'I'm failing in maths, help me to change', 'I can't get on with my mother, help me to change.' A *choice* case occurs when the client is faced with an alternative. 'Shall I take Physics or Chemistry?' 'Shall I leave school now or stay on for A-levels?', 'Shall I leave home or live on unhappily?' In either case we must not try to help until we understand his problem and we can only understand if we allow a period of exploration to take place. We should never assume that the problem or question posed by the client at the beginning of the interview is his main concern or even a real concern. This means that we must give him time to talk about it, to explore the possibilities and to reach a clearer view of what his problem is. There is even more to it than this, Carkhuff says, 'Sometimes the helpee comes to us and presents us with a problem that is not the real problem. It is as if he is testing us to see how good we are. If we cannot sense the real problem then he will not share it with us. And this sharing of the real problem as seen by him is the necessary first goal of helping. When the helpee explores himself he helps the helper to understand his problem better' (p. 168).

Stage Two. The second goal of a counselling interview is to help the client understand his own problem. Following the stage of exploration the counsellor helps the pupil to put his problem into perspective. Here the quality of the communication which has been developed is put to the test. If the counsellor has achieved empathic understanding then the client will begin to understand his own problem which he finds reflected as it were, back to him.

During both these stages the emphasis is upon responsiveness. The counsellor must respond to the words, the emotions, the experiences of the client.

In the second stage, however, the counsellor begins to initiate action. From the relatively passive role he has taken in the early stages he moves into a more active role. He will begin to confront the client with the implications of his behaviour and the likely conclusions of his choices. He will need to tell the client what is going on between them so that he will understand the situation and eventually understand himself.

Stage Three. Finally, the counsellor will help the client to decide upon a course of action. In this stage he is clearly playing an active role. Having helped the client to achieve understanding of his problem he will assist him to act upon this understanding. Very likely the client will have decided what he means to do and the counsellor will support him in his decision and help him to implement it. At other times the counsellor will need to set out the options and help him to choose between them. Yet again the counsellor will need to take action and with the client's approval will make the necessary arrangements. In many instances the decision that is taken will mean further interviews. Perhaps the client will go away with certain tasks to perform, skills to practise, choices to consider and will return to the counsellor to discuss the progress he is making. Perhaps the counsellor will feel that a supporting relationship is necessary and will see the client regularly to support and encourage. Perhaps the problem is one that could be best dealt with by someone else, in or out of the school and the counsellor will discuss this with his client and help him to take his problem elsewhere.

It is clear that there are many different ways of handling counselling interviews and many different outcomes may be expected. Some children may be helped in a single short interview, others will need continuing help. Whatever the length of treatment and whatever the outcomes, however, the chief source of help is the relationship which is developed.

People need close human contacts, 'recognition hunger' Berne (1966) calls it, 'human nourishment' is the term Carkhuff uses. Deprived of this close human contact, babies may be physically as well as emotionally impaired. Deprived of satisfying human relationships, children and adults may become unhappy, anxious depressed, maladjusted. Schools need to provide this basic human nourishment especially when a child is troubled and distressed. Teachers as well as counsellors can satisfy this need when they realise the value of the counselling interview.

12

Helping Children with Problems: The School

In this book we have discussed concepts of guidance and counselling within the context of child study. The point was made early in the book, however, that child study itself is barren unless the knowledge gained of individual children can be translated into effective helping. Some indication of the needs of young people and the problems that they face has come out in the previous chapters while discussing child development and the various ways of studying it. It is necessary at this stage to look a little more systematically at the kinds of needs young people have and the ways in which schools and society at large can try to satisfy these needs.

Human need can be visualised as a pyramid with the most acute, most visible kinds of needs at the top and the most universal, least recognised needs at the bottom (see Figure 22). Children with *gross handicaps* have been recognised as having special needs for a long time. The blind and the crippled were the first to receive special education, the deaf and the mentally handicapped much later. Helen Keller made the public aware of the difficulties experienced by those with multiple handicaps when she, blind and deaf from early childhood, made lecture tours in the early part of this century. In spite of this historical background, however, we cannot feel complacent that extreme handicaps are completely identified and cared for. Autism has only within the last decade been recognised, as distinct from mental retardation on the one hand, and deafness on the other. It has received much publicity during the last few years but there are appropriate special educational facilities for very few of Britain's autistic children.

Brain damage has been recognised for some time as a factor in cerebral palsy, epilepsy and severe retardation. It is only recently, however, that the special needs of brain damaged children, particularly those without severe physical symptoms, have been distinguished and the treatment of these children is still disputed territory. The same applies to dyslexia and developmental aphasia, two conditions associated with minimal brain damage, while less controversial but equally troubling problems exist with the educational treatment of the increasing numbers of children suffering from spina bifida.

What can be said in general terms about the needs of handicapped children? They certainly need special medical and educational

FIGURE 22. A PYRAMID OF NEED

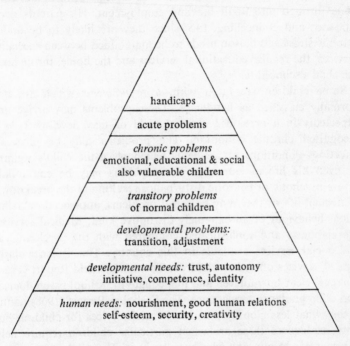

treatment: physiotherapy, hydrotherapy, speech therapy, diagnostic and remedial education. This treatment can be received most effectively in schools catering for the specialised needs of particular groups of handicapped children. On the other hand, one question which has never been satisfactorily resolved is whether there should be a policy of integration or segregation. The tendency over the last decade at least has been towards integration, i.e., to teach handicapped children alongside normal children. The trend has been for smaller special schools, for special classes in ordinary schools and for the integration of handicapped children into ordinary classes. The danger is that, in trying to avoid the danger of institutions, the baby may be thrown out with the bath water. A balance needs to be struck between the two extremes which will ensure that the benefits of special services will not be lost while allowing handicapped children to remain in the community from which they come and to which they must return. Whether he is educated in a special school, a special class or an ordinary class the handicapped child will need more continuous care and guidance than the normal child, and this will need to begin at birth and continue through into adult life and employment. His parents need guidance and councelling, too, since they are likely to be under extreme stress and liaison needs to be maintained between specialist services, the regular educational services and the home, throughout the child's school life.

Some children are faced with *acute problems* which are not normally classified as handicaps. These problems may arrive unexpectedly in a previously normal child or may develop from a recognised chronic condition. The problems may be physical, infectious conditions or accidents which place the child's welfare or even his life in jeopardy. The problems may be emotional; severe psychotic or neurotic disturbance resulting in the breakdown of normal life or they may be social problems, anti-social or delinquent behaviour of an extremely disruptive kind. Medical services are elaborate and sophisticated compared with the psychological and social services available in this country. This is particularly true of services offered to children. The Summerfield Report (1968) makes it clear how uneven and inadequate the school psychological and child guidance services are. The Seebohm Report (1968) paints a somewhat less gloomy picture of social services for children but how inadequate these are when particular children require help is very clear to any one who has sought it. The needs we are considering at this stage are the most extreme that children are likely to reveal. Extremely disturbed children, dangerously aggressive, seriously depressed, incapable of sustaining relationships, precipitating crises wherever they go, present society with some of its most serious problems. Many are not given adequate treatment until they precipitate a crisis. Even then the range of resources is limited and children are often inappropriately placed. When a seriously maladjusted child can no longer be kept at school or home the only answer is a boarding school for the maladjusted – if one can be found. Often the child has to wait months or even years for a place and eventually ends up by travelling hundreds of miles, away from the home and the community to which he eventually must return. If the child has broken the law then other provision is made and again this is frequently inappropriate to the needs of the child.

In order to deal with this level of need a number of small flexible units are needed centred, as far as possible, locally. There should be day units and boarding units, some providing residence only and requiring attendance at normal schools, others being self-contained. Some should be co-educational, others single-sexed. Some should cover a wide age range, others should be limited to a narrow age range. Generally they should cover a range of disabilities, specialist needs being provided by visiting staff and, where appropriate, by pupil visits to other schools and centres. Many studies have made estimates of the number of problem children that may be expected in a normal school population. The estimates have varied from 2 per cent of the school population to 49 per cent according to the age of the children studied, the definition of problem behaviour used, the degree of severity referred to and the country in which the survey took place. An international survey (Wall, 1955) showed that estimates of the total incidence of maladjustment of all levels of severity ranged from 7·6 per cent in New Zealand to 49 per cent in the United States. It was reported that severe maladjustment, which is the level we are considering here, was estimated as ranging from 4 to 12 per cent of the population. Even if we take an even lower estimate of 2 per cent (Martens, 1944) we could expect that in a school population of 50,000 there would be 1,000 severely maladjusted children. This would mean that a local authority, dealing with a school population of this size, could set up 100 small units catering for different ages and types of maladjustment in different ways. There would be scope for permissive environments for children who have been restricted and contained, highly structured environments for children from chaotic home environments, units with a medical bias for children with suspected brain damage, others with behavioural or remedial biases. A generous and stable staff could be supplemented by peripatetic specialists: speech therapists, teachers of the deaf, psychotherapists and remedial teachers. Again there is need for parent counselling. There is nothing so stressful for a family as a maladjusted child and the family reaction to the child's behaviour is an important factor in ensuring that the behaviour is sustained.

The distinction between acute and *chronic problem behaviour* is easier to maintain in theory than in practice. In physical terms we are thinking here of the child with long-term health problems, the asthmatic child, the delicate child, the child with heart disease, who live restricted lives but generally avoid crises. Medical services are well adapted to the needs of recognisable and treatable conditions of this kind. As far as behaviour problems are concerned we can discern three different types: personality difficulties, learning difficulties and social difficulties. The term 'personality difficulties' here refers to those children who are prevented from living a full and effective life by reason of maladaptive personalities. For example, children with excessively high levels of anxiety, children who are driven to seek status through attention-seeking, children who need power and engage themselves in continual power struggle, children who revenge themselves on other people for their own hurt and disappointment and those who withdraw from human contact as the surest way of avoiding further hurt. Children with chronic personality difficulties are even less well served than those with acute problems since sometimes it is only a crisis which initiates treatment. The main service provided for children with behaviour problems or inadequate personalities is child guidance and, as previously mentioned, child guidance is unevenly distributed throughout the country and, even at best, is inadequate to meet the needs.

The kind of treatment offered (see ch. 13) suits certain kinds of problems and certain kinds of children but at best it is likely to be fragmented and sporadic. The appointments at the clinic may be weekly, but, in between appointments, the child is in school and needs to be contained and treated there. The need for a flexible range of education services (as mentioned on p. 173) must be re-emphasised since it is needed for children with personality difficulties as well as those with acute problems. The Inner London Education Authority has gone some way towards establishing such a range of units as this list shows:

(*a*) Tutorial classes for the maladjusted.

(*b*) The Educational Guidance Centre, providing for secondary pupils with acute behaviour difficulties.

(*c*) Additional part-time teachers for children recommended for admission to schools for the maladjusted who are waiting for placement. Such help enables experienced teachers to be brought into schools part-time to give these children individual attention.

(*d*) The School Psychological Service.

(*e*) Child Guidance Clinics.

(*f*) Peripatetic teachers to help infants with particularly difficult and disruptive traits.

(*g*) Experimental Nurture Groups that is 'classrooms' of a semi-domestic nature in which the child's unmet early needs can be at least partly met.

It is easier for a large authority in a concentrated area like London to establish such units than most other local education authorities but the needs at this level are hardly being touched upon even by the ILEA.

It might be expected that children with learning difficulties will receive more adequate treatment than those with emotional difficulties but this is not so. A child who is failing is less disruptive to the life of the school than the child who is disturbed. The child with chronic learning disability tends to be treated by way of streaming and setting which is an acceptance of the disability, a confirmation of it. The more extreme cases are helped through remedial classes, opportunity classes, centres for children with language difficulties and diagnostic and assessment centres. The educational psychologist tends to play a crucial role in assessing and allocating children to these special units. The need again is for numerous small units with different approaches catering for children with different needs and aiming to return children to normal classes. These units should be placed in ordinary schools and the children should be integrated into the life of the school as far as possible.

When we come to social needs the same rule applies. The day of the large orphanage, children's home, or approved school is, or at least should be, over.

Another group of children who can be placed rather loosely into this category of children with chronic problems are vulnerable children. Some children because of circumstances, temperamental or social, are more inclined to be hurt than others. At the physical level there are 'delicate' children and that strange group, the 'accident prone'. There are children who are emotionally vulnerable too, children with higher levels of anxiety than the average or with predispositions to mental illness. Then there is the very wide group of 'socially disadvantaged' children who because of social circumstances, poor housing, unemployment, broken families and a multitude of social ills are more vulnerable to social and psychological hurt. To these should be added immigrant children, a special group, disadvantaged by virtue of language difficulties, cultural differences and what is sometimes called 'culture shock'. Vulnerable children need continual support throughout their school life. Their progress needs to be monitored and periodic checks made on it. It is not sufficient to rely upon the normal vigilance of the school staff. They need to be alerted to the child's vulnerability and should be required to make regular reports on him. The need for positive discrimination for socially disadvantaged children has been constantly emphasised (for example, Halsey, 1972). This means that the curriculum has to be specially adapted and special services have to be provided including that of 'educational visitors' who, on the analogy of health visitors, will call at people's homes to explain good educational practices as the health visitors explain good child-rearing practices. It is not sufficient, however, to rely upon educational services alone. The positive discrimination must be applied to housing, social services, job opportunities, leisure activities. Immigrant children are one group which, given educational priority at the right time, will respond quickly by improved performance.

Foster homes are preferred to even the best endowed institution and small family groups are the rule rather than the exception. Small home-like residences of this kind should be attached to district schools so that children can maintain contact with their families, their school-mates and their community.

This has been a very hasty coverage of the kinds of abiding problems which children have, with some ideas about their treatment. The difference between the 'abnormal' children we have been describing and 'normal' children is a matter of degree. Even those children who are generally recognised as being normal and well-adjusted can pass through periods of stress during which they can show many of the symptoms of the more seriously disturbed child. Very often this stress is externally imposed. Bereavement, illness of a parent, break-up of a home through divorce or separation can all throw intolerable strain upon a child. The reaction to this stress can be excessive anxiety, depression, impaired performance, damaged relationships, self-defeating behaviour like drug-taking. Sometimes the breakdown occurs because of an accumulation of smaller strains, family tensions added to lack of success at school, or absence as a result of illness causing a loss of friends, or difficulties with work brought to a climax by oncoming exams. The symptoms will often resemble those shown by children suffering from acute problems. The difference will be in degree of severity and duration of disturbance. The child suffering from bereavement or responding to stress in the home is likely to recover spontaneously if given no help. If left to himself, however, without support and help during his crisis, his development will be set back perhaps to a serious degree.

Transitory problems of this kind can hardly be predicted. They can be prepared for, however, If the school accepts that it is a caring community, it must organise itself so that it can act like one. It is not enough to say that 'all teachers care'. All teachers must be given the opportunity to care. The caring function of the school needs to be considered closely by all the staff, who will work out its implications and act upon their conclusions. If any aspect of the school – music, art, religious education, sport – is to receive its due emphasis, then it has to receive its due recognition. The same applies to pastoral care. For it to function adequately in a school its importance must be recognised in tangible ways: positions of authority, timetable time, evaluation. Staff meetings which consider these arrangements of pastoral care will discuss such questions as areas of responsibility, methods of communication, record systems, confidentiality, co-operation with parents, liaison with outside agencies. The education officer of the Inner London Education Authority reporting to the Education Schools Sub-Committee says: 'It is of the utmost importance that decisions should be reached as a result of full consultation with the entire staff. *I would like to suggest, therefore, that all secondary schools should take a one-day closure in order to hold a conference of all the staff to discuss organisational and curriculum problems assisted by the district inspector, education psychologist and a representative of the education welfare service'* (ILEA 1971). This is a very good idea but I feel such a conference should be both preceded and followed by staff discussion and that, when the policy details and the organisational structure have been worked out, the meetings should continue as case conferences. Some examples of pastoral care organisations as they have been set up in some comprehensive schools are shown in Figure 23, p. 178. From this kind of approach a caring staff can become a purposefully concerned and vigilant staff and the transitory problems of normal children will not go unnoticed.

When a staff is fully aware of its caring function and all this entails and is organised in such a way as to effectively perform this function, it becomes apparent to the staff collectively that some specialisation is called for. It is at a time like this that the appointment of a school counsellor is natural and inevitable. Not only can a counsellor co-ordinate the guidance activities of a school and maintain liaison with external guidance agencies but he can act as a consultant to his colleagues, and provide for the children an extra source of help introducing a potent therapeutic force into the school itself.

In the primary school the situation is different. Each teacher has responsibility for one class and meets that one group of children for a large proportion of the working day. It is easier to study children under these circumstances, easier to be aware of their problems

FIGURE 23. SYSTEMS OF GUIDANCE OR PASTORAL CARE IN COMPREHENSIVE SCHOOLS

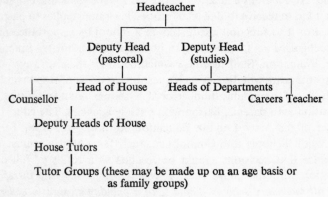

EXAMPLES OF VERTICAL ORGANISATION

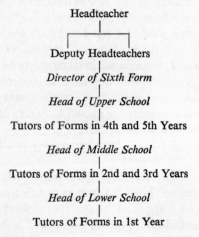

EXAMPLE OF HORIZONTAL ORGANISATION

although not necessarily any easier to help them. The primary teacher as much as the secondary teacher needs the opportunity for individual contact with his pupils and their parents. He needs to be able to get to know the other guidance workers in the district and the kind of help they can offer. What is more he needs assistance within the classroom. This assistance can come not only from specialists who do not just visit to advise but stay to help but also it can come from ancillary workers who should be allowed into the classroom to assist the teacher with troublesome, anxious or handicapped children. Every primary school should, in addition, have one teacher with special responsibility for guidance. This teacher could have extra training to equip him for the position and the appointment of such teachers throughout the country's primary schools would do more to foster good mental health than any other single move.

Caring schools of this kind are able to respond also to the developmental problems met by children. These problems can be predicted from a knowledge of child development and can be anticipated in the life of the school. Problems of transition and adjustment belong to this category. These include transition from home to school, from primary school to secondary school, from school to job or college; adjustment to new teachers, new subjects, new approaches. There are particular problems posed at different age levels, e.g., the pressure of 11+ and public exams, problems associated with physical development at puberty, problems associated with burgeoning independence in the middle teens. The wise school will anticipate that these problems are likely to arise and will arrange the school in such a way as to minimise their seriousness. Take, for example, the problem of transition from primary to secondary school. Liaison between the two schools, co-operation between staffs, visits of secondary pupils to primary school to answer questions about 'our school', return visits by primary school children to the secondary school, the use of sociometric tests to preserve friendship groups, a transition period in the secondary school so that the new pupils can get used to a subject-based timetable after a class-based timetable.

Problems of this kind will arise predictably at various stages of development but will apply to a minority of children only. All children, however will face the same developmental tasks and will share the same developmental needs. The need to develop trust, autonomy, initiative, competence and identity is common to all children. Most will experience little apparent difficulty in acquiring these characteristics but all can be helped, can be facilitated, in their achievement. In addition to the basic requirement of a concerned and vigilant staff the school needs to have a programme to foster positive mental health. Again it is not sufficient that this programme should remain informal, left to all teachers to introduce into their lessons whenever it seems appropriate. There must be a fully worked out curriculum in personal and social education which takes account of what is going on under various subject headings – biology teachers will certainly be giving some sex education, religious education teachers some moral education. Consumer education, vocational education, civics and education for parenthood may be recognised school subjects while community service, anti-pollution projects and education for leisure may be established within the school. The English teachers may be exploring personal relationships through literature and drama, the physical education teachers extending self-awareness through movement and dance. The need is for this to be co-ordinated into a whole which has as its focus the pupil himself, his own development, his own awareness and the way he communicates through personal relationships. A satisfactory syllabus in personal-social education could be based on the concept of developmental tasks and could take account of recent curriculum development in the fields of moral education, vocational education and social studies. There is no time here to go into the details of a satisfactory syllabus in personal-social education. It is sufficient to say at this time that the concept of developmental tasks provides a satisfactory theoretical basis upon which curriculum development can proceed. The methods used by teachers should be appropriate to the subject, which is, basically, training in human relationships. The syllabus should not be a didactic one, 'Chalk and Talk', but an experiential one. Group methods, case study methods, role-playing, simulation should form the basis of the work with individual projects and community service to give it depth.

The base of the pyramid is occupied by human needs, those needs which are shared by all people and not just those shared by all those young people who are growing up in our society. All people need satisfying human relationships; all people need to feel a measure of self-esteem through satisfying interaction with their environment. The need for human nourishment which we all have stems from our social being; the need for creativity stems from our individual being. A school can help to satisfy these needs by being a community in which every child can find the kinds of satisfying relationships which he needs. In such a school the individual, freed from the need actively to seek recognition, will be able to become truly creative, that is he will be able to set free some of the creative possibilities within his own individuality.

Helping Children with Problems:
The External Agencies

Guidance, to be effective, must be a continuous process from conception to maturity and beyond. The school plays a crucial part in this guidance but not an exclusive one. There are numerous services or agencies, statutory and voluntary, aimed at the child from the moment of his conception. It is important for teachers to understand what agencies serve the children they teach and what kind of services they offer. A linear representation of these services is shown in Figure 25. We shall consider these services which are relevant to school-age children beginning with the School Health Service.

The school health service
The principal school medical officer (PSMO), who is also likely to be the medical officer of health, is in charge of the school health service and has under his command a number of school medical officers, a supporting service of school nurses, a school dental service and a range of supporting services including speech therapy, audiometry and peripatetic teachers of the deaf. Sometimes the PSMO has overall control of remedial services, including home teaching, although in other authorities these services come under different departments of the Local Education Authority. The head teacher can expect the SMO to visit the school formally for general medical inspections (see p. 95) but also on frequent occasions to see children with special needs, e.g., asthmatic children, those with heart difficulties, physically handicapped children and to follow up children with other needs, less extreme, observed at medical inspection or referred by the teacher or educational psychologist.

The school nurse will visit more frequently, particularly in the infant school, and will keep contact with the SMO and the child's family doctor. Usually the school nurse will also be the health visitor for the district and will prove a mine of information about the child's background and his social as well as his medical needs. The PSMO is also likely to be in charge of arrangements for special

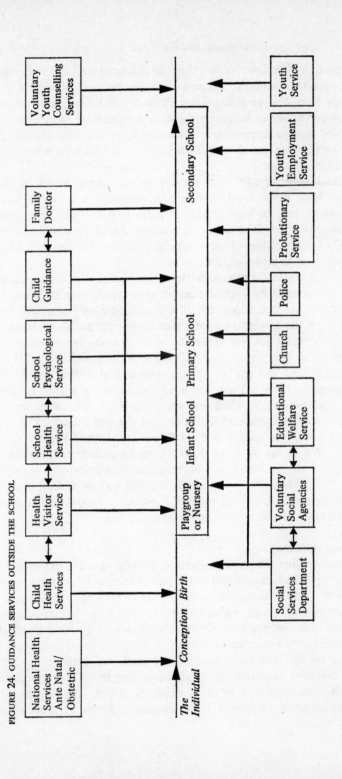

FIGURE 24. GUIDANCE SERVICES OUTSIDE THE SCHOOL

education although this duty may be allocated to a superintendent of special education. Recommendation for special school may come from SMO or Educational Psychologist or may arise from a trial period at an assessment centre. Referral for speech therapy or for hearing assessment is made to the PSMO as are requests for home teachers and the school health service will keep liaison with children in hospital.

SMOs may be employed entirely in the school health service, may have other local authority responsibilities in child health clinics or may be local general practitioners with part-time school duties. In 1969 there were 3,200 school doctors (SMOs) and 8,800 school nurses. Most of these were also employed in the child health clinics and as health visitors.

There has been a general tendency for routine medical inspections to be replaced by special examinations which may be requested by nurse, teacher or parent. 'This throws an even greater responsibility on the teacher to keep under review the health problems of all children in her care and to be ready to bring them forward for discussion with the doctor and nurse' (Pirrie and Dalzell-Ward, 1962, p. 190). The teacher who observes a child with difficulties of a medical kind should ask the head teacher for a chance to speak to the school nurse when next she calls. If the difficulty is serious, of course, the headteacher can contact the SMO directly. The ideal arrangement is spelled out by Pirrie and Dalzell-Ward: 'To be successful in his work the doctor must be an accepted member of the staff of the school and on terms of familiarity with everyone' (p. 190). When this situation applies, and I know at least one SMO who achieved it, formal referral is unnecessary and health needs, both physical and mental, are most easily met.

Child guidance
Responsibility for child guidance is usually vested in the PSMO who employs child psychiatrists and psychiatric social workers to co-operate with educational psychologists in manning the clinic. The overlapping school psychological service is a different matter. Often this too, for administrative purposes, is grouped under the school health service but, more usually the educational psychologists, who provide the main professional staff, are employed directly by the chief education officer although they spend a proportion of their time employed in child guidance clinics. The Summerfield Committee is very clear in its recommendation on this matter,

'Since responsibility both for education and for school health ulti-
mately rests with the education authority we are strongly of the
opinion that it would be logical for all educational psychologists
to be centred administratively on the education departments of
local authorities' (DES, 1968, p. 65).

Cyril Burt (later Sir Cyril Burt) was appointed educational psychologist to the London County Council in 1913, the first appointment
of this kind in this country. Since then psychological services in
schools have developed slowly and in 1966 there were only 396
actually employed in England and Wales (DES, 1968, p. 4). Most
of these were employed in two capacities: as a member of a child
guidance team and as part of the school psychological service.

FIGURE 25. CHILD GUIDANCE AND THE SCHOOL PSYCHOLOGICAL SERVICE

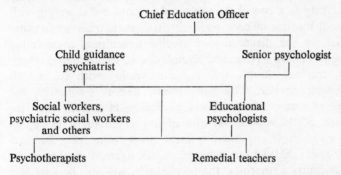

It is hard to describe the work of a typical educational psychologist since there are so many variations throughout the country
and different psychologists emphasise different duties. Ideally,
however, the psychologist will spend much of his time in schools,
working with teachers, diagnosing children's problems, advising on
their treatment, making contact with other agencies, carrying out
remedial treatment and therapy and arranging for transfer to special
classes and schools.

Some of the children seen on his school visits he would recommend
for child guidance. These would be children whose problems were
likely to entail protracted treatment. Other children would be referred
to child guidance by their family doctors or, occasionally, by social
workers. The psychologist would make school visits to see all these
children, preferably before, during and after treatment, in order to
co-ordinate the efforts of school and clinic. Following referral
to child guidance the child and his parents would be invited to the

clinic. There the parents would see the social worker; the child would see the psychologist, if he had not already interviewed him, and the psychiatrist. Following these initial diagnostic interviews there would be a case conference to decide on future treatment. Sometimes a course of treatment with the psychiatrist would be indicated, sometimes one with the psychologist. The social worker would continue to work with the parents, or at least the mother, in the home or in the clinic while the psychologist would maintain the school contact ensuring that the treatment in the clinic was helped by the treatment in home and school. Treatment in the clinic might involve play therapy, painting or other creative work; remedial reading or arithmetic, client-centred or behavioural counselling.

Other duties performed by the educational psychologist are likely to be: acting as a consultant to special schools, collaborating with the school medical officers, audiometrists, paediatricians and other specialists in the diagnosing of specific difficulties, co-operating with the probation services and juvenile courts, lecturing to mothers' groups, teachers, health visitors, collaborating with the Youth Employment Service. The Summerfield Report emphasises the shortage of supply of educational psychologists and the need for expansion of the service. A ratio of one psychologist to 10,000 school children is suggested (present proportions vary between 1:7,000 and 1:30,000) but, even when this figure is reached in all local education authorities, the psychologist will still be stretched too far to work adequately with individual children or to spend enough time in schools to ensure continuity and personal contact. It is for this reason that counsellors have been appointed to schools, although logically the chief need for them is plainly in the primary school. One comment which was made following the Summerfield Report seems to me to sum up what is needed: 'There was a substantial demand from chief education officers that psychologists should help in remedial education, ascertainment of ESN children, group test surveys, advanced education for teachers and educational research. The report takes the view that much of this work must be done by non-psychologists. Unless and until the output of "child guidance psychologists" can be raised – as in Scotland – to such a level that enough are available to provide these extra services – as well as a greater proportion of preventive, advisory and educational work – the logical way to meet these needs is by a body of teachers who have studied the psychology of education beyond the level attempted in their initial professional training for teaching. Many of the Chief Education Officers' demands could be met just as well by a psychologically educated teacher – perhaps better since child guidance psychologists will be increasingly without teaching experience if we accept the recommendation in Chapter 4' (Curr, 1969). The recommendation in ch. 4 of the Summerfield Report, mentioned here is that psychologists in educational services need not be trained teachers.

Social Services departments

The Social Services departments have changed considerably over the last few years and are still in process of change. This is the result of the Seebohm Report (1968) and the 1970 Social Services Act which followed it. Figure 26 illustrates the organisation of local authority social work before and after the Act. As can be seen all social work services have been centred under one director except for social work in child guidance and the Probation Service. The Education Welfare Service is still disputed territory. Seebohm recommended its inclusion in the Social Services department but this recommendation was not accepted by the government. In some areas social work services for schools have been incorporated directly into the Social Services department under the director of social services but in most areas they remain a separate service under the chief education officer. I shall describe the work of the Education Welfare Service (EWS) in some detail and shall follow it by a less detailed description of the children's services offered by the Department of Social Services.

Education Welfare Service

The EWS has grown principally out of the need for attendance enforcement but it also developed as a means of organising the provision of welfare benefits to school children such as shoes or free meals. Although it has had no legal definition or recognition it has become a way of helping and supporting families and has provided a link with existing social welfare agencies. Most education welfare officers have had no specific training in social work and they have been lacking in adequate status or pay, but they have been operating in the role of educational social workers and as Seebohm says, 'Over the years it [EWS] has made an indispensable contribution to the welfare of school children' (1968, para. 223). The EWO usually operates from the Education Offices (or the District Offices where

FIGURE 26. THE ORGANISATION OF LOCAL AUTHORITY SOCIAL WORK BEFORE AND AFTER THE 1970 ACT.

I *Organisational structure of social work services prior to Local Authority Social Services Act (1970)*

1. *Within the local authority setting*

County or County Borough Council

Education Committee	Children's Committee	Health Committee	Welfare Committee
Chief education officer	Children's officer	MOH (sometimes combined)	Chief welfare officer
Psychiatric social workers in child guidance clinics	Child care officers	Mental welfare officers	Welfare officers working with the old, the handicapped and the homeless
Education welfare officers			

2. *Outside the local authority setting*

Medical social workers in hospitals. Probation officers attached to courts or prisons. Social workers in voluntary organisations.

II *Organisational structure of social work services consequential upon L.A. Social Services Act (1970)*

1. *Within the local authority setting*

County Council or County Borough Council

Education Committee	Social Services Committee
Chief education officer	Director of Social Services
Psychiatric Social Workers in child guidance clinics	Social workers providing services principally to: children deprived of a normal home life or otherwise at risk, families at risk, the old, the homeless, the physically and mentally handicapped
Education Welfare Officers	

2. *Outside the local authority setting*

Medical social workers in hospitals. Probation officers attached to courts or prisons. Social workers in voluntary organisations.

N.B. (1) The location of this chart refers only to *social work* and not to the full range of *services* provided by the agencies identified.
(2) The Local Government Act (1972) which reformed the structure of local government also provided for the incorporation of medical social workers into L.A. Social Services Departments as from 1st April, 1974.

such exist) and is responsible for co-operating with a number of schools. Other duties, administrative and welfare (e.g., the escort of handicapped pupils to special schools) are divided out among the team. The EWO's first concern is still likely to be the problem of avoidable absence from school. Truancy, irregular attendance and school refusal are growing problems (see Tyerman, 1968) and the realisation by all concerned with children that enforcement by way of the law is not necessarily the best treatment of problems of absence throws increasing strain upon the education welfare officer. He is likely to be the person who visits the home to discover the reasons for absence. This may lead to extended case work with the family and liaison with the social services; it may lead to the EWO providing practical help of some kind or negotiating some change in the school; it may lead to referral to child guidance or in some cases to bringing the child or his parents before the court.

There are three main categories of 'avoidable' absence which is the term used to include all absence from school for which acceptable reasons have not been provided (e.g., illness, holiday). Truancy is when the child stays away from school without his parents' knowledge. Usually the truant leaves for school in the morning but never reaches it. He is often at great risk then because of the opportunities for delinquent behaviour that are afforded. Irregular attendance usually occurs when parents are uninterested in their children's school attendance. They may keep them home to look after the baby, let them stay home on the slightest pretext; they are not concerned about occasional truancy and are often prepared to provide notes of excuse. School refusal tends to take place with the parents' knowledge but against their wishes. Their child may refuse point blank to go to school, may simulate illnesses, or may become hysterical whenever attempts are made to send him. He may have developed an acute phobia or fear of school or some aspect of it (bullying children, embarrassing situations, scolding teachers, frightening subjects). He may be suffering from separation anxiety and become extremely anxious when he has to leave home or when he leaves mother. It may not always be clear what is causing the child's refusal to go to school. One boy showed obvious signs of anxiety when taken in a car from his home towards the school. This anxiety increased the closer he came to the school until it became unsupportable. When the car was turned round and headed back for home the anxiety diminished. Was this a clear case of school phobia? When the driver continued past the house and drove away in the

opposite direction to the school the anxiety again increased. This
was separation anxiety! (See ch. 14). The most extreme cases of
school refusal need to be dealt with by child guidance but even then
the EWO is likely to be involved in many ways and in cases of irregular
attendance and truancy he is often the only one who can act. His
duties do not end here, however, since he provides the main liaison
between school and social services. This means that he becomes
concerned with the prevention of delinquency and, through the
parents, with children having behaviour problems. Often the EWO
is the first person to discover family problems, poverty, poor
housing conditions, illness, and marital problems, and he is often
called upon to act as mediator. At other times he provides much
needed liaison between health services, educational services and
social services.

Social Services Department

It is because of the confusion of social workers who may be working
with one family that the Seebohm Report recommended the cen-
tralisation of services under one director. To prevent the establishment of 'monolithic departments', deployment into local offices
has been taking place. Each of these offices deals with a comparatively
small geographical area and contains a staff of social workers with
different specialisms but devoted to the idea of 'generic social work'.
That is, they will not take on a case load of all children, all handicapped adults, for example, or all old people but will take on a
cross-section of the community, with the emphasis on helping whole
families rather than individuals. The advantages of this scheme
are plain to see. It will eliminate much unnecessary duplication of
services since child care visitor, mental health officer and family
welfare officer will be combined in the person of one local authority
social worker. During the re-organisation period, however, many
difficulties have arisen. Old lines of communication have been
broken, new ones have not been connected; old teams have been
broken, new ones have not been built up. In addition, the social
services department have had to tackle new duties and these have
not always run smoothly. This has happened particularly in the
area of court work. The Probation Service fell outside the terms of
reference of the Seebohm Committee since it was not a local authority
service. This meant that it was not possible to integrate all the social
work carried out with children before the courts with other social
work. Social Services, as a result of the Act, took over from magi-

strates the responsibility of deciding what happens to young offenders on care orders, including the power to send them to approved schools. Since social workers are loath to take children from their families the number of young offenders in approved schools has been dropping since the implementation of the Act. The magistrates have retained the power to send young offenders to detention centre or borstal and, feeling that the Social Services are misusing the care order, have increasingly done so. A report of the Magistrates Association says: 'With depressing regularity juveniles who have been placed in the care of local authorities reappear on fresh charges, sometimes quite soon. The legal provisions for their disposal are extremely limited but the situation is aggravated when it is found that after being placed in care they are permitted to remain at home' (*The Guardian*, 8 Dec. 1972). At the time of this report attempts were being made to heal the breach between courts and social services.

In those areas where the Social Services departments have taken over education welfare services other difficulties have arisen. The school can no longer make easy contact with a familiar EWO and, while new methods of liaison will no doubt be laid down, it will take time before they are as effective as the best of the old. This illustrates the necessity for developing and maintaining close and easy communication between school and external agencies. The Seebohm Report went so far as to suggest: 'the establishment on an experimental basis of a recognised post of special responsibility in some schools for liaison with outside social agencies particularly with the Social Services department. Such a post might be combined with counselling or with remedial teaching. It might also be linked with direction of school community services' (para. 221). Where counsellors have been appointed to schools this liaison work has been seen as part of their responsibility. In a few places counselling has been combined with school community services and here again effective liaison has been developed. Other secondary schools have built up systems of pastoral care and guidance and teachers with key positions in the school, head of house or head of year, for example, have the responsibility for liaison. No doubt other schools have established their liaison, as Seebohm suggests, via the remedial teacher, but I do not know of any in which this operates. In primary schools it is most often the responsibility of the head teacher. What is important is that whoever takes on the job in a school should take it seriously. He needs to be well informed about the work of his opposite numbers in the Social Services department and should develop personal contact with them. This will mean introducing himself to the social workers and proving to them, not only that he provides an efficient point of contact for them but that he understands their language and the way they operate and also that he conforms to the same ethical standards of confidentiality as they do. When liaison operates on a first-name basis of professional trust it is likely to provide the co-ordinated effort on behalf of children in trouble that the Seebohm Report looked forward to.

The Probation Service

Before the Children and Young Persons' Act of 1969 the Probation Service was responsible for a wide range of children's services including the supervision of all children and young people placed on probation, carrying out most social enquiries for juvenile courts, aftercare of children from approved schools and some adoption work with children. Much of this work has been transferred to the Social Services Departments and the Probation Service has consequently less to do directly with young people. Under the new Act a child brought before the court may have one of the following orders made:

A Supervision Order ⎱ supervised by local authority social
A Care Order ⎰ workers

A Hospital Order   under the Mental Health Act.

In some cases the parents will be 'bound over' to take care and exercise proper control of their children under pain of forfeiture of a bond.

The juvenile court still has the power to commit young people to Quarter Sessions for sentencing to a period of training in a Borstal institution. When the young person is released from Borstal he is likely to be kept 'on licence' under the supervision of a probation officer. Again the court has retained some of its pre-1969 powers as an interim measure and this leaves the probation officer with some work with young people. It is true, however, that the Probation Service has a diminishing responsibility for children.

The approved school system is being restructured so that each independent unit will support a much smaller number of children, and these, together with all the residential children's establishments previously administered by the children's department, are to be known as 'community homes'. These will be available to all children in the care of the authority and will provide a range of specialised care according to the needs of the children. New forms of 'intermediate' treatment are being introduced under the supervision order. These will include a range of activities on a part-time or residential basis, such as adventure camps, dramatic and artistic activities, community service, educational classes which may be practical or academic, swimming and sporting activities, remedial and recreational activities, field studies, local history and archaeology. Most of these will not be set up especially to cope with young offenders but will be existing services, activities and organisations such as the Boy Scouts. They will have agreed to co-operate in providing intermediate treatment, will have been included in a scheme prepared by the Children's Regional Planning Committee of the area and will have been chosen by the child's supervisor from that scheme as being suited to his needs (DHSS 1972).

The Youth Employment Service

The Youth Employment Service in March 1971 was operated by 143 of the 197 local authorities in Great Britain. In the rest of the country the service was provided by the Department of Employment. There were 4,000 careers officers each serving on average 420 15-year-olds. (NYEC 1971). These officers provide a service to the schools which complements the work being done by careers teachers, personal tutors and school counsellors. Where careers education is begun early, is integrated into the curriculum of the school and is aimed as much at the 'examination' pupils as those leaving without passing examinations the careers officer can be most effective. Otherwise it is difficult for him to be much more than a crisis counsellor in the vocational field. The picture throughout the country is an uneven one. 'While many schools are developing careers education as an important part of their role, in the majority of schools the pattern of co-operation with the YES reflects much older and outdated concepts of the guidance process while in a very few schools the value of co-operation with careers officers is still not recognised' (NYEC 1971, p. 11). If guidance is to be a continuous process throughout school life then the careers officer must not be thought of as a placement officer for the school leavers but as an important member of the school's vocational guidance team (e.g., see TES, 8th March 1974).

G

14

Helping Children with Problems:
A Strategy for Teachers

In this final chapter it is necessary to bring together the different threads of studying and caring for children into a plan of action which may be followed by teachers. Such a strategy is shown in summary form in Figure 27. The four stages represent a natural focus of the pastoral care of the school on the individual child with the evaluation stage representing much needed feed-back into the organisation of the school.

Stage one: Becoming aware of problems
The efficacy of any help rests, in the first instance, upon the identification of a need. This means that teachers need to possess the qualities of vigilance, curiosity and accessibility. What is more, these qualities need to be reflected in the ethos of the school and implemented in its organisation, curriculum and teaching methods. Vigilance suggests efficient observation on the part of individual teachers and an effective record system. It has been a continual source of surprise to me how often teachers can be unaware of children with problems or how information about children's difficulties can fail to reach the consciousness of individual teachers. A counsellor was telling me only recently how he circulated information about a child's hearing handicap to all his colleagues only to find some weeks later that the child was sitting idly at the back of the classroom. What is needed therefore is continual scrutiny of school children by all teachers, together with a method of collating information, observations and hunches and disseminating all this in effective ways to all interested teachers. Since the aim is the welfare of each individual child there need be no unnecessary piling up of information for its own sake but there has to be some way of getting the information to each teacher so that the individual child in the classroom can be helped. Each school needs to develop its own system of communications, but whatever the methods used the different aspects of the communication system (e.g., curriculum

FIGURE 27. A STRATEGY FOR TEACHERS

Stage One: Becoming aware of problems
This demands three qualities on the part of the teacher:

Vigilance: efficient observation and efficient records. This is most effective when linked to a well-organised pastoral care system in a caring school.

Curiosity: asking the right questions; using the right screening procedures. The teacher needs to be actively concerned about the welfare of his pupils and to use child study methods to discover their problems.

Accessibility: being available to children and parents; being seen to be available. If the teacher is accessible to his pupils and their parents they will come to him with their problems.

Stage Two: Investigation
There are three stages of diagnostic investigation:

Set up hypotheses based on observation or pupil self-exploration.

Check hypotheses using further observation or continued exploration with the client of his problem. Check against normative data.

Adopt a working hypothesis when an hypothesis seems to be supported by all available evidence base action upon it although continuing to test it against further evidence.

Stage Three: Appropriate action
Selection of appropriate action will depend upon the working hypothesis adopted and the resources available within the environment. Three types of action may be taken:

Involve other people. Involvement of colleagues within the school, parents or other pupils. Referral to extra-mural professionals in the helping services.

Change the environment. The pupil's group within the class, his class or stream or his school may need to be changed. At other times his work, his diet or other aspects of his physical environment should be changed.

Change behaviour. Behavioural modifications can be used to change specific behaviour. Counselling can be used to induce changes in attitude, particularly self-attitude, and combinations of counselling and behavioural modification can give help in more complex behavioural problems.

Stage Four: Evaluation
Continual assessment of the effects of helping action needs to be made.
If the action seems to be appropriate continue or confirm.
If the action seems inappropriate change or check working hypothesis.

communications, social communications, pastoral care communications) each need to have a co-ordinator. Most secondary schools these days are too big for the headmaster to manage all the necessary co-ordination. In the matter of pastoral care co-ordination, I believe that a school counsellor or someone trained in counselling is best fitted for the role. Such a post could be set up as head of guidance services or head of pastoral care. Housemasters or year-masters could take on these duties although, again, overall co-ordination is necessary and ideally a co-operative system with counsellor, housemasters and careers teachers in a guidance team should be set up. Primary schools are not as yet so big as to make communications complicated, and the head or deputy can take on the role. Ideally, he should seek counselling training or similar experience.

Communications within a school need to be informal as well as formal and this is most likely to happen when it is not only individual teachers who are concerned about children but the staff as a collective body. I have been in schools in which talk about pupils is discouraged as 'shop' and where deep concern for the welfare of children is hidden behind a superficial veneer of cynicism.

This brings me to the second quality 'curiosity'. We ought to be curious about the children we teach, to want to understand them. Some people discourage this as 'nosiness' and resent well-meaning curiosity about their own or other people's business. Real concern lies, however, in real interest and, if we are interested in other people, we want to know all about them. If there were more nosy neighbours, for instance, there would be fewer old ladies dying alone, fewer battered babies, fewer crimes. National stand-offishness and love of privacy can cover up lack of concern for our fellow-men. The teacher needs to have an active concern for the welfare of each child in his class. This means asking himself the right sort of questions and it is hoped that the earlier chapters will have been helpful in formulating these questions. It will be necessary to use screening devices: tests, questionnaires, observation schedules and to know what to look for in the results. For example, the teacher will be concerned to know whether any of his pupils are under-achieving. The question to ask is, 'Are any of my pupils performing in my subject at a level below what might reasonably be expected from other evidence?' The other evidence could be the pupils' performance in other subjects, their oral as compared to their written behaviour, evidence from records of earlier performance, status among peers, leisure activity (see, 'Things done on your own', Appendix C3). Screening methods can be adopted for all problem areas. (A book that does this well is *Identifying Children with Special Needs* by Kough & DeHaan.) What is being recommended here is an active curiosity. The teacher does not wait until problems are manifest but tries to anticipate their occurrence and to adopt a preventative approach.

This brings up the question of the teacher's accessibility. Children will talk about their problems to a sympathetic adult if they have the opportunity. It is not always easy for them to find such an opportunity. The more sympathetic the teacher, the more likely he is to be surrounded by other children at those rare times when he is not actively involved with their learning activities. The shy or troubled child will find it difficult to talk to a teacher at times like this and other opportunities must be allowed. This does not end with the children. Parents, too, will bring the problems of their children to the teacher if they feel that he is easy to reach and easy to talk to. Too often, however, parents will be encouraged verbally to come to the school but will be discouraged by the sheer practical difficulties involved. This is another very good reason why a school needs a counsellor. He can be seen by parents as the person in the school with the main responsibility for the welfare of pupils, because of his freedom from the timetable he is much more accessible and counsellors are usually prepared to see parents in the evening or to make home visits when necessary. If teachers in a school are genuinely concerned to be accessible to parents, similar kinds of arrangements must be made whether there is a counsellor in the school or not. The test of the accessibility of teachers is not their own readiness to hear the problems of children but the pupil's readiness to bring these problems to them. It is not sufficient to be accessible; one must be seen to be accessible.

Stage two: Investigation

Teachers becoming aware of their pupils' problems need to investigate further in order to gain a clear picture of the pupils' needs in relation to their pupils' own resources. During this stage a full range of child study techniques needs to be employed in order to collect data which will help in setting up and testing hypotheses about the nature of the problem. The first step arises naturally from Stage One, as we become aware that a child is experiencing difficulties, we begin to look for explanations. If these explanations are stated in ways which allow them to be tested we can call them hypotheses. Let us take an example. A teacher observes a child over a number of occasions dropping books and pens, tripping over feet, bumping into other children, knocking furniture over. What kind of explanations may be offered for this clumsy behaviour? A number of possible hypotheses will come to mind immediately. These can be summarised as:

1. *visual difficulties:* poor eyesight may result in apparent clumsiness
2. *orthopaedic difficulties:* there are several muscular and skeletal conditions which may result in clumsiness
3. *neural conditions:* serious illnesses such as muscular dystrophy begin with lack of co-ordination
4. *brain damage:* lesions in the brain which may originate from prenatal conditions or may happen at birth, or later from accidents or infection, can bring about muscular dysfunction
5. *puberty:* at adolescence rapid growth can cause clumsiness
6. *lack of confidence:* personality difficulties such as extreme anxiety and self-consciousness can make young people behave clumsily.

These conditions vary greatly in seriousness, of course, but initially they must be considered as possible explanations of clumsiness. Each of these hypotheses needs to be tested and eliminated if we are to be certain that we have arrived at the most adequate explanation of the difficulty. Some hypotheses can be eliminated very quickly. We need not consider number 5 on our list if the pupil is well outside the age of puberty. Others need to be checked by further observation, reference to record cards, interviews with the child concerned and checks with colleagues. Are there other indications of visual handicap? As suggested on p. 93 teachers can often be reliable observers of sight difficulties. Subtle orthopaedic and neural disorders are not so easy to spot and it may be thought unlikely that teachers could discover them where parents and doctors have failed. The truth is, however, that schools are often the first place where children are discovered to have such difficulties, whether they be of recent origin, e.g., degenerative diseases, brain tumours or long-standing such as epilepsy or cerebral palsy. Personality disorder as an explanation of clumsiness may be ruled out by other observations of good adjustment, of freedom from anxiety, of self-confidence and may be checked in interviews with the child.

As a result of this hypothesis-checking activity a working hypothesis should be adopted. This may be that the child appears to be short-sighted, or seems to have difficulty in maintaining balance, or more generally is clumsy because of some unknown physical condition. In all these cases it may be necessary to test our observations against any available standards or norms. Some of these will be established norms, like those for eyesight, intelligence or reading ability. Others will be informal norms that we adopt from our own experience, e.g., the standard of co-ordination that we should expect from a child of a given age (even here, in fact, we could use a visual-motor test to check our judgment, e.g., p. 97 and p. 245).

Stage three: Appropriate action
Having adopted a working hypothesis we can decide upon a course of action to follow. What action we take will depend on the hypothesis we have adopted and the resources that are available to us. If our hypothesis is that the child is suffering from a physical disability we shall wish to make a referral to the school medical service. We may need first to contact the parents to discover if any medical action has already been taken and to elicit their co-operation in any action we feel we have to take. Even if we have adopted the idea of personality disturbance as a working hypothesis it may be wise to make sure that there is no physical disability by asking for a medical examination.

Referral of this kind represents one type of action, that is, involving other people. This will be discussed more fully a little later.

Another kind of action we could take would be to change the environment. We might feel that the apparent clumsiness is the result of embarrassment and the child would be better working with another group of children. (Clumsiness is often quoted as a symptom of falling in love.) The third kind of action involves changing behaviour. It may be felt that counselling interviews will help to eliminate negative feeling about the self, that a position of responsibility in the classroom will lead to an increase in self-confidence, that dance, drama or physical activity will increase motor co-ordination. We could adopt one or all of these methods of helping our clumsy child.

Stage four: Evaluation
The final stage is one that is frequently omitted. Evaluation of the outcome of helping action is rarely carried out in any systematic way but if help is to be effective it needs to be continually assessed. This will demand further child study, further liaison with parents and external agencies and further discussion with other members of the staff. If the action we have decided upon seems to be helpful then we should continue with it. If the action seems inappropriate, then the treatment should be changed or the working hypothesis

should be checked to find if we have made a mistake. Evaluation should also serve as feed-back to the school. Information on children, their problems, their response to different modes of treatment is valuable in assessing the changes needed in the school organisation, its pastoral care, its curriculum and its teaching methods. Information about our clumsy child might cause changes in the school record systems, the liaison with the school medical service or social organisations within the school.

Guidance strategies

In trying to explain this strategy by reference to one particular problem, some dangers are run. No one problem can adequately fit the model which is being described and, in attempting to make it fit, the whole exercise may appear artificial and superficial. It is necessary now to look at the possible courses of action which a teacher can take to help children in more detail. In the first chapter these different kinds of help were discussed under the general term, 'guidance'. Counselling was mentioned in that chapter, and subsequently in Chapter 12, as one of these modes of help particularly appropriate to the school, which works mainly through the quality of the communication between counsellor and client. Most counselling encounters, however, will in addition include more specific kinds of action and when we look at the situation as a whole we can see that intervention of all kinds is made both in and out of school in order to help children. I feel that the term 'guidance' is a useful one to cover this variety of help but it is necessary to specify in detail the kinds of ways in which children with problems may be helped. For convenience the different kinds of guidance have been summarised in Figure 28. The focus of attention at any particular time, whether it be the individual pupil on his own, the individual as a member of a group, the environment in which the individual acts or the particular aspects of his behaviour with which he needs help, is listed on the left while the diagram is divided vertically into three columns to contain the areas of concern of the teacher, the counsellor and the external agencies. This gives twelve squares in which different kinds of helping action, education, counselling, psychotherapy and social work are listed. Many of these methods of help have already been mentioned, some in detail. Others like psychotherapy and social work are beyond the scope of this book. What must be dealt with in this concluding chapter, if only in a cursory manner, are the varieties of help which can be

FIGURE 28. GUIDANCE

Focus of attention	The concern of the teacher	The concern of the counsellor	The concern of the external agencies
The individual	pastoral care educational guidance vocational guidance	counselling educational guidance vocational guidance	psychotherapy case work vocational guidance
The individual *in a group*	social education group work	group counselling group guidance	group therapy
The individual's *environment*	modifying the classroom environment	modifying the school environment (sometimes modifying the home environment)	modifying the home environment (through social work and social action)
The individual's *behaviour*	behaviour modification in the classroom	behavioural counselling	behavioural therapy

given by the teacher and the teacher/counsellor in the everyday
school situation.

Multiple reference theory and guidance

Most ways of helping a person depend upon direct interaction with
that person. Theories of counselling and psychotherapy tend to
emphasise the importance of the one-to-one relationship in producing help and, traditionally, the interview is the main helping
format. This raises questions about the relevance of such an approach
to young children since it is based upon assumptions about the
level of articulation possible in young children and the degree of
individual autonomy which they have achieved. Adults may be
helped without the helper making any reference to other important
people in their lives, spouses, for example, or employers or colleagues. In fact this may be the only way to help that particular
adult since any other approach, such as trying to arrange better
working conditions for him, may seem patronising and may ulti-
mately prove degrading to the person we are trying to help. With
children it is not so straightforward. The young child cannot be
considered autonomous in the way the adult is and, the younger the
child, the more dependent upon his parents he is likely to be. The
age of the pupil seeking help is, therefore, one consideration. Another
is the source of referral. If someone comes to you of his own free
will to seek your help then he is your client and it would be inappropriate for you to involve other people in his problem without
his expressed permission. This applies whatever the age of the child
although the older he is the more likely it is that he will actively
seek your help.

Figure 29 represents an attempt to reconcile these two factors
and to explain the basis of different treatment. The term 'client-
centred counselling' is used to describe the first phase of the counselling process (see p. 167) since the approach adopted during this
phase is best exemplified in the client-centred counselling of Carl
Rogers. It must be pointed out, however, that as stressed in Chapter
11, the respect of the counsellor towards his client is a necessary
condition of all helpful action so that, even when a child is caught
red-handed pilfering and is sent to the counsellor because he needs
help, he still has his rights as an individual and these exclude his
being treated like a chattel and moved about without his understanding. The younger the child, the more necessary it is to adopt a
multiple reference approach. This recognises that the individual's

behaviour at any time is to a large extent the result of the combined influence of the behaviour of a number of other people on that individual. Child Guidance takes account of this by treating both the child and his family. When family therapy takes place the whole family is the subject of treatment and is interviewed at the

FIGURE 29. AGE AND REFERRAL BASIS IN GUIDANCE

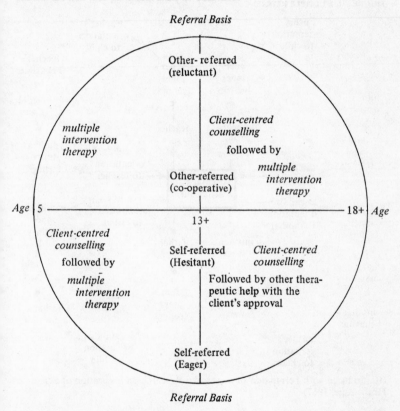

same time. Then the individual child ceases to be the patient with his parents co-operating with the therapist to help him; the family as a whole is the patient and when this happens it often becomes clear to all concerned that one member of the family is being forced into the role of scapegoat. The way in which an individual's behaviour is determined by the 'significant others' in his environment is illustrated in Figure 30. This has been taken from the book *The In-betweeners* (Center for Research on Utilization of Scientific Know-

ledge, 1967) which describes an action-research programme carried
out in Michigan on emotionally handicapped children. It is possible
to intervene, or enter into these cycles, at many different points.
Let us take the example of a child who is always in trouble with his
teachers, the ring-leader in noisy, disruptive behaviour. Through

FIGURE 30. MULTIPLE REFERENCE

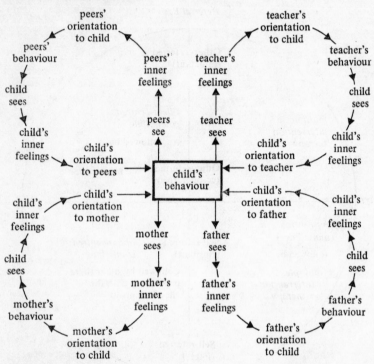

(Reproduced with permission of Center for Research on Utilization of Scientific
Knowledge, 1967)

individual counselling he can be helped to recognise his own behaviour as self-defeating and unproductive and can learn strategies
to make it more effective. Following the counselling session, however, the child will return to a classroom where his peers will expect
him to behave in certain familiar ways, where his status in the
group may well depend on his behaving in that way. His teachers
will expect him to behave predictably too and will be rather dis-
concerted when he does not do so. Let us take an example:

Richard's need for attention from his peer group led to his behaving in disruptive ways in the classroom. He was the ring-leader of unruly behaviour and made it very difficult for his teachers to maintain a satisfactory environment for learning. In three counselling sessions he was helped towards a greater understanding of his own actions and the effect they were having upon his own school attainment. He decided to change his behaviour and worked out with the counsellor ways of coping in the classroom which would satisfy his need for attention and yet would be socially acceptable. The new Richard, however, did not meet with the approval of his class-mates. They tried in various ways to provoke him so that he would provide the entertainment they were accustomed to. His teachers were suspicious of the silent, conforming boy he had become. They thought he was using new, more sophisticated ways of causing trouble and were relieved when his class-mates manoeuvred him into the familiar situation where he was representing them against the teacher. If Richard was to be really helped he needed backing up in his efforts to change his behaviour. At the very least his teachers should have been told so that they could have supported him and interpreted his new behaviour to the class. Inclusion in a group where he could have discussed his desire to change with his age-mates or even some general discussion in his class about stereotyping and the need that individuals have to break out of the mould would have helped to alert his friends to what he was doing and hopefully could have elicited their support. This would have been a 'multiple entry' approach and would have had more chance of long-term success than counselling alone. At other times home conditions may be the chief reason for anti-social behaviour and the conditions under which this behaviour has developed will persist unless some intervention is made in the home.

The multiple interventions which need to be made in a child's life space to support his own efforts at change can be of many different kinds. Class or group or even school can be changed, work arrangements and syllabuses can be altered so that different social groups can develop and different expectations arise. Sometimes the whole class can be brought into the treatment by eliciting co-operation, at other times only a few 'significant others' in the classroom may help. With older children in particular, the peer group may be left untouched but the child can be helped to recognise his school friends' reactions and can be prepared for them. The teachers involved with the child should be brought into the treatment from the beginning and their co-operation sought at every stage so that they can reinforce the child's attempts at rehabilitation. Parents can also assist by being kept in the picture and by having the child's behaviour explained to them in ways they can accept. It is often possible to enlist the parents' help in re-inforcing the child's attempts at new social learning. The kinds of intervention which are appropriate will depend on many factors including the organisation and climate within the school, the role of the teacher/counsellor, the age of the client and the conditions of the referral. Generally they will arise naturally during the action phase of a counselling relationship and will take place with the full knowledge and agreement of the client.

What we have just described has taken in many of the different kinds of help which were listed in Figure 28: counselling, modifying the school environment, modifying the home environment, behaviour modification in the classroom and behavioural counselling. I feel that there is a need to go through Figure 28 more systematically so as to explain the different forms of treatment mentioned in it, emphasising especially those which have received little attention up to now. These will include group work and behaviour modification.

The individual in the group

Teachers are concerned with groups and need to have some knowledge of how groups behave if they are to be effective as teachers. Such knowledge is even more essential for the guidance side of a teacher's job. Just as interviews may be classified according to the degree to which they are structured (see Figure 19) so may different kinds of groups be classified along a dimension according to their objectives (see Figure 31).

Groups are particularly appropriate in social education and guidance. These activities are especially concerned with feelings and attitudes and it is in groups that this kind of learning takes place most easily. Any programme of social education in personal

FIGURE 31. GROUP WORK

teaching groups				helping groups			
Mainly didactic ——————— Objectives ——————— Mainly therapeutic							
formal lecture group	lecture—discussion group	discussion group	guidance group	sensitivity training group	encounter group	counselling group	therapeutic group

relationships will need to include group work of all kinds. Educational and vocational guidance, too, will often be most effective when carried out in groups. For example, problems of vocational choice and decision-making or discussion of aptitudes and interests following the administration of tests are appropriately carried out in groups. Common problems of adolescence may be discussed freely in small groups whereas the same problems would be too loaded emotionally for the whole class and might never come to light in individual interviews. Groups discussing common problems come very close to group counselling in their therapeutic purpose but the term 'group counselling' is properly retained for groups which are brought together to share their problems as a way of obtaining help. Each member of the group will have been interviewed individually first to determine their readiness. The counsellor in such a group is in the same relationship to each member as the counsellor is to his client in the counselling interview. When it is properly done group counselling is a very powerful way of giving help. One reason for this is that attitudes are learned initially in groups, are practised in groups and will only change when brought out and examined in a group. Adolescents are particularly affected by the attitudes of their peers and are often suspicious of adult control so that the group is an appropriate place for them to learn adequate social attitudes. Another reason for the power of the group in affecting change is that it enables hidden assumptions to be brought out into the open and gives the opportunity for experimenting in new modes of behaviour. In a group each individual is able to experience himself as a helping person. Group counselling should not be undertaken as an economic measure to save the time involved in individual counselling but as an effective method of help in its own right. Some other kinds of group activity which have become popular recently are aimed at the emotionally healthy rather than those with specific problems. The intention in sensitivity training groups is to improve communication, to make the individual more aware of his own feelings and those of others and of the effect that his own behaviour has upon his fellow group members. The emphasis in the *encounter group* is upon personal growth especially in the areas of openness and honesty. The aim is to help people to live more fully and completely. Centres for group experiences of these kinds are springing up all over the country and seem to answer a need for improvement in personal relationships and self-knowledge. Teachers interested in extending their guidance role will find such experience useful in improving their sensitivity towards others and some of the procedures used by encounter groups can be used effectively in human relations training in schools.

The individual's environment

The concept of adjustment has for a long time dominated thinking about child development and problem behaviour. The child was judged according to his degree of conformity to social norms. If he deviated from them he was considered to be atypical, abnormal or maladjusted. Efforts were to be directed at bringing the individual back on to course, adjusting him to society, helping him to fit into his class or his school. It was always the individual who was felt to need the change, rarely the environment. Thinking about human behaviour has, however, altered in recent years and the emphasis is much more upon social action. At one time social workers accepted that there were 'Things we cannot change', to quote the title of a film on this subject; very few young social workers would accept this as a working premise these days. They would feel their priority to be changing housing conditions rather than helping people to adjust to them. The same thinking should influence teachers concerned with the guidance and welfare of children. Conditions in school often contribute directly to children's unhappiness, their 'maladjustment'. Streaming can produce 'delinquescent' classes (Hargreaves, 1967), corporal punishment can produce aggressive behaviour in children (Clegg and Megson, 1967), constant failure can produce maladjustment (Fernald, 1943), stress when beginning new schools, or at exam time can produce anxiety, extreme deviations from the norm (even when it is extreme brightness) can cause unhappiness and distress (see Pringle, 1970). Many of these circumstances can be altered if teachers in the school feel it to be worth while. Streaming can be abandoned for arrangements which are educationally more desirable, concepts of punishment and discipline can be replaced by concepts of remedying and self-discipline, failure can be reduced by fitting the work to the child rather than trying to fit the child to the work, stress can be reduced by anticipating its likely occurrence and planning to avoid it and children can be taught to welcome individual differences rather than to mistrust them. In other words, teachers should try to make schools what they try to make their homes, warm, accepting places in which no one is rejected or neglected.

More specifically changes can be made in the individual's environment when it appears to be hindering a child's development. Small but important changes like arranging the seating so that he may see and hear properly, or arranging it in such a way that he sits next to someone who is helpful and supportive rather than someone who is unfriendly or unreliable. Where group work is used there are many such opportunities. The peer group is particularly important to teenagers, and classroom groups or school teams can provide the kind of relationship which the child needs. By changing the group membership we can help provide the kind of social environment which can be most helpful. Direct help may often be given through the curriculum; change of work, reading-book, assignment, homework load, subject or set course can all provide the kind of relief or the kind of stimulus a child needs. Sometimes the changes need to be made in the school, rather than the classroom and changes in class, stream or band may have to be arranged. Perhaps the trouble will necessitate a change in school, to boarding-school, ESN school, School for the Maladjusted or School for the Delicate.

Modifying the home environment is very much more difficult and is properly the province of the Social Services Department. It often falls to other helping agencies, however, to intervene in the home environment of a particular child. The psychiatric social worker in a child guidance team will, for example, try to back up the therapy offered to the child by changing the attitude of other members of the family towards that child. Suggestions made by the psychiatrist or the educational psychologist about the way the child needs to be treated in the home will be interpreted by the PSW to the parents. The PSW will often find herself being asked for help in home management, the treatment of children or marital problems and as far as she can she will try to be helpful. The educational welfare officer often finds himself cast in the same role. Officially he represents the liaison between education services and individual families, and teachers should call upon his services whenever appropriate. The need to intervene in the child's life in as many places as possible, the need to modify the home environment in some important respect, the need for information about the child's home or simply the need to keep parents informed about the child's progress will call for liaison with parents and very often the EWO is the most appropriate person for this job (see Chapter 13). At other times, however, the school itself must undertake it and the parents should be invited to the school. If the parents cannot come to the school a teacher, or the counsellor representing the teacher, must make a home visit. Tact and diplomacy must be added to the other helpful characteristics of warmth and respect; for parents are, rightfully, suspicious of people who seem to be telling them how to look after their own children. The school can, however, do a lot to reconcile the conflicting claims of home and school, to explain the opportunities offered by the school, to avoid the child playing off one against the other and to interpret to puzzled parents the behaviour of a teenage child who no longer communicates with them.

Modifying individual behaviour
When children misbehave in the classroom, acting aggressively or seeking attention, the teacher needs to determine whether the behaviour is the result of the individual's own problems or the consequence of group feelings. If it arises from the dynamics of the group, if the class as a group, for example, are in conflict with the school or a particular teacher, if the class is testing out the teacher or if the children as a group feel frustrated or thwarted, then there is likely to be aggressive reactions. When, however, an individual with a problem acts in an uncontrolled way, offers violence to teacher or class-mates or pushes beyond acceptable limits in other ways, then the teacher is faced with the problem of helping the individual to overcome his problem while at the same time preventing him from 'infecting' the others with his misbehaviour. Redl and Wineman (1962) have offered a number of suggestions about the 'first-aid' treatment of deviant behaviour in the classroom on the principle that some immediate steps have to be taken even when the problem is a long-term one. A summary of their suggestions is made below:

1. Planned ignoring. This is the skill needed in sizing up surface behaviour and in seeing that much of it, unless reinforced, will peter out of itself. Interference is then limited to those behaviours which are too disruptive or are unlikely to stop from their own exhaustion. This technique of planned ignoring applies to most attention-seeking behaviour.

2. Signal interference. Much wild behaviour occurs, not because the child has no judgment about the danger implied or its unacceptability but because the danger signals given from his inner controls are too weak or the attractions of the behaviour are too great. At such times the observant teacher can anticipate his reaction and can signal his disapproval. For example, a child fiddling with a ruler can be observed to be tempted to use it as a missile. A shake of the head from the teacher can reinforce the child's own resistance to the temptation. The teacher needs to have a good relationship with the child and to act at an early stage in the behaviour if this technique is to be effective. Two boys squaring up for a fight can be calmed down merely by the teacher calling their names. Once they have exchanged blows, however, it is much harder to interfere.

3. Proximity and touch control. The nearness of an adult can have a calming effect on many children. Moving a child to a seat near the teacher is a recognition of this fact. Similarly the teacher, by moving round the classroom during activity periods can calm down many incipient disturbances. With many children, however, proximity is not enough. The teacher needs to touch the child, and to put a gentle hand on his shoulder or to pat his back. Some very disturbed children need to be held tightly to help them to control their behaviour but with most the lightest of contacts is sufficient.

4. Involvement in interest relationship. This is an expansion of the 'distraction' technique used with small children ('Look at that dog over there!' to a naughty small boy in a car). With older children, a well placed question or an interest expressed in their activities can serve to reduce tension and divert antisocial attention-seeking.

5. Hypodermic affection. This is simply to say that there are many times when what the child needs to help him control his behaviour is some extra display of affection from an adult. If the teacher can show that he cares for him at such times, he can help to reduce destructive or disruptive behaviour.

6. Tension-decontamination through humour. It is possible to reduce tension in problem behaviour by a judicious use of humour. This humour should, however, never be aggressive. It would be wrong to use sarcasm or cynicism for example.

7. Hurdle-help. Much problem-behaviour is the result of frustration and builds up when the child meets obstacles or 'hurdles'. The alert teacher can anticipate these hurdles and can help him over them so avoiding the behaviour disturbance. This should not be extended to become overprotective, but, used wisely, is a valuable way of ensuring that behaviour does not get out of control.

8. Direct appeal. Too often interference is through threats, punishment and prohibitions where direct appeal might work. Appeals related to group progress can be particularly useful where group loyalties are still present but appeals for consideration by the adult are effective with most children at some time. Examples of appeals are:

   (a) to personal relationship: 'that's not fair to me'.

   (b) to physical reality implications: 'that's dangerous'.

   (c) to group codes: 'the other boys won't think that's fair'.

9. Antiseptic bouncing. This is not to be seen as an angry adult throwing out a boy with a display of hostility, aggression, anger and triumph, but the removal of a child from a scene of conflict in an emergency. This can happen in a crisis when the child's behaviour has reached an intensity but also as a preventive step.

This technique has to be used with care and not at all if it means the breakdown of rapport between teacher and child. It is also important that the situation into which the child is removed is a satisfactory one.

10. Physical restraint. This is not to be confused with physical punishment since there is no evidence that the latter is effective in changing behaviour in any positive way. It is necessary sometimes with very disturbed children to restrain them physically to prevent them harming themselves and others. The adult in such a situation must remain calm, friendly and affectionate. This is not easy but the importance of a nonpunitive attitude during periods of restraint cannot be overemphasised.

These are examples of ways of modifying behaviour in the classroom. Let us look more closely at the ways in which individual children may be helped by such methods.

Behaviour modification sounds a rather sinister activity like something out of *1984*. The term, however, covers all attempts to change behaviour and this includes bringing up children, training and education. Behavioural psychologists have analysed classroom behaviour according to learning theory and behaviour modification is the scientific application of procedures which teachers use in unscientific ways all the time. One of the basic concepts of learning theory is 'reinforcement'. Learning takes place or, in other words, a response is more likely to recur, when that response is followed by a satisfying event – a reinforcer; a response is less likely to recur when it is followed by an unsatisfying event. This means that reinforcement can be positive or negative. Positive reinforcements consist of rewards of all kinds: verbal rewards such as praise, smiles, encouragement, interest, attention; more tangible rewards like good marks, stars, merit awards, privileges; object rewards like sweets, coins and tokens; and promises of reward or privilege. Negative reinforcement includes punishment: corporal punishment, scolding, sarcasm, bad marks, being put on report, detentions and, also, the withdrawal of reward, interest, encouragement or privilege. Now, if learning is to take place, it is important that reinforcement be given as close to the act which is to be learned as possible, at least in the early stages of any new learning. It is important, too, that reinforcement should be consistent, that is, it should occur as far as possible after each occurrence of the response, although again this is most true in the early stages of learning. This means that learning takes place most easily when the reward follows closely behind the event, e.g., when a teacher marks a child's work as soon as he completes it, when he praises good behaviour whenever it occurs, when he punishes bad behaviour every time it happens. Now there are many difficulties about this. Consistent, immediate reinforcement is not easy in a classroom and this applies particularly to social behaviour rather than academic or intellectual behaviour since it occurs in less controlled ways. There is a particular difficulty in the use of punishment in suppressing undesirable behaviour. What is likely to happen is that, when punishment is given, the pupil does something to avoid that punishment. This avoidance behaviour is not necessarily desirable behaviour, e.g., the child could hide things, do things on the sly, run away, play truant. Since the teacher does not see this behaviour it is not punished and this means that it is reinforced. Thus the consequence of punishment is that the avoidance behaviour is reinforced rather than the misbehaviour suppressed. Again it is very difficult to give immediate negative reinforcement to misdeeds. Instead other responses become reinforced, e.g., the child learns to distrust the teacher, to hate arithmetic or to dislike school. Redl and Wineman say this about punishment. 'If you ever thought of using punishment . . . because it "saves trouble" . . . give that daydream up in a hurry' (1962).

One example of the way in which reinforcement maintains undesirable behaviour is attention-seeking. Here the child's attempts to gain attention are reinforced every time the teacher takes some notice of him. Even if the teacher scolds or punishes, the attention-seeking behaviour is still being reinforced and will, therefore, be strengthened. To reduce attention-seeking to acceptable levels one must use 'planned ignoring' of the undesirable attention-seeking while reinforcing other more desirable means of achieving notice. Shouting out answers or leaving the desk to come to the teacher are ignored while plenty of attention is given to quiet work, and 'putting up hands' or other approved ways of obtaining attention are praised. If the attention-seeking is more disruptive it may be necessary to use 'antiseptic bouncing', that is, removing the child from the scene to a place where he cannot cause trouble, but even this is reinforcing to a certain degree and it certainly increases the child's need for attention. In general the modification of seriously disturbed behaviour is helped by bringing the child concerned into his own treatment. It is better for him to know that his behaviour is disruptive and to understand that he will be ignored when he shouts out in class so that he will co-operate with the treatment and will learn to control his own behaviour. Some children, however, react to discouragement and frustration by withdrawal rather than by attention-seeking. If they characteristically employ avoidance reactions then they do not develop the social skills necessary for everyday living. They need to be helped to develop new methods of coping, new skills in communication, new ways of responding to other people. In the classroom the teacher will draw the withdrawn child into the classroom society in as many non-threatening ways as possible. He will need to be asked direct questions where he is certain to know the correct answer. He will be encouraged to read out loud if only for a few minutes at a time, to take part in plays if only in non-speaking parts, to take a constructive role in group work. The secret is to go slowly in this socialising process and to make sure that no step forward into social contact is too big for him, and that when the step is taken it is reinforced promptly. If we ask him to perform a social task for which he is not yet ready, he is likely to retreat again into his non-demanding world of silence. Sociometric studies will have helped to identify the social structure of the classroom and the isolate can be helped by assigning him to warm, accepting groups. Not only must the escapist be encouraged to communicate within the classroom but also he needs to be given tasks to perform which allow him to achieve significance within the school community.

It is difficult to help the withdrawn child by counselling techniques which depend upon verbal interchange. The counsellor needs to use various ploys which will encourage the pupil to talk. It does not matter initially if this talk seems irrelevant to the pupil's problems. Talk of any kind should be encouraged and reinforced whenever it appears. It may help to ask the pupil to describe his day in great detail, reinforcing with approval every statement he makes. It may be useful to have him talk about his school work, read out loud, draw pictures and talk about them, respond to simple projective techniques like interpreting pictures, telling a structured story (see p. 156) or completing sentences (see p. 155). What is important is that the counsellor does not content himself with talking to the pupil nor allow himself to become discouraged by lack of progress. The withdrawn child makes slow progress into human relationship but every step he takes is important.

Besides reinforcement techniques other methods of behaviour modification are known as 'desensitisation' or 'reciprocal inhibition'. They are based on the principle that it is impossible to be relaxed and anxious at the same time and are effective over a wide range of difficulties, including phobias and other conditions producing anxiety. Very often relaxation techniques are employed to remove the fear of particular situations; at other times affection, feeding or social reassurance are used to counteract anxiety. Let us take school phobia, for example. Many cases of school refusal are the result of home circumstances and cannot properly be called a phobia, but some children are genuinely anxious about school. A simple treatment of such a problem would be the systematic desensitisation of the anxiety. The child would be helped back into the school by a series of gradual stages. Woody (1969) describes ten such stages which might be set out in this way:

1. Watching children pass his house on their way to school.
2. Walking out of his house with school books.
3. Walking the route to school.
4. Seeing the school in the distance.
5. Standing in front of the school.
6. Standing alone on the playground.
7. Standing on the playground with other children.
8. Standing at the doorway of the school.
9. Standing in the hallway of the school.
10. Standing in the classroom.

Step No. 1 is the least anxiety-producing and Step No. 10 the most, and these steps will have been determined in a counselling relationship with the child. The person helping the child (EWO, educational psychologist, school counsellor or teacher) would begin by standing with the child at the window watching the children going to school. He would discuss his feelings, giving him reassurance and help him to feel relaxed. He would then accompany him through the different stages, giving him help and encouragement all the time. This may well be spread over many weeks and the child may stay at some stages for a considerable time. Woody in fact feels that many more steps (at least twenty) would be needed. Eventually the affection and social approval he has received at each stage will counteract the anxiety and he should be able to face school again. This may sound a long, drawn-out treatment but, if successful, it is much shorter than the protracted treatment of school refusal called for by other methods used at present. Sometimes the counsellor will treat the phobic person without leaving the interview room. The hierarchy of fear-producing situations will be decided upon within a counselling relationship after which the client will be taught relaxation techniques. Then gradually he will be taken in imagination through the stages while remaining relaxed. His level of anxiety will be carefully observed and the experience stopped as soon as he feels uncomfortable. By taking the child gradually through the hierarchy of situations and by teaching him techniques of relaxation he can be helped to tackle the real situation. Other problems for which this treatment can be used are: fears of snakes, spiders, cats, etc., fear of speaking in public, fear of water, fear of exams. At a simple level my wife and I used it on our baby daughter when she developed a fear of her bath water. On the principle that she could not be fearful and relaxed at the same time we gave her a bottle to feed from while she was in her bath. At first she drank apprehensively and her bathtime was a hurried occasion but, as she learned to associate the water with the pleasures of drinking, she began to enjoy her bath again and very soon she could enjoy her bath without her bottle. Desensitisation procedures of this kind are usually very time-consuming and for this reason are probably outside the province of the teacher. The counsellor, working with the child guidance clinic, the educational psychologist, or, in cases of school refusal, with the EWO can use these techniques, however, and may give help to children who appear to be beyond other forms of help.

Other occasions on which desensitisation or relaxation training may be used include excessive fear of exams, fear of speaking before a class, fear of travelling on a school bus. Sometimes the relaxation training itself can be helpful and the pupil who becomes so anxious during examinations that the panic interferes with his answers or forces him to leave the room can be taught to relax, to slow his breathing, to think of pleasant things until he has sufficient control to continue. It is better, however, to rehearse the situation beforehand so that the pupil has reduced the anxiety by associating the situation with a pleasant relaxed state.

Another way of modifying behaviour depends on the use of role-playing. Teachers will be familiar with this technique as a way of helping children to understand another person's role. At its best role-playing can give training in empathy, that is, it can help the participant to put himself inside another's skin, to feel as he feels. This is obviously relevant to the particular problems of children who may need to understand someone else's point of view, that of their parents for example, their teachers or their friends. Another use for role-playing is to teach particular social skills – how to talk to people, how to behave in a job interview, how to respond to provocation. Children can be helped by role-playing in the classroom during English lessons, for example, or social education. Various role-play situations can be introduced and roles can be assigned to different children. This will enable the teacher to make sure that children can practise the particular skills they most need to learn. Children with more serious problems can play roles in small groups or in the individual counselling interview. Take, for example, the child whose repertoire of social skills is so limited that he can never think of any verbal response to teasing and so responds with aggression. In the safety of the counselling interview the pupil can try out the kind of social situations in which he fails and can learn to respond in more socially appropriate ways.

Social modelling is another method of behaviour modification which is frequently employed by schools. Imitation has always been seen to be an important way of learning and social modification is a favourite technique of the advertisers. The model may be the teacher himself, the counsellor, older pupils or filmed models. It is important that the models used should be prestigious ones in the eyes of those who are to be helped. The modelling can be made more effective by discussion of the behaviour modelled to draw attention to the significant features to be copied. For example, older pupils can demonstrate social behaviour, job interviews, talking to policemen or public servants, talking to the opposite sex. Following the demonstration the spectators can discuss the demonstrated behaviour with the actors.

This chapter can give only the briefest introduction to methods of behaviour modification which may be used in helping children with problems. It should be sufficient to demonstrate that, when children have been studied and their needs understood, appropriate help can be selected from among a large number of approaches and specific techniques.

The purpose of this book has been to describe child study in the context of child development, emphasising in particular those methods of study which seem best suited to the needs of students, teachers and counsellors. The final chapters have attempted to relate the discovery of information to the process of helping. In order to achieve confidence in the use of either methods of observing or methods of helping children supervised practice is necessary. This should be part of the initial training process and should be the subject of in-service courses. Teachers in school could get this practice through case conferences to which could be invited educational psychologists, remedial teachers, social workers and school medical officers. In this way greater understanding of children could be added to greater confidence in helping them with their problems.

Bibliography

ALLPORT, GORDON W., *Pattern and Growth in Personality* (London, Holt, Rinehart and Winston, 1963).

ALMY, MILLIE, *Ways of Studying Children: a manual for teachers* (New York, Bureau of Publications, Teachers College, Columbia University, 1959).

AMERICAN COUNCIL ON EDUCATION, *Helping Teachers Understand Children* (ACE, Washington D.C., 1945).

ARGYLE, MICHAEL, *The Psychology of Interpersonal Behaviour* (Harmondsworth, Penguin, 1967).

AUSTRALIAN COUNCIL FOR EDUCATIONAL RESEARCH, *The Adjustment of Youth.* ed. by Cunningham, K. (Melbourne, Melbourne University Press, 1951).

BALDWIN, A. L., KALHORN, J., and BREEZE, F., 'Patterns of parent behaviour', *Psychol. Monogr.* (1945), pp. 58–73.

BARKER, R. G., and WRIGHT, H. F., *Midwest and its Children: the psychological ecology of an American town* (New York, Harper and Row, 1955).

BELLAK, L., and BELLAK, S. S., *Manual of Instruction for the Children's Apperception Test* (New York, CPS, 1949).

BENE, E., and ANTHONY, J., *Family Relations Test: an objective technique for exploring emotional attitudes in children* (London, NFER, 1957).

BERDIE, R. F., LAYTON, W. L., *The Minnesota Counseling Inventory* (New York, The Psychological Corp., 1957).

BERNE, E., *The Games People Play: the psychology of human relationships* (London, Deutsch, 1966).

BESSELL, ROBERT, *Interviewing and Counseling* (London, Batsford, 1971).

BINET, A., and HENRI, V., 'La Psychologie individuelle', *L'Année psychologique* (1896), II.

BINET, A., and SIMON, TH., 'Le Developpement de l'intelligence chez les enfants', *L'Année psychologique* (1908), XIV.

BLOCHER, R. D., *Developmental Counseling* (New York, Ronald Press, 1966).

BLOCHER, D., *et al., Guidance Systems: an introduction to student personnel work* (New York, Ronald Press, 1971).

BOLGER, A. W., 'KOISK – A new vocational counselling instrument', *Brit. J. Guidance and Counselling* (July 1973), Vol. 1, No. 2, pp. 91–5.

BOWLEY, A., *The Natural Development of the Child* (Edinburgh, E. and S. Livingstone, 1942; reprinted 1963).

BOWLEY, A., and GARDNER, L., *The Handicapped Child: educational and psychological guidance for the organically handicapped* (Edinburgh, Churchill Livingstone, 1972).

BRAITHWAITE, E. R., *To Sir with Love* (London, Bodley Head, 1959).

BRUNER, J. S., GOODNOW, J. J., and AUSTIN, G. A., *A Study of Thinking* (New York, Science Edns, 1956).

BRUNER, J. S., *Toward A Theory of Instruction* (Cambridge, Mass., Harvard Univ. Press, 1966).

BULL, NORMAN J., *Moral Judgement from Childhood to Adolescence* (London, Routledge, 1969).

BUROS, O., *The Sixth Mental Measurements Year Book* (New Jersey, Gryphon Press, 1965). *The Seventh Mental Measurements Year Book* (2 vols, New Jersey, Gryphon Press, 1972).

BURT, C., *The Young Delinquent* (London, University of London Press, 1938).

BURT, CYRIL, *The Subnormal Mind* (3rd ed., London, O.U.P., 1955).

CARKHUFF, ROBERT R., *Helping and Human Relations: a primer for lay and professional helpers.* Vol. I, *Selection and Training.* Vol. II, *Practice and Research* (London, Holt, Rinehart and Winston, 1969).

CARKHUFF, ROBERT R., *The Development of Human Resources* (London, Holt, Rinehart and Winston, 1971).

CARKHUFF, ROBERT R., and BERENSON, BERNARD, G., *Beyond Counseling and Therapy* (New York, Holt, Rinehart and Winston, 1967).

CARMICHAEL, L., *Manual of Child Psychology* (2nd ed., New York, Wiley, 1965).

CATTELL, R. B., *Personality and Motivation Structure and Measurement* (New York, World Book Co., 1957).

CATTELL, R. B., *The Scientific Analysis of Personality* (Harmondsworth, Penguin, 1965).

CATTELL, R. B., 'The theory of fluid and crystallised general intelligence checked at the 5–6 year old level', *Brit. J. Educ. Psychol.* (1967), 37, 209–24.

CATTELL, R. B., *Handbook for the High School Personality Questionnaire (HSPQ)* (Illinois, IPAT, 1962).

CENTER FOR RESEARCH ON UTILIZATION OF SCIENTIFIC KNOWLEDGE, *The Inbetweeners: participants' manual* (Reading, Mass., Addison-Wesley, 1967).

CLARKE, E. J., 'Teachers and their evaluation of objectional pupil behaviour', *J. Ed. Res.* (1951).

CLEGG, ALEC, and MEGSON, BARBARA, *Children in Distress* (Harmondsworth, Penguin, 1968).

CLOSS, S. J., *et al., The A.P.U. Occupational Interests Guide* (London, ULP, 1970).

COLE, L. W., *Psychology of Adolescence* (6th ed., New York, Holt, Rinehart and Winston, 1964).

COMMISSION ON TEACHER EDUCATION, *Helping Teachers Understand Children* (Washington, D.C., American Council on Education, 1945).

CONNOLLY, T. G., *Connolly Occupational Interests Questionnaire* (Cambridge, CRAC, 1970).

CRANE, A. R., 'The pre-adolescent gang', *J. Gen. P.,* VIII (1952).

CROWLEY, A. D., *Crowley Occupational Interests Blank* (Cambridge, CRAC, 1970).

CURR, W., 'Psychologists in education services – a critical notice', *Brit. J. Educ. Psychol.* (February 1969), Vol. 39, Part 1.

DEHAAN, ROBERT F., and KOUGH, JACK, *Helping Children with Special Needs* (Chicago, S.R.A., 1956).

DEPARTMENT OF EDUCATION AND SCIENCE, *The Health of the School Child in 1964–65* (London, HMSO, 1966).

DEPARTMENT OF EDUCATION AND SCIENCE, *The Health of the School Child in 1966–68* (London, HMSO, 1969).

DEPARTMENT OF HEALTH AND SOCIAL SECURITY, *Intermediate Treatment* (London, HMSO, 1972).

DOBZHANSKY, T., *The Biological Basis of Human Freedom* (New York, Columbia University Press, 1956).

DOLL, EDGAR A., *Measurement of Social Competence* (Circle Pines, Minnesota, American Guidance Service Inc., 1953).

DOMAN, C., *Teach your Baby to Read* (London, Cape, 1964).

DOUGLAS, J. W. B. *et al., All our Future: a longitudinal study of secondary education* (London, Davies, 1968, and Panther, 1971).

ERIKSON, E. H., *Childhood and Society* (New York, Norton, 1963).

EVANS, W. M., *Young People in Society* (Oxford, Blackwell, 1965).

EYSENCK, H. J., *Fact and Fiction in Psychology* (Harmondsworth, Penguin, 1965).

EYSENCK, H. J., *Sense and Nonsense in Psychology* (Harmondsworth, Penguin, 1958).

FERNALD, GRACE, *Remedial Techniques in Basic School Subjects* (New York, McGraw-Hill, 1943).

FISHER, J. F., 'Indicators of creative ability in craft students' (University of Keele, unpub. M.A. thesis, 1972).

FLAVELL, J. H., *The Developmental Psychology of Jean Piaget* (New York, Van Nostrand, 1963).

FLEMING, C. M., *Cumulative Records*, Educational Research Pamphlet (London, University of London Press, 1945).

FORDER, ANTHONY (ed.), *Penelope Hall's Social Services of England and Wales* (London, Routledge and Kegan Paul, 1971).

GARRY, RALPH, *Guidance Techniques for Elementary Teachers* (Columbus, Merrill, 1963).

GILSON, E., *History of Christian Philosophy in the Middle Ages* (London, Sheed and Ward, 1955).

GOLDMAN (1963) quoted in GORDON, I. J., *Studying the Child in School* (New York, Wiley, 1966).

GOODENOUGH, F. J., and HARRIS, D. B., *Goodenough–Harris Drawing Test* (New York, Harcourt, Brace, Jovanovich, 1963).

GORDON, I. J., *Studying the Child in School* (New York, Wiley, 1966).

GUILFORD, J. P., 'Three faces of intellect', *American Psychologist* (1959), 14, 469–79.

GUNZBURG, H. C., *The Progress Assessment Charts of Social Development* (Birmingham, SEFA Publications, 1969).

HALSEY, A. H. (ed.), *Educational Priority*. Vol 1. *EPA Problems and Policies* (London, HMSO, 1972).

HAMLEY, H. R., *et al., The Educational Guidance of the School Child* (London, Evans Bros., 1936).

HAMLEY, H. R., 'Research and reconstruction', *The Schoolmaster* (10 Aug. 1944).

HARGREAVES, DAVID H., *Social Relations in a Secondary School* (London, Routledge and Kegan Paul, 1965).

HARGREAVES, DAVID H., *Interpersonal Relations and Education* (London, Routledge and Kegan Paul, 1972).

HARRIS, A. J., *The Harris Test of Lateral Dominance* (Windsor, NFER, 1958).

HAVIGHURST, R. J., *Human Development and Education* (London, Longmans, 1953).

HEBB, D. O., *The Organization of Behavior* (New York, Wiley, 1957).

HECHINGER, G., and F., *Teenage Tyranny* (London, Duckworth, 1964).

TRAUX, C. B., and CARKHUFF, R. R., *Toward Effective Counseling and Psychotherapy: training and practise* (New York, Aldine, 1967).

TYERMAN, L. M., *Truancy* (London, University of London Press, 1968).

TYLER, LEONA E., *The Work of the Counselor* (3rd ed., New York, Appleton-Century Crofts, 1969).

VALENTINE, C. W., 'Temperamental traits, the specific nature of and a suggested report form', *Brit. J. of Educ. Psychol.,* Vol. X (1940).

VERNON, P. E., 'The psychology of intelligence and G', Ch. 17 in *Readings in Psychology* (London, Allen and Unwin, 1964).

VERNON, P. E., *Intelligence and Cultural Environment* (London, Methuen, 1969).

WALKER, A. S., *Pupils' School Records* (London, NFER, 1955).

WALL, W. D., *Education and Mental Health* (London, UNESCO/ Harrap, 1955).

WATSON, T. J., *The Education of Hearing-Handicapped Children* (London, University of London Press, 1967).

WATSON, T. J., *The Manchester Picture Vocabulary Test. The Manchester Sentence Test* (Department of Audiology and Education of the Deaf, University of Manchester).

WECHSLER, DAVID, *Wechsler Intelligence Scale for Children. Manual.* (New York, The Psychological Corporation, 1949).

WEPMAN, J. M., *The Auditory Discrimination Test* (London, National Institute for the Deaf, 1958).

WILSON, GLENN D., and PATTERSON, JOHN R., *The Conservatism Scale.* (London, NFER, 1970).

WISEMAN, S., and FITZPATRICK, T. F., *The Devon Interest Test* (London, Oliver and Boyd, 1955).

WITSEN, BETTY VAN, *Perceptual Training Activities Handbook* (New York, Teachers College Press, 1967).

WOODY, ROBERT H., *Behavioral Problem Children in the Schools* (New York, Appleton-Century Crofts, 1969).

WRIGHT, HERBERT F., *Recording and Analyzing Child Behavior with Ecological Data from an American Town* (New York, Harper and Row, 1967).

YAMATOTO, K., *Scoring Manual for Evaluating Imaginative Stories* (Minneapolis, Minn., Bureau of Educational Research, University of Minn., 1961).

YOUNG, M., and MCGEENEY, P., *Learning Begins at Home: a study of a junior school and its parents* (London, Routledge and Kegan Paul, 1968).

Addendum

RICH, J., *Interviewing Children and Adolescents* (New York, Macmillan Co., 1968).

Appendix A. Training Courses in Counselling, Guidance and Pastoral Care

---

This does not represent a complete list of all the courses in Guidance and Counselling which are available in this country but only those of which I am aware at the present. Further information may be obtained from the Standing Conference for the Advancement of Counselling, Bedford Square, London.

One-year full-time courses emphasising counselling

University of Aston in Birmingham	Diploma in Counselling in Educational Settings Emphasises *College* Counselling
University of Keele	Diploma in Advanced Study in Education (with special reference to Counselling) Options in *School* and *College* Counselling
University of Exeter	Diploma in Education (Guidance and Counselling)
University of Newcastle	Diploma in Advanced Study in Educational Studies (Counselling)
University of Swansea	Diploma in School Counselling
University of Reading	Diploma in Guidance and Counselling in Education
New University of Ulster at Coleraine	Diploma in Guidance and Counselling in Education
Queen's University Belfast	Diploma in Education (Counselling)
North-East London Polytechnic (Barking)	Diploma in Counselling (with special reference to schools)

In general these courses are open to qualified teachers with at least three years' experience although exceptionally non-teachers may be accepted.

One-year full-time courses emphasising aspects of guidance and pastoral care

University of Manchester	Diploma in Educational Guidance
University of Bristol	Diploma in Advanced Study in Education (Pastoral Care)
University College of Swansea	Diploma in Adolescent Development
University of Keele	Diploma in Advanced Study in Education (with special reference to the education of Deprived and Maladjusted Children) A course aimed at training teachers for guidance and counselling in primary and special schools and for pastoral posts in secondary
Edge Hill College of Education	Diploma in the Education of Children under Social Handicap

Part-time courses emphasising aspects of guidance and pastoral care

University of Leicester	One-year part-time course in Pastoral Care and Guidance
Association of Psycho-therapists	A range of part-time courses in counselling skills and pastoral care
Westminster Pastoral Foundation (London SW1)	A range of part-time courses in counselling skills and pastoral care
Richmond Fellowship College (London W14)	Human Relations Course, two days per week over two years – Pastoral Care and Counselling
Dundee College of Education	Courses for serving teachers
Jordanhill College of Education	Courses for serving teachers

One-year full-time courses combining counselling with some other study

Edge Hill College of Education	Diploma in Counselling and Careers
City of Birmingham College of Education	Certificate in Health Education and School Counselling

Part-time courses emphasising counselling

University of London Extramural Department	Two-year part-time course in Student Counselling
S.W. London College	Four-term part-time Certificate course in Counselling and Welfare Three-term advanced course in Counselling and Welfare
Middlesex Polytechnic	Two-year part-time Diploma in Counselling
Tavistock Institute of Human Relations	One-year part-time course on Aspects of Counselling in Education
National Marriage Guidance Council (Rugby)	Short residential courses in Counselling
University of Durham	Parts of MA and BEd courses emphasise Guidance and Counselling
University of Sussex and Brighton Polytechnic	Part of In-service BEd on 'The Teacher as Counsellor'
Middlesex Polytechnic	Educational Guidance and Counselling in Secondary Schools
Clinical Theology Association (Nottingham)	Two-year advanced course for Pastoral Counsellors

Appendix B. Examples of School Record Forms

The following notes are appended with the permission of the Headmaster, Tolgus School, Redruth.

They describe the administration of a 'two-tier' record system established to fill the needs of a 'family tutor' system of pastoral care. They are two-tier in that confidential material is reserved for the tutor's card which is kept and maintained by the tutor. The school card shows only the information which is needed by secretarial staff and subject teachers. The latter would need to refer to the pupil's tutor for further information.

This record system is not fully cumulative since it does not take account of primary school records. A fully cumulative record card would be too bulky to show in this book.

Tutor system
To give some initial guidance in operating the tutor system we have set out below specimens of
    1. The school card   2. The tutor's card
and how these cards may be completed. The filling of these cards will be a continuing process over the whole of the pupil's career. Information on the tutor's card will be transferred periodically to the school card.

The specimens are only a guide; the details entered will depend on the individual tutor as to content and depth.

1. School card—Side A

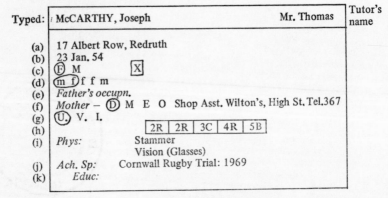

(a) Address and, where possible, telephone number.
(b) Date of birth: Note 23 Jan 54, not 23.1.54.
(c) F(ather) M(other) – to be ringed if deceased. In the case of a broken home or other family difficulties – housing, income, etc. – place a red cross in the box.
(d) Brothers and sisters to be set out m, male, f. female. Pupil to be ringed. In example given pupil has twin sister, 2 younger sisters, 1 younger brother.
(e) Father's occupation and, if possible, name of employer and tel. no. for emergency.
(f) If mother is working ring appropriate symbol D – daily; M – mornings only; E – evenings only; O – occasional; and give occupation and tel. no. on which she may be contacted in an emergency.
(g) Ring the symbol which applies to the pupil's environment: U – Urban; V – Village; I – Isolated.
(h) Enter the forms of which the pupil is a member, year by year.
(i) Physical limitations.
(j) Sporting achievements – usually of some note, e.g. representing county.
(k) Educ. or related achievements esp. extra-curricular.

Side B

Medical Accident '66 Oct.						Parents Visits 1965 Oct. M.I.	
Special Notes						Mar. 67 Gen. behav. Parents Mtgs. √ √	
Vocational Aim Police Brewery – final placing.						Feb. '69 YEO	
Speech √	Hear- ing	Vision √	Child Guid.	Juv. Ct.		Cloth- ing √	Free Meals √

Medical – Illnesses of long duration, affecting school performance; Accidents.
Special Notes: Important matters at tutor's discretion not included in other sections.
Vocational Aim – Not normally to be filled in until the 3rd year at earliest. Should also show what pupil has finally gone on to do – Tech. College etc. – nature of course or, if working, employer's name and address.
Parents Visits – with note of occasion.
Boxes at foot of card – A tick to be placed in any applicable box if pupil has treatment or has appeared before Juvenile Court. Whether in receipt of clothing grant or free meals. This information to be expanded if necessary on tutor's card.

2. Tutor's card

Side A

(a)	McCARTHY, Joseph

(b)	17 Albert Row, Redruth	Bicycle
	23 Jan. 54 Adm. Sept. 55. Leav. D: Easter 69.	
	Last School Trewirgie.	
(c)	*Parents* Father died in accident Jan. 1966.	
	Mother Sept. 1966 adm. St. Lawrence's.	
	April 67 Mother working regul. WILTON's shop asst.	
(d)	*Family* Twin sister (Tolgus). 3 younger chn. f f m	
	(Trew.)	
	Gen. Free meals. Clothing Grant.	
	Often late 66–7. (Mother leaves home 7.45).	
	No pocket money. Occ. paper round.	
(e)	*House.* Council. 3 bedrooms. Shares room with	
	younger brother.	
(f)	*Friends*	
(g)	*Hobbies* etc. Plain-an-Gwarry Youth Club. Gardening.	
(h)	*Absences* Winter 66 frequent (Illness of Mother)	

Side B

Discipline   On Report Easter Term 1967. 1, 1, 1, unruly in class
Summer Term 1967. 1,   unruly in class
Health, Personal and Social Problems   1966 Accident Rugby
Broken Collar bone.
1966 *Very* sensitive about father's accident and family poverty.
Resentful.
General Notes
Sports etc. Rugby: U 13, U 15 Cornwall Trial 1969
Vocational Aim and Result   1968 Police or Army.
Easter 1969 – Brewery. October 1969 – Army.
Parents Visits   M.I. – 65, Mar. 1967 – General behaviour.
Parents meeting Nov. 67, Nov. 68. Feb. 69 Y.E.O.

(a) Standard information as on school card; also state method of pupil's travel to school, e.g. Grenville Motors (S.T.)

(b) Dates – of birth – of admission to Tolgus – of earliest leaving date. School from which admitted. Any overseas education to be indicated. Any erratic pattern to be shown.

(c) *Parents* – Full details – names; whether child is adopted, fostered, has step-parent. If parents are non-English-speaking. Whether child comes from broken home. Any circumstances likely to affect behaviour of child.

(d) *Family* – Full details of other members of family – brothers, sisters, ages; details of careers etc. Whether other members of family – e.g. Grandparents – live with them. General financial position – whether child has pocket money, how much.

(e) *House* – Type of house, incl. no. of bedrooms. Whether pupil shares. Whether room for quiet work.

(f) *Friends* – in and out of school, with some details if friends do not attend Tolgus.

(g) *Hobbies etc.* – personal hobbies and interests. Out-of-school activities in sport, membership of clubs, choirs, societies etc. What participation in school camps, holidays abroad etc.

(h) *Absences* – Whether any serious record of absenteeism. If so reasons for absence – i.e. personal, medical or family – social. Whether parents give co-operation or not.

Discipline – Any disc. trouble. Record of serious action agst. pupil e.g. often on report; any record of anti-social behaviour – e.g. proved pilfering in school.

Health – most obvious problems – e.g. asthma. Any new entries under this head must be drawn immediately to the attention of P.E. Staff and H.M.

Problems of personal or social adjustment will be such as pupil raises or those perceived by an understanding adult. If it seems necessary they should be referred to H.M. for possible consultation with Child Guidance.

General Notes. Tutor's own impressions on matters not covered elsewhere. Any responsibilities undertaken by pupil.

Sports – Achievements in school and representative sport.

Educ. – Extra-curricular interests – Music, typing, classes etc.

Vocational Aim and Result – Voc. aim should not be entered before the third year. Part-Time job. Hours of work, name and address of employer. What pupil does on leaving school, i.e. Nature of Technical College Course; whether pupil has an apprenticeship; name of employer and some indication of starting wage etc.

It is suggested that, though the tutor may wish to get his group to complete a pro-forma giving name, address, etc., the more detailed and intimate information can only be obtained over a long period by tactful conversation. The tutor should not normally record these details under the eye of the pupil.

Appendix C. Examples of Observation Schedules and Checklists

---

1. Keele school behaviour screening form
This screening device is aimed at identifying those children in a class who have extreme behaviour difficulties. It is still in an experimental form and reports on its use would be welcomed by the author.

Underline any statements which apply to children in your class writing their names in the space alongside.

Underline observed problems	*Names of children*
1. Frequently absent with very little reason, truants, malingers or frequently late.	
2. Aggressive, squabbles frequently, fights, argues, bullies or uses bad language.	
3. Restless, poor concentration, fidgety or inattentive.	
4. Shy, withdrawn, solitary, no friends, timid in new situations, suspicious or rejects attention.	
5. Seeks attention, needs approval or sympathy, over-talkative or constantly asks for help	
6. Sad, depressed, worries a lot, fearful, irritable or moody.	
7. Tells lies, has stolen from children or teacher, has no respect for property, destructive.	

Underline observed problems	Names of children
8. Stammers, extremely poor speech, has mannerisms, twitches, tics, bad nail biting, rapid eye blinking, frequent thumb sucking.	
9. Overcareful, meticulously neat or very careless and untidy, works erratically or as little as possible.	
10. Unconcerned, has no appreciation of consequences, openly flouts rules etc.	
Children mentioned three or more times	

2. Keele problem checklist – amended version

Please tick the column which you think says most clearly how worried you are about these problems.

	often	*sometimes*	*never*
I am worried because:			
1. I have lots of headaches.			
2. I have many colds or sore throats.			
3. I am not good looking enough.			
4. I am overweight.			
5. I don't get enough sleep.			
I am worried because:			
6. I am afraid of tests.			
7. I am afraid of failing in my school work.			
8. I can't keep my mind on my studies.			
9. I'm not clever enough.			
10. I often feel restless in class.			
I am worried because:			
11. I am failing in so many things I try to do.			
12. I feel nervous.			
13. I take things too seriously.			
14. I cannot make up my mind.			
15. I am afraid of making mistakes.			
I am worried because:			
16. I often get low marks.			
17. I am not getting along with a teacher.			
18. I am afraid to speak up in class.			
19. I'm not spending enough time on study.			
20. I don't like school.			

	often	sometimes	never
I am worried because:			
21. I am always getting into trouble.			
22. I am sometimes not as honest as I should be.			
23. I should like a more pleasant personality.			
24. I am not having as much fun as other children.			
25. I am trying to stop a bad habit.			
I am worried because:			
26. I have bad dreams.			
27. I am always worrying about something.			
28. I find it hard to talk about my troubles.			
29. I sometimes wish I was never born.			
30. I am lacking in self-confidence.			
I am worried because:			
31. I get into fights.			
32. I lose my temper.			
33. I am very stubborn.			
34. I hurt other people's feelings.			
35. I keep getting into arguments.			
I am worried because:			
36. I am always daydreaming.			
37. I am being lazy.			
38. I feel ashamed of something I've done.			
39. I sometimes tend to be careless.			
40. I keep on forgetting things.			

	often	sometimes	never
I am worried because: 41. I talk back to my parents. 42. My parents do not understand me. 43. I am missing someone very much. 44. I am not telling my parents everything. 45. My family is worried about money.			
I am worried because: 46. I want things my parents won't give me. 47. I don't get along with my brother or sister. 48. I feel I am disappointing my parents. 49. I don't seem to be able to talk to my parents. 50. My parents seem to prefer my brother or sister.			
I am worried because: 51. I need a job in the holidays. 52. I need to know more about jobs. 53. I need to know what I shall do after school. 54. I have nothing interesting to do in my spare time. 55. I don't get enough pocket-money.			
I am worried because: 56. I have no real friends. 57. I am bothered about my boy friend. 58. I am bothered about my girl friend. 59. I wished people liked me better. 60. I have no one to tell my troubles to.			

	often	sometimes	never
I am worried because:			
61. I think too much about the opposite sex.			
62. I get embarrassed by talk about sex.			
63. I don't like swearing or dirty stories.			
64. I wish I knew more about sex.			
65. I wonder if I shall ever get married.			
I am worried because:			
66. My feelings are so easily hurt.			
67. I sometimes tell lies.			
68. I dislike someone very much.			
69. I feel jealous.			
70. There seems to be no future for the world.			
I am worried because:			
71. I have trouble with arithmetic or mathematics.			
72. I have trouble with spelling, grammar or writing.			
73. I have trouble in doing all my homework.			
74. I am in a low stream in school.			
75. I don't like P.E. or Games.			

I should like to talk to someone about my problems. Yes . . . .

No . . . .

Here is a space for writing any other problem which bothers you:

GO BACK OVER THE PROBLEMS AND UNDERLINE ANY
WHICH PARTICULARLY BOTHER YOU

I

3. Things done on your own

Name............ Grade...... School.......... Date........

Directions: Below is a list of activities boys and girls sometimes do on their own. Indicate which ones you have done during this school term by checking the blank at the left. Include only the things you have done on your own, not the things you have been assigned or made to do.

( ) 1. Wrote a poem.
( ) 2. Wrote a story.
( ) 3. Wrote a play.
( ) 4. Kept a collection of my writings.
( ) 5. Wrote a song or jingle.
( ) 6. Produced a puppet show.
( ) 7. Kept a diary for at least a month.
( ) 8. Played word games with other boys and girls.
( ) 9. Used *Roget's Thesaurus* or some other book in addition to a dictionary.
( ) 10. Recorded on a tape recorder an oral reading, dialogue, story, discussion, or the like.
( ) 11. Found errors in fact or grammar in newspaper or other printed matter.
( ) 12. Acted in a play or skit.
( ) 13. Directed or organised a play or skit.
( ) 14. Made up and sang a song.
( ) 15. Made up a musical composition for some instrument.
( ) 16. Made up a new game and taught it to someone else.
( ) 17. Pantomimed some story.
( ) 18. Acted out a story with others.
( ) 19. Wrote a letter to a member of family or a friend away from home.
( ) 20. Made up an original dance.
( ) 21. Played charades.
( ) 22. Visited a zoo.
( ) 23. Explored a cave.
( ) 24. Read a science magazine.
( ) 25. Read a science book.
( ) 26. Mixed colours.
( ) 27. Invented a new game.
( ) 28. Printed photographs.

( ) 29. Grew crystals.
( ) 30. Made a leaf collection.
( ) 31. Made a wildflower collection.
( ) 32. Made an electric motor.
( ) 33. Made a musical instrument.
( ) 34. Planned an experiment.
( ) 35. Dissected an animal.
( ) 36. Grafted a plant or rooted one from a cutting.
( ) 37. Distilled water.
( ) 38. Used a magnifying glass.
( ) 39. Made ink.
( ) 40. Made leaf prints.
( ) 41. Started a fire with a lens.
( ) 42. Used a magnet.
( ) 43. Raised rats, mice, rabbits, or guinea pigs.
( ) 44. Collected insects.
( ) 45. Collected rocks.
( ) 46. Kept a daily record of weather.
( ) 47. Been a bird watcher.
( ) 48. Kept a science notebook.
( ) 49. Kept a science scrapbook.
( ) 50. Attended a science fair or display.
( ) 51. Used a chemistry set.
( ) 52. Produced static electricity.
( ) 53. Constructed a model aeroplane.
( ) 54. Designed a model aeroplane.
( ) 55. Counted annual rings in a log.
( ) 56. Made a stamp collection.
( ) 57. Made a collection of post marks.
( ) 58. Organised or helped to organise a club.
( ) 59. Served as officer in a club organised by boys and/or girls.
( ) 60. Thought out a way of improving a game we play at school or home.
( ) 61. Thought out a way of improving the way we do something at home.
( ) 62. Thought out a way of improving the way we do something at school.
( ) 63. Thought out a way of improving the way we do something in a club, Scouts, etc.
( ) 64. Solved a problem about getting along with my parents.

( ) 65. Solved a problem about getting along with other boys and girls.
( ) 66. Helped act out some historical event.
( ) 67. Found out about the history of my city or town.
( ) 68. Found out about the way some government agency (post office, court, etc.) operates.
( ) 69. Wrote a letter to someone in another country.
( ) 70. Wrote a letter to someone in another county or city.
( ) 71. Made a map of my community.
( ) 72. Made my own decision about the use of money.
( ) 73. Asked questions about the way some business operates.
( ) 74. Made a poster for some club, school, or other event.
( ) 75. Organised or helped organise paper drive, rummage sale, etc.
( ) 76. Sketched landscape with pencil and/or charcoal.
( ) 77. Designed stage settings for play or skit.
( ) 78. Developed a design for jewelry,
( ) 79. Developed a design for cloth.
( ) 80. Illustrated a story of my own or one in a book.
( ) 81. Took colour photographs.
( ) 82. Took black and white photographs.

(From E. Paul Torrance, *Guiding Creative Talent*, © 1962 pp 251-3. Reprinted by permission of Prentice-Hall Inc., Englewood Cliffs, New Jersey.)

Appendix D. Tests for Studying Aspects of Intellectual Development

TYPE	USE	AGE-RANGE	NAME	SUITABILITY	AVAILABILITY
General Intelligence	Individual	4–6½	Wechsler Pre-School and Primary School Intelligence Scale (WPPSI)	Five verbal and five performance tests giving verbal IQ, performance IQ and full-scale IQ. American Norms 1966	Usually Psychologists Level Q
		5–15	Wechsler Intelligence Scale for Children (WISC)	Five verbal and five performance tests giving verbal IQ, performance IQ and full-scale IQ, a deservedly popular test American Norms (+Scottish) 1949	Psychologists only. Teachers need to be able to interpret reports Level R
		2–18	Stanford-Binet (1960 rev.)	A series of varied tests arranged in age steps, non-reading at infant level; deviation IQs. The newest revision of the oldest intelligence test. 1960	A difficult test to administer, used by Psychologists Level R

TYPE	USE	AGE-RANGE	NAME	SUITABILITY	AVAILABILITY
General Ability or Intelligence	Group	1½–15	Intelligence Tests for Children (Valentine)	A small book using Binet type tests; some apparatus needs to be assembled. Most useful for infant school level 1958	Published by Methuen, generally available
		5–15	Goodenough-Harris Drawing Test	Child draws a man, a woman and himself. Untimed (20 minutes or so) non-reading test, quick scoring. American Norms (not necessarily applicable here). 1963	Published by Harrap as *Children's Drawings as Measures of Intellectual Maturity*
	Individual or Group	5½–11	Coloured Progressive Matrices (Raven)	Untimed (20 minutes or so), non-reading easy and attractive. British Norms (small sample). 1958	Lewis and Co., generally available (can be given with Crichton Vocab. Scale)
		8–14	Progressive Matrices ABCDE	Untimed (50 minutes or so). 1956	Lewis and Co. (Can be given with Mill Hill Vocab. Scale)

10–16	Figure Reasoning Test	Timed (30 minutes) non-reading test. 1962	Published by Crosby and Lockwood, generally available
5–7	S.R.A. Primary Mental Ability Test	Five sub-tests, three timed (total time 60–80 minutes). American Norms. 1954	Published by SRA Generally available
6–7	Carlton Picture Intelligence Test A and/or B	Non-reading eight timed sub-tests (32 minutes). 1962	Published by ULP
8–12	Verbal Tests, BC, CD, C and D	(30–35 minutes) A series of tests covering 2 yr. age ranges containing arithmetic, analogies, sequences, codes, etc. 1959–66	Published by Ginn for NFER
11–adult	AH4	Times (20 minutes) Verbal or non-verbal. 1969	NFER Level P

Group

TYPE	USE	AGE-RANGE	NAME	SUITABILITY	AVAILABILITY
Special Aptitude	Individual or Group	11–adult	Morrisby Differential Test Battery	A battery of test used in vocational guidance general norms, grammar school norms, University norms, e.g. Mechanical Ability Test (15 minutes timed). 1955	Available from J. R. Morrisby Education and Industrial Test Services, 85 High Street, Hemel Hempstead, Herts, UK
		13–adult	ACER Mechanical Reasoning Test	Australian norms (20 Mins.) 1951–54	NFER Level P
		15–adult	Modern Language Aptitude Test	Administered by tape-recording (except short form) Norms in percentiles. Complete test 1 hour; short form 30 minutes. Elementary edition also available.	NFER Level P
		7–adult	Measure of Musical Ability	Produced on long playing record. British Norms. 1966	Harrap. Generally available

Attainment and Diagnostic	Individual	6–12	Neale Analysis of Reading Ability	Scores for Speed, Accuracy and Comprehension. A series of six short stories graded in difficulty followed by comprehension questions. 3 parallel Forms, Diagnostic record sheets. 1958	Macmillan Generally available
		6–9½	Simple Prose Reading (Test R2)	A simple test by Schonell. The pupil reads a short story and answers questions. Scores for accuracy, speed, comprehension. 1945	Oliver and Boyd Generally available
		5–15	Graded Word Reading (Test R1)	A test of word recognition, 100 graded words, untimed. The most commonly used reading test. 1938	Oliver and Boyd Generally available
		2–9	Standard Reading Tests	A series of diagnostic tests, including an attainment test. Especially useful where a phonic approach is to be taken. 1958	Chatto and Windus Generally available

TYPE	USE	AGE-RANGE	NAME	SUITABILITY	AVAILABILITY
Attainment and Diagnostic	Individual	2–10	Illinois Test of Psycholinguistic Abilities	Used to diagnose language difficulties in young children (45–60 minutes). American norms. 1968	NFER Level P
		3–8	Marianne Frostig Developmental Test of Visual Perception	Five sub-tests of visual perception or motor co-ordination (30–35 mins.). Allied to a programme for training in visual perception. 1964	NFER Level P
		5–8½	Word Recognition Test (Carver)	Child underlines word in row dictated by teacher – gives diagnostic information. Standardised in Manchester. 1964	ULP Generally available
		6–7½ 7–8·11	Southgate Group Reading Tests	Two overlapping tests, parallel forms of second test. 1959, 1962	ULP Generally available

Attainment and Diagnostic				Oliver and Boyd or NFER
Group Reading	6·9–12·8 6·7–13·7	Silent Reading Tests A and B (R3 and R4)	Useful group tests of reading comprehension. Test A (R3) best with younger slower readers. (R3 9 mins.; R4 15 mins.) 1945	
	13·6–15·2	Manchester Reading Comprehension Test (Senior)	A good test for this age group. 8 sub-tests (45 minutes).	ULP Generally available
	6–15	Gates MacGintie Reading Tests	A series of six overlapping tests with equivalent forms. British norms in process of collection. 1965	NFER Level A (T)
Group English	8–14	English Progress Test A–F	A series of overlapping tests, averaging 45 minutes in length, testing a range of English skills. 1952–55	Ginn for NFER
	7–14	English Progress Tests A–F A2–F2 G B3 D3 F3	A similar series to above but designed for the more modern approach to English with emphasis on free response answers. 1960	Ginn for NFER

TYPE	USE	AGE-RANGE	NAME	SUITABILITY	AVAILABILITY
Attainment and Diagnostic	Group English	8–13·11	Bristol Achievement Test (English)	A series of overlapping tests, each one made up of 5 sub-tests (50–55 mins.). NB. Tests in Maths and Study Skills too. 1968	Nelson Generally available
	Individual Maths	7–21	Graded Arithmetic – Mathematics Test (Vernon)	A concise useful test, decimal version available. 1963	ULP Generally available
		7–8·6, 8·6–9.8	Maths attainment Tests (Oral) A and B	New tests following modern approaches. 1965	Ginn for NFER
	Group Maths	9·3–13·0	Maths Attainment Tests C1, C3, DE1, DE2, EF, H1	A series of tests each suitable for a narrow age range. Most test concepts rather than computation. 1965–72	Ginn for NFER
		8–13·11	Bristol Achievement Tests (Maths)	A series of overlapping tests, each one made up of 5 sub-tests (50–55 mins.). NB. tests in English and Study Skills also 1968	Nelson Generally available

Appendix E. A Perceptual Survey Rating Scale

(Adapted from Kephart, Newell C., *The Slow Learner in the Classroom*)

TEST 1. Balance
Use a walking board 8–12 feet long 2×4 inches thick

	Stepping off no. of times	Stop- ping no. of times	Bilateral stepping off on each side yes/no	Unilateral stepping off on one side left/right
(a) *Forward* walk to other end of board, feet straight on board				
(b) *Backward* walk backward to other end without looking back				
(c) *Sideways* rt right angles to board, step up and walk sideways in each direction left				

TEST 2. Control over large muscles

	yes	no
Jumping (a) *Both feet* forward one step		
(b) *Right foot* Stand on right, (left foot off floor), jump forward 1 step using right foot only, (left foot does not touch floor).		
(c) *Left foot* Stand on left, (right foot off floor), jump forward 1 step.		
Skipping (d) Skip across room using feet alternately		
Hopping (e) Hop 1/1 Stand feet together, hop on right lifting left, hop on left lifting right, alternate hopping, first on right then on left.		
(f) Hop 2/2 as (e) but twice on right, twice on left etc.		
(g) Hop 2/1 hop twice on right, once on left, etc.		
(h) Hop 1/2 ditto, sides reversed.		

TEST 3. Identification of body parts
Child stands at a distance of 10 feet. Teacher says 'Touch your shoulders' etc.

	yes	no
1. Shoulders		
2. Hips		
3. Head		
4. Ankles		
5. Ears		
6. Feet		
7. Eyes		
8. Elbows		
9. Mouth		

Evaluate by checking where a child responds appropriately to command.

TEST 4. Obstacle course
Test child's awareness of the space occupied by his body in various positions.

		yes	no
1.	Step over yardstick, knee high (stick across 2 chairs)		
2.	Duck under yardstick 2 inches lower than shoulders (stick across back of 2 chairs)		
3.	Squeeze through narrow opening (chairs back to back)		

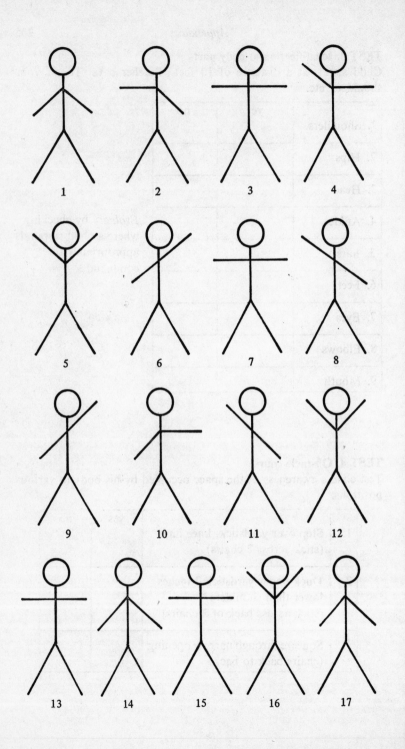

TEST 5. Imitation of movements

Child stands 8–10 feet away facing examiner and far enough from walls to move hands without obstruction. Hands loose at sides. Instruct to do whatever examiner does. Follow patterns in order:

Evaluate – ability to control upper limbs independently and in combination;
translation of visual pattern into a motor pattern which will reproduce it.
Difficulty indicated by hesitancy, lack of certainty, error in executing patterns.

	L	*R*	*Note*
1.			
2.			
3.			
4.			
5.			
6.			
7.			
8.			
9.			
10.			
11.			
12.			
13.			
14.			
15.			
16.			
17.			

TEST 6. Angels in the snow

Child to lie on his back on the floor, arms at side, feet together. Moves arms over his head, keeping them on the floor. Should feel floor with wrists as he moves arms. Then moves feet wide apart, also along floor. When he understands he follows these directions:

1. Move just this arm (points to right arm). Now put it back.
2. Move just this arm (point to left arm). Now put it back.
3. Move just this leg (point to right leg). Now put it back.
4. Move just this leg (point to left leg). Now put it back.
5. Move both arms. Now put them back.
6. Move both legs. Now put them back.
7. Move this arm and this leg (point to left arm and left leg). Now put them back.
8. Move this arm and this leg (point to right arm and right leg). Now put them back.
9. Move this arm and this leg (point to right arm and left leg). Now put them back.
10. Move this arm and this leg (point to left arm and right leg). Now put them back.

Do not identify limb except by pointing.

Evaluate – control of parts of body individually or in prescribed combinations. Inadequate performance shown by (1) marked hesitancy in beginning movements, (2) restriction of extent of movements. (3) overflow to limbs not required, (4) inability to initiate movement or identify limb by visual clues alone (use of factual or Kinaesthetic information), (5) inability to carry out any pattern.

TEST 7. Stepping stones

Use six-inch squares of cardboard (10 black, 10 red) placed according to pattern below:

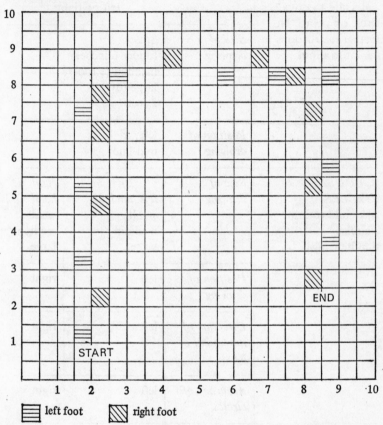

Child has black ribbon on left foot, red ribbon on right foot. Instruct 'Put foot with black ribbon on this first square.' Help him. 'Now put red foot on next square. Now walk round all squares putting your black foot on black squares and red foot on red squares. Always step on the very next square and do not back up. Do not step on floor, only on the squares.' (Demonstrate first six only; child places ball of foot on squares.)

Evaluate – eye-foot co-ordination, laterality and directionality.

Difficulty shown by child failing any of steps, stepping off stones or altering prescribed foot placement.

TEST 8. Chalk board

A. *CIRCLE* Ask child to draw a circle on board. No further instructions or demonstrations.		Preferred hand: left or right	
	Size of drawing	Small (under 6 inches) medium (1 foot) large (over 2 feet)	
	Position of drawing	left right mid-line	
B. *DOUBLE CIRCLES* Ask child to draw 2 circles simultaneously	*Size of drawing*	*left hand* small medium large	*right hand* small medium large
	Position of drawing	left	right
	Direction of movement of hands	left	right
	Accuracy of circles	left	right
C. *LATERAL LINES* Ask child to turn around so that he cannot see board. Put X 18 inches to left of centre and X 18 inches to right. Ask child to turn around and draw a straight line from one X to another.	*Use of body*	walking across	
		changing feet	
		excess tension	
	Use of hands	changing hands	
		inaccurate lines	
		false starts	

D. *VERTICAL LINES* Ask child to draw 2 parallel vertical lines simultaneously from top to bottom	*Use of body*	general balance	
		excess tension	
	Use of hands	unequal lines	
		inaccurate lines	

Evaluate – on child's handling of mid-line problem.

Test 9. Ocular pursuits
This technique investigates ability of child to control ocular movements.

A. Lateral Put a drawing pin into end of pencil. Child follows movements of pin in a semi-circle 18–20 inches from his eyes. Head is held still and eyes should follow movements. *Observe:* eye movements working of eyes together, behaviour when crossing mid-line.
Evaluate – ocular control. Difficulties shown by losing target, not being able to follow it easily or moving of head.
B. Vertical Move pencil vertically in arc of circle 18 inches from child's eyes.
C. Diagonal Move pencil in diagonal direction from lower left to upper right and from upper right to lower left, 18 inches from eyes.
D. Rotary Move pencil in a circle directly facing the child and with a radius of 18 inches.
E. and F. Right and left eyes. Repeat tasks A–D with one eye covered each time.
Evaluate – all these tasks as for A.

TEST 10. Visual Achievement Forms
The copying of simple geometric shapes with attention to the manner
of production as well as the product. Child sits at desk. Forms are
presented one at a time in a straight vertical/horizontal orientation.
Say: 'I want you to copy these seven drawings (flip through pages)
on this sheet of paper.' Begin with circle, 'Make one like this.'
(7 years old, 7 forms, 6 years old, 5 forms, 5 years old, 4 forms, 4
years old, first 3 forms.)

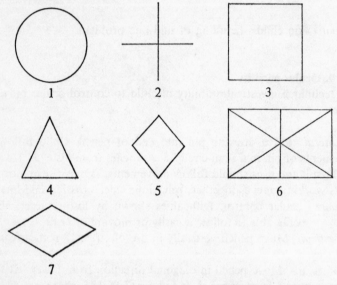

Evaluate – Child's ability to perceive and manipulate forms. Weakness shown by unrecognisable form in one or more
drawings or gross segmentation.

Kraus-Weber Tests

Test 1   Child lies flat on back, hands behind head, legs outstretched. Examiner holds his feet to floor, child pulls up to sitting position without using hands.

Test 2   Child lies on back, hands behind head, knees bent. Examiner holds feet to floor. Child sits without using hands.

Test 3   Child lies on back hands behind head, legs out straight. Child raises feet 10 inches from floor while keeping legs straight and holds this for 10 seconds.

Test scored if legs raised without bending knees and held for 10 seconds.

Test 4   Child lies face down, hands clasped behind neck, small pillow under hips. Examiner holds feet to floor. Raises head, shoulders and chest off floor and holds for 10 seconds.

Test 5   Similar position. Legs raised off floor without bending knees, feet 10 inches from floor.

Both tests scored passed if held for 10 seconds.

Test 6   Child (without shoes) bends hips, knees and feet together and touches floor with finger tips.

Score passed if child can touch floor without bending knees or 'bouncing' and holds for 3 seconds.

Evaluate – general postural and gross motor co-ordination, related to school achievement.

Name Index

Allport, G. W., 136, 145, 150
Almy, M., 219
Anthony, J., 33, 34
Argyle, M., 165
Austin, G. A., 11
Ayres, N., 52, 53

Bacon, Francis, 21
Baldwin, A. L., 54
Barker, R. G., 51
Bellak, L. and S. S., 154
Bene, E., 33, 54
Berne, E., 118, 169
Bessell, R., 158
Binet, A., 22, 99
Blocher, D., 14, 140, 141, 142
Bogardus, E. S., 149, 150
Bolger, A. W., 152
Bowley, A. H., 29, 30
Braithwaite, E. R., 125
Braly, K., 149
Breeze, F., 54
British Psychological Society (BPS), 79
Bruner, J., 99, 100, 111
Bull, N. J., 119
Buros, O., 77
Burt, Sir Cyril, 44, 101, 185

Carkhuff, R. R., 118, 162, 164, 167, 169
Carmichael, L., 136
Cattell, R. B., 34, 102, 105, 144, 146
Center for Research on Utilization
  of Scientific Knowledge, 203, 204
Church, J., 88
Clarke, E. J., 120
Clegg, Sir Alec, 58, 208
Closs, S. J., 150
Cole, L. W., 18
Commission on Teacher Education, 39
Connolly, T. G., 150, 151
Crane, A. R., 121, 125
Crowley, A. D., 150, 151
Curr, W., 187

Dalzell-Ward, A. J., 184
DeHaan, R. F., 196
Department of Education and

Science, 92, 95, 96, 185
Department of Health and Social
  Security (DHSS), 193
Dobzhansky, T., 135
Doll, E., 122, 123
Doman, G., 49, 139
Douglas, J. W. B., 87, 88, 91

Erigena, 20
Erikson, E. H., 140
Eysenck, H., 120, 137, 146, 147, 149

Fernald, G., 208
Fisher, J., 112
Fiske, G., 149
Fitzpatrick, T. F., 150
Fleming, C. M., 45, 150
Freud, S., 139

Galen, 20
Galton, F., 22
Garry, R., 162
Gesell, A., 139, 143
Gilson, E., 20
Goldman, R., 108
Goodenough, F. L., 31
Goodnow, J. J., 111
Gordon, I. J., 108
Griffiths, R., 143
Guardian, The, 191
Gunzberg, H. C., 123, 124

Halsey, A. H., 176
Hamley, H. R., 35
Hargreaves, D. H., 13, 56, 125, 208
Harris, A. J., 31, 91
Havinghurst, R. J., 138, 139
Hebb, D. O., 102, 138
Heim, A. V., 101, 105, 151
Henri, V., 22
Hines, B., 125, 164
Hippocrates, 20
Howe, G., 21
Huarte, Juan, 20

Inner London Education Authority
  (ILEA), 177

Institute of Child Study, University of Maryland, 63
Isaacs, S., 118

Jackson, B., 58
Jackson, S., 77, 104, 115
Jacobson, L., 57
James, F. E., 93
Jersild, A., 18, 54, 120, 136
Johnson, W., 94

Kagan, J., 111
Kalhorn, J., 54
Katz, D., 149
Keller, H., 170
Kephart, N., 89, 97
Kough, L. J., 196

Lawrence, D., 162, 163, 164
Lifton, M., 128
Lippitt, R., 120
Locke, J., 21
Lodwick, A. R., 108, 109
London Institute of Education, 44

McClelland, D., 144, 145, 149, 154
McGeeney, P., 37, 58
Maguire, U., 145, 147
Marsden, D., 58
Martens, E. H., 173
Martin, R. L., 57
Mead, G. H., 117
Megson, B., 58, 208
Merrill, M. A., 99
Miller, K., 150
Moreno, J., 129
Morris, G., 63, 70
Moss, J. A., 111
Murphy, G., 104

National Foundation for Educational Research (NFER), 14, 44, 45, 77, 78, 79
National Youth Employment Council (NYEC), 44, 77, 79, 92

Opie, I. and P., 125, 127

Patrick, J., 121
Patterson, J. R., 149
Pavlov, I. P., 138
Piaget, J., 100, 107, 108, 110, 139
Pickard, P. M., 18
Pirrie, D., 184

Plowden, Lady Bridget, 103, 120
Plowden Report, The, 9, 10, 12
Postman, N., 10, 11
Prescott, D., 64, 65, 68
Pringle, M. K., 208

Quintilian, 9

Raven, J. C., 101, 155
Redl, F., 210, 211, 212, 213
Reed, M., 94
Rhode, A. R., 154
Rich, J., 158, 166
Richardson, E., 51, 125
Robertson, J., 30
Rogers, C., 163, 164, 202
Rosenthal, R., 57
Ross, J. M., 91
Rothwell, J., 150
Rotter, J. B., 154
Rowe, A., 14, 57
Rutter, M., 91, 149

Science Research Associates (SRA), 30, 32
Seebohm Report, The, 187, 190
Sheldon, W. H., 90, 144
Sigel, I., 111
Simmonds, V., 151
Simon, Th., 22, 99
Simpson, H. R., 91
Smith, V. H., 93
Sorenson, A. G., 12
Sprott, W. J. H., 117
Stendler, C. B., 120
Stone, L. F., 88
Stott, D. H., 30, 125
Strang, R., 63, 70
Summerfield, A. (*Summerfield Report, The*), 184, 185, 186, 187

Tanner, J. M., 86, 87
Taylor, G., 52, 53
Terman, L. M., 99
Thompson, A. J. M., 58
Times Educational Supplement, 193
Tizard, J., 91
Torrance, E. P., 102, 112, 113, 114
Truax, C. B., 162
Tyerman, L. M., 189
Tyler, L., 163, 164

Valentine, C. W., 45
Vernon, P. E., 102

Vinci, Leonardo da, 20
Vives, 20

Walker, A. S., 44
Wall, W. D., 173
Watts, K. P., 151
Wechsler, D., 115
Weingarten, C., 11
Wepman, J. M., 94
White, R., 120
Whitmore, K., 91

Wilson, G. D., 149
Wiltshire Education Committee, 44
Wineman, D., 210, 211, 212, 213
Wiseman, S., 150
Woody, R. H., 215, 216
Wright, H. F., 52, 63

Yamamoto, K., 113
Young, M., 37, 58
Young, N., 120

Subject Index

Achievement (attainment), *see* Tests
Adjustment, 208; social, 125
Administration, of tests, 81, 82
Adolescence, 59, 88, 140, 142, 198, 207
Agencies, helping agencies outside
  the school, 17, 18, 182–93
AH 4 Test, 27
Aims, of school, 13, 57
Allport-Vernon study of values, 150
Anecdotes, anecdotal records, 61, 70;
  examples of, 70–3
APU, Occupational Interest Guide,
  150, 151
Art in child study, 31
Attainment tests, *see* Tests
Attendance problems, 189, 190, 215,
  216
Authoritarianism, in parents, 54; in
  group leaders, 120
Autism, 170
Autobiography, in child study, 33
Autonomic Nervous System, 138

Behaviour, as object of study, 19, 20,
  21; modification of, 210–18;
  problems, 172, 173, 174, 176
Bias, in observation, 26, 75
Binet Test (Terman-Merrill and
  Stamford-Binet), 22, 29
Blindness, 170
Body build, 89, 90
Bogardus Test, 150
Bristol Social Adjustment Guides, 30,
  125, 149
Brook Reaction Test, 151, 153

Careers Officer (*see* Youth
  Employment Service)
Case conference, 186
Child, guidance, 17, 184, 185, 186;
  psychiatrist, 184, 185; society,
  125–7; study, 12, 14
Children, needs of, 171–81;
  problems of, 172–80
Children's Apperception Test (CAT),
  154
Children's Personality Questionnaire
  (CPQ), 144, 145

Clinic, child guidance, 184, 185, 186
Community service, 180
Confidentiality, and records, 40, 41
Connolly Occupational Interest
  Questionnaire, 150, 151
Controlled Projection Test, 155
Correlation coefficient, 80
Cotswold Personality Assessment, 150
Counselling, 16, 17; interview,
  162–71; stages in, 167–9
Counsellor, 41; attitude of, towards
  client, 163–4; towards self, 164,
  165; communication of, with
  client, 165, 166
Court, Juvenile, 41, 191
Creativity, 112, 113, 114
Crowley Occupational Interest Blank,
  150, 151
Culture, influences on tests, 81, 82
Cumulative records (*see* Records)
Curriculum, 180

Deafness, 170
Delinquency, 56, 191–3
Democratic attitudes, in parents, 54;
  in group leaders, 120
Desensitisation, 215–17
Development, emotional, 135–58;
  intellectual, 98, 117; physical,
  84–98; of personality, 135–58;
  social, 117–35; vocational, 43, 150–2
Developmental, tasks, 139, 143;
  problems, 179, 180; scales, 143
Devon Interest Test, 150
Discussion groups, 206, 207
Dossier, *see* Records

Ecology, as applied to human
  behaviour, 51–3
Education, aims of, 9; personal and
  social, 16, 180; vocational, 16, 180
Education, welfare service, 17,
  187–90
Educational psychologist, 184–5,
  186, 187
Emotional development, 136–8
Empathy, 51, 77; in counselling, 165,
  166, 167

Environment, 59, 208; modifying the, 208–10
Expectations, pupil, 57; teacher, 56, 57
Experiments, 32
Eysenck Personality Inventory (EPI), 146

Family, background, 53–5; climate, 54; counselling or therapy, 203
Family-Relations Test (the Bene-Anthony), 33, 54, 55
Film record, 30
Friendship choices, 129, 130

Genetic inheritance, 84, 85, 102, 103
Group, relationships, 127, 128; tests, 75, 76; work, 206–8
Guidance, 12, 14, 15, 201; child, 184–6; and counselling, 16; in comprehensive schools, 178; educational, 16; and multiple reference, 202–6; personal, 38, 194–200; strategies in, 200; and referral, 203; vocational, 16, 150, 151
Gunzburg Progress Assessment Charts (PAC), 123

Habitat, of the child, 51–61; the home, 53–5; the school, 55–9
Handicapped children, 170, 171
Health, history, 86–7; of mother, 85
High School Personality Questionnaire (HSPQ), 144–6
Home, as part of the child's habitat, 53–5
Human, needs, 180; relationships, 180
Hypothesis checking, 195, 197–9

Immigrant children, testing of, 81
Intelligence, concept of, 100–2; tests of 99, 101, 106, 245–53; and personality, 105
Interview, 158–70; as a technique of child study, 159–62; directive, 158–62; non-directive, 162–9; orientation, 159, 167; counselling or helping, 162–9
Ipsative tests, 151

Junior Eysenck Personality Inventory (JEPI), 146

Keele Occupational Interest Sorting Kit, 152
Keele Problem Checklist, 238–41
Keele School Behaviour Screening Form, 236, 237

Lateral Thinking, 91
Learning disability, 125

Maturity, social, 122–5; tests of, 122, 124
Measurement, 32, 74–6
Medical, officer, *see* School health service; record cards, 95, 96; service, *see* School health service
Mental retardation, 170
Minnesota Counseling Inventory, 145, 147
Mood cues, 65–9
Moral development, 119
Mother, 135, 136
Motor co-ordination, 198, 199; tests of, 96, 97

Narrative records, 28, 29
Needs, children's, 170–81; human, 180
New Junior Maudsley Inventory (NJMI), 146
Norms, normative data, 75, 81, 245, 253

Observation, 23–34; in the study of personality, 144; without control of situation, 28, 29, 30, 31, 62, *see also* anecdotal records; with control of situation, 32, 33, 34, *see also* measurement
Organisation, of pastoral care, 177, 178; of social work, 188; of school, 57

Parallel forms of tests, 82
Parents, 53, 54, 55, 59; schools' attitude towards, 58, 59; parent-teacher associations, 58; parent-teacher contacts, 37, 70; interviews with, 37, 43, 44; liaison with, 37; and child, 136; attitudes of, 54
Pastoral care, 12, 58, 177, 178, 201
Perceptual factors, 98
Personal products, 31
Personality, 117; development of, 135–43; study of, 143–57; of counsellor, 163–6

Phrenology, 21
Physical factors in development, 84–94
Probation Service, 192, 193
Problems of children, 170–80; acute, 172, 173; chronic, 173–5; developmental, 179–80; transitory, 176
Projective techniques, 33, 152–6
Psychologist, educational, 182–7; reports of, 46
Punishment, 213

Questionnaires, 34, 196

Rapport, 81, 82, 161
Rating scales, 30, 31, 34, 148, 149
Reading, as a developmental task, 139; remedial, and counselling, 164; tests, 106, 107, 114–16
Reciprocal inhibition, 215–17
Records, anecdotal, 61–74; characteristics of, 41–3; confidentiality in, 40, 41, 44; cumulative, 35–51; forms of, 45–9; need for, 35–7; opposition to, 39; uses of, 37–41, 49, 50
References and testimonials, 38, 39
Reinforcement, 212, 213
Reliability, 80, 81
Remedial work, 16, 164
Respect, in counselling, 164
Role-playing, 217
Rorschach Test, 154
Rothwell-Miller Interest Blank, 150, 151

School, as part of the child's habitat, 55–7
School Health Service, 182, 184
School Medical Officer, School Doctor, 182, 184
School Nurse, 182
School Phobia, school refusal, 215, 216
Scores, 76; accuracy of, 81, 82, 86; normative, 32
Self-Reports, 34

Senses, sensory development, 91–4, 100
Sentence completion tests, 154, 155
Sincerity (genuineness), in counselling, 164, 165
Social modelling, 217
Social Services Department, 17, 188, 190, 191, 192
Social stereotypes, 149
Social work and social workers, 190–2
Sociometry, sociometric devices, 34, 129–34
Standardisation of tests, 75
Study of values, 151

Tell-a-story Test, 156
Tests, aptitude, 106, 107; attainment, 78, 106, 107; creativity, 111–14; diagnostic, 107; group, 75, 76, 82; individual, 76, 82; intelligence (ability), 78, 99, 100–2, 105–7, 107–8; interpretation of, 82; non-verbal, 76; performance, 76; projective, 79; psychometric, standardisation of, 75, 81, 82; verbal, 76; vocational, 150, 151, 152
Therapy, and counselling, 202, 203; family, 203; group, 206–8; outside the school, 17
Time sampling, 30
Truancy, 189

Under-achievement, 115, 116
Understanding in counselling, 165–7

Validity, 79–80; concurrent, 79; content, 79; predictive, 79
Vineland Social Maturity Scale, 122
Vocational guidance, 16, 150, 151; interest tests, 150, 151, 152

Warmth, 161; in counselling, 163
Wechsler Intelligence Scale for Children, 105

Youth Employment Service, 17, 193

HEIM, A. W., WATTS, K. P., and SIMMONDS, V., *Brook Reaction Test* (London, NFER, 1969).

HEIM, ALICE, *Intelligence and Personality* (Harmondsworth, Penguin, 1970).

HINES, BARRY, *Kestrel for a Knave* (London, Michael Joseph, 1968).

HOLT, JOHN, *How Children Fail* (New York, Pitman, 1964).

ILEA, 'Children with special difficulties'. A report by the Education Officer to the Education Schools Sub-Committee (8th July 1971).

JACKSON, S., *A Teacher's Guide to Tests and Testing* (London, Longmans, 1968 and 1971).

JACKSON, B., and MARSDEN, D., *Education and the Working Class* (London, Routledge, 1962).

JERSILD, A. T., *Child Psychology* (4th ed., New York, Prentice-Hall, 1954).

JERSILD, A. T., *Child Psychology* (6th ed., London, Staples Press, 1969).

JERSILD, A. T., *The Psychology of Adolescence* (New York, Macmillan, 1963).

JOHNSON, W., *Children with Speech and Hearing Impairment* (Washington DC, Office of Education, Bulletin No. 5, 1959).

KAGAN, J., MOSS, H. A., and SIGEL, I., 'Psychological significance of styles of conceptualisation', Society for the Research in Child Development Monographs, 86 (1963), 28 : 73–112.

KEPHART, NEWELL C., *The Slow Learner in the Classroom* (Columbus, Ohio, Chas. E. Merrill, 1960).

KOUGH, J., and DeHAAN, R. F., 'Identifying children with special needs', *Teachers' Guidance Handbook* (Elementary School Edition, Vol. 1. Chicago, Science Research Associates Inc., 1955).

LAWRENCE, D., 'The effects of counselling on retarded readers', *Educ. Research* (Feb. 1971), Vol. 13, No. 2, 119–24.

LAWRENCE, D., 'Counselling of retarded readers by non-professionals', *Educ. Research* (Nov. 1972), Vol. 15, No. 1, 48–51.

LIFTON, WALTER M., *Working with Groups: group process and individual growth* (2nd ed., New York, Wiley, 1966).

LIPPITT, R., and WHITE, R., in Maccoby, E. E., Newcombe, T. M., and Hartley, E. L., *Readings in Social Psychology* (3rd ed., New York, Holt, Rinehart and Winston, 1958).

LODWICK, A. R., 'An investigation of the question whether the inferences that children draw in learning history correspond to the stages in mental development that Piaget postulates' (unpublished dissertation Dip.Ed., University of Birmingham, 1957).

MAGUIRE, U., 'The effectiveness of short-term counselling on secondary school pupils' (unpublished thesis, University of Keele, 1971).

MARTENS, E. H., *Needs of Exceptional Children* (US Office of Education, Leaflet No. 74. Washington DC, US Government Printing Office, 1944).

MARTIN, R. L., 'An investigation into the effects of class nomenclature on performance, attitude and intelligence' (unpublished dissertation, University of Keele, 1973).

MCCLELLAND, O., *Personality* (New York, The Dryden Press, 1951).

MEAD, GEORGE H., *Mind, Self and Society* (Chicago University Press, 1934).

MILLER, K. M., *The Rothwell-Miller Interest Blank* (British Edition) (London, NFER, 1968).

MORENO, J., *Who Shall Survive? Foundations of sociometry, group psychotherapy and sociodrama* (2nd ed., New York, Beacon House, 1953).

MURPHY, GARDNER, *Human Potentialities* (London, Allen and Unwin, 1958).

MCGEENEY, P., *Parents are Welcome* (London, Longmans, 1969).

NFER, *Statement of Policy* (London, National Foundation for Educational Research in England and Wales, 1953).

NORTHWAY, M., *A Primer of Sociometry* (Toronto, University of Toronto Press, 1952).

NYEC, *The Work of the Youth Employment Service 1968–1971* (London, HMSO, 1971).

OCKHAM, WILLIAM of, *Philiosophical Writings*, trans. P. Boehner (Edinburgh, Nelson, 1957).

OPIE, I. and P., *Children's Games in Street and Playground* (Oxford, OUP, 1969).

OPIE, I. and P., *The Lore and Language of Schoolchildren* (Oxford, Clarendon Press, 1959).

PATRICK, JAMES, *A Glasgow Gang Observed* (London, Eyre Methuen, 1973).

PICKARD, P. M., *Psychology of Developing Children* (London, Longman, 1970).

PIRRIE, D., and DALZELL-WARD, A. J., *A Textbook of Health Education* (London, Social Science Paperbacks, 1962).

PLOWDEN, LADY BRIDGET (chairman), *Children and their Primary Schools*, Vol. 1 (London, Central Advisory Council for Education, HMSO, 1967).

POSTMAN, N., and WEINGARTEN, C., *Teaching as a Subversive Activity* (Harmondsworth, Penguin, 1971).

PRESCOTT, D., *The Child in the Educative Process* (New York, McGraw-Hill, 1957).

PRINGLE, KELLMER, *Able Misfits: a study of educational and behaviour difficulties of 103 very intelligent children* (London, Longmans, 1970).

QUINTILIAN, *On Education* trans. Wm. Snail (Oxford, Clarendon Press, 1938).

RAVEN, J. C., *Controlled Projection for Children* (2nd ed., London, H. K. Lewis, 1951).

RAVEN, J. C., *The Progressive Matrices Test and the Coloured Progressive Matrices Test* (London, H. K. Lewis, 1956 and 1963).

REDL, F., and WINEMAN, D., *The Aggressive Child* (Glencoe, Free Press, 1957).

REED, M., *The Picture Screening Test of Hearing* (London, National Institute for the Deaf, 1960).

RICHARDSON, ELIZABETH, *The Environment of Learning* (London, Nelson, 1967).

ROGERS, CARL, *Client-centered Therapy: its current practice, implications and theory* (Boston, Houghton Mifflin, 1951 and London, Constable, 1965).

ROHDE, AMANDA R., *The Sentence Completion Method* (New York, Ronald, 1957).

ROSENTHAL, R., and JACOBSON, L., *Pygmalion in the Classroom: teacher expectation and pupils' intellectual development* (New York, Holt, Rinehart and Winston, 1968).

ROTHNEY. JOHN W. M., *Methods of Studying the Individual Child – the psychological case study* (Waltham, Mass., Blaisdell Pub., 1968).

ROTTER, J. B., and RAFFERTY, JANET E., *Manual: The Rotter Incomplete Sentence Blank* (New York, Psychol. Corp., 1950).

ROWE, ALBERT, *The School as a Guidance Community* (Hull, Pearson, 1971).

RUTTER, MICHAEL, 'A children's behaviour questionnaire for completion by teachers: preliminary findings', *Journal of Child Psychology and Psychiatry* (1967), 8: 1–11.

RUTTER, M., TIZARD, J., and WHITMORE, K., *Education Health and Behaviour. A Report on the IOW Survey* (London, Longman, 1970).

SEEBOHM, F., Committee on Local Authority and Allied Personal Social Services: *The Seebohm Report* (London, HMSO, 1968).

H

SHELDON, W. H., *The Varieties of Temperament: a psychology of constitutional differences* (New York, Harper and Row, 1942).

SHERIDAN, MARY D., *The 'Stycar' Hearing Tests* (Revised ed., Windsor, NFER, 1969).

SMITH, V. H., and JAMES, F. E., *Eyes and Education* (London, Heinemann, 1968).

SORENSON, A. G., HUSEK, T. R., and UY, C., 'Divergent concepts of teacher role: an approach to the measurement of teacher effectiveness', *Journal of Educ. Psychol.* (1963), Vol. 54, pp. 287–94.

SPROTT, W. J. H., *Human Groups* (Harmondsworth, Penguin, 1958).

STENDLER, C. B., and YOUNG, N., 'Impact of beginning first grade upon socialisation as reported by mothers', *Ch. Devel.* XXI (1950).

STONE, L. J., and CHURCH, J., *Childhood and Adolescence: a psychology of the growing person* (New York, Random House, 1957).

STOTT, D. H., *The Bristol Social Adjustment Guides* (London, University of London Press, 1956; 2nd ed., 1971).

STRANG, RUTH, *An Introduction to Child Study* (3rd ed., New York Macmillan, 1951).

STRANG, RUTH, *The Role of the Teacher in Personnel Work* (New York, Bureau of Publications, Teachers College, Columbia University, 1953).

STRANG, RUTH, and MORRIS, G., *Guidance in the Classroom* (New York, The Macmillan Co., 1964).

SUMMERFIELD, A., Department of Education and Science: *Psychologists in Education Services, report of a working party* (London, HMSO, 1968).

SUTTIE, IAN D., *The Origins of Love and Hate* (Harmondsworth, Penguin, 1960).

TANNER, J. M., *Education and Physical Growth* (London, University of London Press, 1961).

TAYLOR, GEORGE, and AYRES, N., *Born and Bred Unequal* (London, Longmans, 1969).

TERMAN, L. M., and MERRILL, M. A., *Stanford-Binet Intelligence Scale* (Boston, Houghton-Mifflin, 1960).

THOMPSON, A. J. M., 'An investigation into the work performed by some trained counsellors in English secondary schools'. Final report to the SSRC (Keele, Institute of Education, University of Keele, 1970).

TORRANCE, E. P., *Guiding Creative Talent* (Englewood Cliffs, N.J., Prentice-Hall, 1962).